STUDENTS OF THE DREAM

STUDENTS OF THE DREAM

RESEGREGATION IN A SOUTHERN CITY

 Ruth Carbonette Yow

Harvard University Press

Cambridge, Massachusetts & London, England

2017

Library of Congress Cataloging-in-Publication Data
Names: Yow, Ruth Carbonette, author.
Title: Students of the dream : resegregation in a Southern city / Ruth Carbonette Yow.
Description: Cambridge, Massachusetts : Harvard University Press, 2017. |
Includes bibliographical references and index.
Identifiers: LCCN 2017016822 | ISBN 9780674971905
Subjects: LCSH: Segregation in education—Georgia—Marietta. | School
integration—Georgia--Marietta. | Discrimination in education—Georgia—Marietta. |
Marietta (Ga.)—Social conditions.
Classification: LCC LC214.23.M3 Y69 2017 | DDC 379.2/6309758245—dc23
LC record available at https://lccn.loc.gov/2017016822

CONTENTS

STUDENTS OF THE DREAM

INTRODUCTION

ON AN AUGUST AFTERNOON, Jan Robles, the Marietta Blue Devils' only Latino starter, and Kenny Norwood, a talented black wide receiver, folded their long legs under the table and tucked into their chicken sandwiches. They sat with their shoulders touching, but having crammed together into bus seats for countless away-game trips, they didn't seem to mind the close quarters. Their boyishness made their bulk less menacing; they stepped on each other's sentences, cackled at and corrected each other's accounts, and narrated each other's best games to the ethnographer across the booth from them. Jan and Kenny had been close since they met in middle school, back when Jan was still learning English, still missing his hometown of Bayamon, his friends there, his old life. In Puerto Rico, Jan's father worked in telecommunications, and his mother, a homemaker, raised Jan and his sister. But the family was called—both his parents worked in their church's youth ministry—to move to Georgia where they had no family or connections, and they suffered a hard landing. "It was like starting from zero. It was like I was just born, all new," Jan said.[1] His well-educated, highly skilled father struggled to find a job; the financial security and comforts of Bayamon vanished into the heat of their first Georgia summer. Looking for a community, Jan picked up a sport no one played back home—football.

"When I first tried out," Jan recalled, shaking the ice in his drained lemonade, "I was the only Hispanic [on the team] . . . I didn't know anybody

1

and with my [language] barrier, I was set apart. So I didn't make friends that well." In a just a couple of years, though, Jan was playing varsity ball. He found a home on the team, where he was still one of only two Latino players, but where, he said, no one was white, or black, or Latino. They were Blue Devils: "Not once was there ever a racial comment. We were all a family, not only the football team, but in the school—the faculty, the lunch ladies—they knew the football players, so they'd give us extra pizza in the pizza line. . . . [T]hat's how it is at Marietta. We're really close— we're a family." "Family" meant a lot at Marietta High School—it could expand widely, and it could also exclude fiercely.

Some months later, at the much-anticipated Homecoming game, I followed Jan's bobbing helmet as he and his team burst onto the field through a huge "Go Blue Devils" banner. He and Kenny described that moment, emerging into the stadium lights on Friday nights, as "euphoric," the crowd's roar so loud that it solidifies into "pure silence." "It's like you're looking down on yourself," Kenny told me. Yet by the first whistle, "you're so concentrated," recalled Jan, "you don't care about the crowd." Kenny was a slender, lithe asset to the Blue Devil offense; Jan, a powerful defensive end. The thrill for the spectator was in Jan's tackles; he sought the hardest hits—the ones that make you suck your breath in and hold it until everyone gets up and trots away like nothing happened. In the "Senior" section of the 150-page full-color commemorative program, Jan is pictured cradling a football beside the big white bell that clanged after every home-field win. Unlike many of his teammates who are bearing stoic frowns in their photos, Jan is grinning broadly.

WHAT KIND OF PLACE is Jan's Marietta? Like Atlanta, Marietta rose from the rails. Railroads like the Western and Atlantic—which proved a critical artery in the Civil War—spurred Marietta's growth and that of Cobb County, the economically segregated and densely populated suburb in which Marietta is nestled. Through the nineteenth and twentieth centuries—from tanneries to cotton mills to factories churning out war planes—Marietta played its part in the industrializing South.[2] By the middle of the twentieth century, as civil rights activism transformed the region, Marietta's population of around 25,000 was 15 percent black.[3] Although Marietta did not experience the civil rights battles that convulsed some of its Southern neighbors, the local White Citizens for Segregation fought to preserve Jim Crow.[4] Beyond the indignities of, for example, the "S" for segregation the WCS encouraged local businesses to post loomed entrenched structural inequality: Marietta's white population was, on average, four years more educated and twice as wealthy as their black counterparts.[5] But by the 1970s, gains for black citizens across the South registered in black Marietta, too. The decade brought increased representation in city government as well as incomes and education levels more competitive with those of white Mariettans.[6]

Throughout the 1980s and 1990s, Marietta's black population swelled, until the city had regained the numbers of black denizens it lost to the Great Migration north. During the same period, the suburban boom that demographically remade the Sunbelt South expanded Marietta's white middle class and its black population; in the year 2000 black Mariettans once again made up one-third of the city's total. That share—about 33 percent of the city population—did not change much between 2000 and 2015, when Marietta's population hovered just under 60,000.[7] In recent decades, the city has tried to preserve its old South charm—distinguished by the historic square and Civil War battlefield—as shopping plazas and business parks multiplied and enfolded Marietta into the bustle and heterogeneity of twenty-first-century suburbia.

Deep South in character, Marietta was as shaped by white supremacy as its neighboring cities, but it was not a hub of racial violence in the nineteenth or twentieth centuries. The city's only well-known incident of white vigilantism was the lynching of Jewish pencil-factory owner Leo Frank in 1915. The sign for Frey's Gin Road, where Frank was hanged from a tree by a group of some of Marietta's most prominent white citizens, still stands, innocuous and a little weathered, off Highway 41.[8] Formerly surrounded by farmland, today, Marietta is bisected and defined by Highway 41. To see Marietta from 41 is to see little more than shabby shopping plazas; down-at-the-heels businesses, motels, and churches; and of course, the fifty-foot-tall Big Chicken—surely the country's most flamboyant KFC restaurant—its red, four-foot-tall comb and the whites of its mechanically rolling eyes visible for miles.

Marietta could be deemed a dowdy little sister with nothing on Atlanta's glittering, grimy, harlequin allure. But that's not seeing the Marietta that denizens like Jan love. It's a town where the Fourth of July parade on the square attracts thousands, where several generations of Blue Devils turn out for big games, and where many graduates return to their alma mater as teachers, coaches, and mentors. At the same time, like so many American cities, it is a place of métissage—of Dominican hair salons, Lebanese cafes, mosques and synagogues, *supermercados, pastelerías,* and roti stands amid the Presbyterian churches, antique stores, and ice cream shops that used to dot the town square and define the cultural and physical geography of the city. It is a place where immigrants from the Caribbean, Middle East, South Asia, and, especially, Latin America are making a new Marietta and demanding a stake in the political, economic, and educational order.

DURING A LULL in the action of the game, I glanced around the stands and tried to imagine, somewhere in their chaos, the delicate pleats and careful coifs of the studious and shy black tenth graders who integrated Marietta High School in 1964. Although Treville Grady transferred out of MHS that same fall, her friend, Daphne Delk, stayed. The bright, ambitious sophomore knew a very different Marietta High than Jan and Kenny do: for Delk, there were no Friday nights at Northcutt Stadium, no Homecoming dances, no marching band. Her isolation was a different kind of "pure silence": she was much talked about, but seldom spoken to. She moved through the din of lockers slamming and laughter rippling along the hall looking down on herself and the strange quiet of her exclusion. "My intent was scholarly," she told me when we met, almost fifty years later.[9] "You're so into [just doing] it that you can't see left or right; you're in the middle, and you're dealing with it, because it is what it is." So she pressed ahead— blocking out the epithets and threats, the reality of what integration would mean for her former high school, her peers, her community—all the way to graduation. I searched the stands again, contemplating what Delk's sacrifices signified in the twenty-first-century South, where school integration had flourished and where many now fear it may die.

Daphne Delk had described Marietta as a kind of "Mayberry," a small town where there was not much "dissension" between white and black residents. It was a segregated place, of course, and yet, in the closeness of black and white neighborhoods, in the constant presence of black Mariettans in white homes, it was not "that separated," as Delk said. "[When] we were smaller," she recalled, [black and white children] would meet in the branches, in the wooded areas where water was running and we would play across the water. It wasn't until [we] started growing up that the difference would come." During her first year at Marietta High, when she had long stopped playing by the creek with white neighbors, Delk was not afraid. She was, instead, "in a real place of questioning and challenging what was happening and what was going to happen next."

Outside Northcutt a clutch of black teenagers, observed by a white officer of the Marietta Police Department, cheered the team through a chain-link fence. Across the street, stadium-side homeowners had mown bold "M"s into the grass of their lawns. Inside the fence, a crowd worthy of glossy promotional pamphlets—adorned in blue, diverse in race and nationality, spanning generations from toddler to doddering patriarch—roared their approval at the presentation of the black, white, Latino, and Middle Eastern members of the Homecoming Court. To the joy of the fans—and the even greater glee of Jan and his teammates—Marietta prevailed that evening. Such clear victories are hard to come by in twenty-first-century Marietta; for the public schools especially, football season's ritualizing of Blue Devil identity offers welcome proof that schools are powerful unifiers in transforming communities and that Marietta's historical struggle against educational injustice is a "long arc" indeed.

Integration has many registers—church pews, office breakrooms, pool halls, and neighborhood pools—in which Americans negotiate community and identity every day. This story, though, focuses on school integration. Through the history of one Southern city and its flagship high school, I explore integration's role—past, present, and future—in shaping students into citizens who demand more of their schools, their communities, and by extension, their democracy. Underlying many of the reflections, doubts, and hopes of Mariettans are ideas about race, class, and opportunity that dramatically influence the contemporary challenges of producing and sustaining integrated schools.[10]

Integration—the condition that results from a successful desegregation process—was institutionalized slowly and stumblingly in the two decades after the 1954 Supreme Court decision in *Brown v. Board of Education*; it encompassed more than black and white students and stretched far beyond school walls. School integration of the 1960s and 1970s cultivated not just a tolerance of race- and income-mixed schools but also a belief in the importance of values that were foreign, if not anathema, to the previous generation of white Southerners, such as an appreciation of diversity and the importance of judging people on character not color—a notion whose shorthand, "colorblindness," masks its cultural complexity. While many white Mariettans used the term colorblindness to describe a personal value or attitude, both black and white interviewees discussed diversity at the institutional register—the team, classroom, or workplace—using it as a kind of index for progress in such particular arenas. Where, though, did colorblindness and diversity as values in public schooling come from? How did a segregated and openly racist society become one in which so many Americans claim to prize diversity and to hope their children will value and benefit from it too?

After decades of litigation, both in and beyond the South, integration was legally enshrined as a core principle of American public schooling with the Supreme Court's ruling in *Brown v. Board of Education*.[11] In May of 1954, Thurgood Marshall and his NAACP Legal Defense Fund colleagues celebrated the decision they had long sought. The Court's unanimous opinion declared segregated education unconstitutional and ordered the nation's segregated schools desegregated with (in the now infamous phrase) "all deliberate speed." Yet public education was a site for the contestation of our American dilemmas, to borrow Gunnar Myrdal's phrase, long before 1954. In the nineteenth century, before the Civil War, a cadre of zealous school reformers, all white men and mostly Protestant, sought to secure the future of the republic and its moral moorings by creating centralized, standardized, free public schooling.

The "common school" reformers of the early republic were not interested in cultivating racial or cultural diversity in education—just the opposite: they sought uniformity. They saw the one-room schoolhouses hosting toddlers up to teenagers; the circuit-riding teachers, in one season, out the next; and the brought-from-home spellers as evidence of chaos and moral turpitude, not the makings of a great Christian republic. Consequently, reformers like Horace Mann, Henry Barnard, John Pierce, and famed antislavery senator William Seward exhorted their constituents to consolidate their disparate districts, to elect state superintendents of education, and to tax themselves in order to sustain a system of free public schools.[12]

That nineteenth-century vista, so vastly different from the landscape of public education today, offers some landmarks for mapping out the legacy of the period for present-day public schooling—landmarks like the school building itself. Especially in rural places where gathering spots were few and far between, the school served as the community's theater, its meeting house, its competition hall, and its celebration venue.[13] The school was at the center of public life, rivaled only by the church, and it is important to note that this quality of the school, especially the high school, has endured in many ways into the twenty-first century. Sociologists such as Katherine Newman and Douglas Foley have written about the school's role as a metaphorical "public stage" for community-making; they suggest that the status, power, and identity of local families are negotiated through their students at the local school.[14] Correspondingly, the school produces outsiders and insiders in ways that have an enduring impact on the community itself.[15]

The history of public schooling is as fraught with contradictions and injustice as the history of our democratic experiment.[16] Over the nineteenth and first half of the twentieth centuries, schools proved to be central sites for entrenching racial segregation and attendant prejudices and customs. Yet public schooling and the institution of the public school also proved to be ideal levers for outsiders—groups previously marginalized, oppressed, and excluded—to call out hypocrisy and insist upon representation and rights.[17] Although a wellspring of resistance to white supremacist schooling and capitalist exploitation had been gathering for several decades in communities of Native Americans, black Americans, and Latinos, during the decade following the *Brown v. Board* decision, what was taught, by whom, and to what end was fiercely contested in cities across the country.[18]

The position of public schools at the forefront of this dramatic cultural transformation is a fact of consequence for the longer trajectory of racial integration. In districts—mostly in the border South—where public schools desegregated in the first few years after *Brown,* they represented the first public venue, apart from the military, in which black and white Southerners socialized, played, ate, and learned together.[19] Not at lunch counters, in movie theatres, in amusement parks, or even in church pews could integration as a democratic ideal and social value become so successfully entrenched as in the institutions where nearly all American children spent more than a decade of their lives.

Integration has indeed been successfully institutionalized, and as a social value it exerts enduring influence on Americans' ideas about education: in how people talk about what they want from public schools and what kinds of citizens public education should produce. As researchers have documented, many Americans believe that public schooling should "prepare students for a diverse work-world" by cultivating both colorblindness and an appreciation for diversity.[20] Although colorblindness often describes a personal attitude that denies complicity with structural racism and injustice, it can also indicate a willingness to challenge one's previous beliefs or those of one's family or social group. This willingness had a very real role in shaping how black and white students negotiated distrust, fear, and vicious stereotypes in order to make sense of newly desegregated environments. Institutionalization has also, however, undermined integration as a lever for equity because although colorblindness and "diversity" may be ways of understanding changing racial attitudes, they are not useful legacies of desegregation or revelatory lenses on public education's contemporary challenges.[21] In the current context of intensifying racial and economic inequality, the institutionalizing of diversity and colorblindness elucidates why a new integration movement is necessary—one that actively disavows these values as final victories and interrogates their complicity in entrenching the status quo and, increasingly, legitimating free market education reform.

Although the integration efforts of the 1960s and 1970s in the Deep South focused on black and white students, the fight for integration today must encompass growing populations of immigrant students, especially those who are undocumented.[22] For students without documents, the legal barriers to college admission and the job market constitute the material, political, and cultural context for a justice movement, a movement that has been growing in cities and school systems across the country where mostly Latino students stand together "undocumented and unafraid."[23] The struggles and the marginalization of poor students of color and undocumented students testify to the need for a new integration era. Tribulations unique to undocumented students reveal that an integration movement that does not encompass whole communities—and their linked issues of low graduation rates, endemic discrimination and criminalization, high deportation rates, and deepening poverty—will not serve the needs of the coming generations, generations that will be increasingly Latino.

Integrated education did not solely unfold in cafeterias and classrooms; it was also built through teams, youth groups, political and civic organizations, service clubs, and other networks. That is to say, integration was a radical reform with consequences far beyond school walls.[24] This book offers a look into how integration became institutionalized in and outside local schools and how students, teachers, activists, and community members have understood the stakes of integration and translated that knowledge into school reform, city legislation, and collective action.

Marietta's story also reveals the ways that students and community members have sought to de-institutionalize racism, classism, and ethnocentrism and transform rhetoric about diversity and colorblindness into material and political support for marginalized students. The dramas of desegregation and resegregation related here—that is, the ongoing effort to institutionalize integration—center on Mariettans' myriad efforts to achieve integrated schools and on the beliefs, values, and fears that have guided community members toward some strategies and away from others.[25] Organizing, service, activism, and civic engagement in the contemporary moment in Marietta illuminate the critical role community building will play in counteracting how the law, the local government, and local corporations institutionalize discrimination against and disfranchisement of the undocumented and people of color in metro Atlanta and across the country. What is happening in Marietta's most marginalized communities testifies to the power of collective action through community building to redefine integration for a new era and for the students who have the most at stake.[26]

ON A SPRING DAY, when the redbud trees and dogwoods are flowering and the faint sounds of orchestra rehearsal and basketball practice lace the late afternoon, Marietta High School seems "pristine" indeed and suited to the small town that desegregator Daphne Delk recalled. But just as the rumbling of the Civil Rights Movement shook the foundations of that "Mayberry" in the 1960s, so too does resegregation threaten to unmoor the Marietta High of the twenty-first century. A new integration era is necessitated not only by the limitations and incompleteness of the first, but also by the rapid resegregation of once-integrated public schools across the South and across the country. In schools like Marietta High, which experienced decades of integration, contemporary students are tapping the capacity to imagine and engineer a new integration era. To explore the possibility of that new movement and the urgent necessity for it, we need to look to the desegregation of Marietta High in 1964 and trace its trajectory toward resegregation in the twenty-first century.

Marietta High desegregated a full decade after the ruling in *Brown*. The elementary and middle schools desegregated during the following two years. The town's small black population constituted little threat to the large white majority, and as in other Georgia counties where the black population was small, in Marietta there was little support for school closures or organized resistance to desegregation.[27] White Mariettans took pride in the calm civility with which they finally met *Brown*. In Atlanta, desegregated schools resegregated within just a few years due to massive white flight.[28] By contrast, Marietta whites neither relocated nor sought refuge in private schools. In 1970, there were proportionally fewer white students in private schools than ten years earlier, before *Brown* came to Marietta.[29]

In the years that followed desegregation, the city's black population grew gradually, and MHS was, for a period beginning in the mid-1970s and enduring into the early 1990s, a racially balanced, fully integrated high school. A yearbook photo from 1977 depicting two black and two white hands in a crisscross grip captures the esprit de corps of that period—a time when the belief in, if not the social reality of, racial harmony was central to school identity. Integration was institutionalized during this period through students' negotiations around race, representation, and belonging at school. School leaders, teachers, and in limited, specific ways, students, too, institutionalized integration through an ethos of colorblind camaraderie, in which black and white clasped hands—instead of a more accurate portrait of confrontation, exclusion, and power—offer desegregation's central lessons and essential truths. Understanding desegregation through the lens of colorblind camaraderie has had consequences for school and local politics in Marietta, because it is a limited tool for implementing new, effective strategies for integration in Marietta's resegregating schools.

Resegregation in the South represents, in the words of desegregation scholars Gary Orfield and Chungmei Lee, a "historic reversal."[30] When the public schools of the Deep South eventually desegregated, the impact was profound. At the high-water mark in 1988, 44 percent of Southern black students were in majority white schools, versus less than 3 percent in 1964.[31] The North never saw such high levels of interracial schooling.[32] Where it was implemented well and equitably—often through metropolitan remedies bridging city and suburb, like those of Orlando, Tampa, Nashville, and Charlotte—desegregation worked.[33] Academic outcomes for children of color improved and racial attitudes were remade among the generations of students who began their educations in integrated schools.[34]

Yet seminal Supreme Court cases of the 1970s and 1990s undermined the capacity of communities to integrate their schools effectively. In the 1974 *Milliken v. Bradley* decision, the Court considered cross-district busing in Detroit; this form of busing was deemed critical in desegregating metropolitan areas where residential segregation, instead of *de jure* segregation, had produced white and black schools. The Supreme Court struck it down. In 1991, in the *Board of Education of Oklahoma City Public Schools v. Dowell* ruling, the Court discredited the idea that maintaining integration was a permanent responsibility and a moral obligation of local school districts and thereby released districts from the court orders that had made them desegregate.

In the new century, *Brown* saw its clearest repudiation by the 2007 Supreme Court's decision in *Parents Involved in Community Schools v. Seattle School District No. 1,* which dramatically weakened the ability of districts to use race in desegregation plans. Education scholar David Kirp called Seattle's plan and that of Louisville, Kentucky—which was also being examined by the court—"modest" in their use of race.[35] Seattle and Louisville had desegregation plans that allowed students to rank schools in order of preference; race was used as a factor among others—such as where siblings were enrolled—to determine which students would be admitted to a school that received more number-one rankings than it had slots for students. If the oversubscribed school required more black students to maintain the school's racial balance, a black student could be given preference over a white student. As legal scholar Jonathan Entin put it, the Seattle and Louisville-Jefferson County school boards "based their policies on the notion that integration was legally and morally a worthy goal and that considering race for that beneficent purpose was vastly different from using race as a device to promote segregation."[36] The Court disagreed. In the Roberts Court's construal, students and parents are consumers unmarked by race or class—to assert that such structural positions materially and dramatically impact public schooling is, to quote Chief Justice Roberts, "discriminating on the basis of race."[37]

In the aftermath of the *Seattle* decision, scholars and policymakers debated the importance of race as a factor in creating integrated schools; some pointed to districting and attendance zone strategies that were attentive to socioeconomic status and to universities that shifted their focus to class-based affirmative action in states that banned using race in college admissions.[38] Gary Orfield and other leading desegregation scholars argue that class-based strategies will not accomplish what race- *and* class-based strategies can.[39] Further, socioeconomic integration in secondary education is not always popular, as critics claim that it, too, abrogates the rights of parents and their children. In Eden Prairie, Minnesota, for example, an income-based integration plan proposed in 2011 prompted local parents to threaten a lawsuit and organize the termination of the superintendent responsible for the plan.[40] The sanctity of individual choice over the sacrifices entailed by collective action and the Supreme Court's enshrining of those principals have dramatically damaged the fortunes of school desegregation, even in places where many parents prize integrated education.

The unwillingness of the Supreme Court or of the Nixon, Reagan, or Bush administrations to support new desegregation strategies or maintain those plans already in place coincided with the growth of Latino populations in schools across the Southeast. What had before been a civil rights struggle over educational equity for black students has been transformed by Latino immigration in the decades since the 1980s.[41] By most measures, California, New York, and Texas led the way through the aughts in the segregation of Latino students in majority-minority schools, but on their heels were Georgia and North Carolina.[42] A decade before most of its Deep South peers, Georgia was a destination for Mexican immigrants who sought jobs in agriculture, construction, and the carpet industry. Provisions in the Immigration Reform and Control Act of 1986 had resulted in the redirection of immigrants toward "nontraditional" destinations such as Alabama, North Carolina, and Georgia. In 1994, the ratification of the North American Free Trade Agreement (NAFTA) further fueled immigration into the United States from Mexico.[43] By 2016, Georgia had the tenth largest Latino population in the United States and some of the nation's most rapidly resegregating schools.[44] Alarmingly, even as resegregation continues apace, especially in areas with large and ever-growing immigrant populations, and as the nation's children get poorer, desegregation has receded from education policy debates and from the rhetoric of mainstream education reform. Despite decades of research demonstrating the profound dangers of racial isolation for low-income students of color (including that which produced the unanimous decision in *Brown v. Board*) and the benefits of integrated education, school *re*segregation has not yet been taken up with any seriousness by policymakers.[45]

Integration has always been a difficult-to-quantify reform, and education policymaking is hindered by what Cuban and Tyack diagnose as "amnesia" about the positive impacts of long-term transformation.[46] As scholar Susan Eaton put it, "desegregation . . . created a generation of people for whom diversity was the norm."[47] In fact, as the story told here suggests, it created more than one generation—the institutionalizing of integration cemented racial diversity as an educational value, if a complicated one. And yet desegregation is out of step with the contemporary search in education policy for a curricular or administrative silver bullet that will raise the scores of American students and render American schools more "globally competitive."[48] Effective desegregation is an elegant proof in which each and every factor is critical and complex in its own right: class and race demographics, local leadership, parental investment, relationship between metro area and urban center, funding, curriculum, historical precedent, and political will.

Desegregation's crises have been spectacular and its successes under-documented. Although few Americans argue with the idea that public education should ensure an "equal chance to succeed" for children of different backgrounds, equally few will support the comprehensive programs—like busing—that actually produce equally resourced, integrated schools.[49] Education scholar Jennifer Hochschild asserts that "few people want [comprehensive desegregation and] most districts do it poorly . . . [but] when coupled with deep systemic reform of educational governance and content, it is our only available option for ending racial isolation."[50] Integration is our only hope for ending the educational inequality that pervades resegregating systems. But valuing the collective good over individual advantage is a great deal to ask of parents. This is especially true when institutions such as the church or the community center that might prize such an ethos are facing the powerfully individualist and market-centered ideologies institutionalized in government policy and programs, from No Child Left Behind to NAFTA.[51]

The rhetoric and strategies of No Child Left Behind, the Bush administration's education reform act, reshaped the landscape of public education between 2001 and 2012 but have done nothing to confront the rapid resegregation of public schools. Test scores have come to stand for the success or failure of American schools and communities, and the consequences have been profound. Along with major cheating scandals, school closings, and teacher firings, the centerpieces of twenty-first-century school reform—standards, accountability, and market-oriented solutions—have damaged Americans' dialogue around race, poverty, and educational equity.[52] The same cultural attitudes that have denuded the landscape of desegregation possibilities are also exacerbating resegregation in places like Marietta, where school choice has been the system's primary response to increasing racial isolation in the schools.

Suburban schools are the perilous frontier of resegregation. There are now more low-income students in suburbs like Cobb County than in large cities. Yet the expansion of resegregation from large cities into American suburbs has not been widely documented nor are its implications for educational equity fully understood.[53] Metro Atlanta has seen particularly rapid resegregation and little public discussion about it. As scholars Erica Frankenberg and Gary Orfield write, "In a high stakes accountability era, there is no significant accountability for integrating schools. . . . [M]any communities have re-segregated without ever having a significant public discussion about what is happening and what could be done."[54] In Cobb County, the percentage of black and Latino students in desegregated schools decreased by more than 10 percent just between 2000 and 2005.[55]

As the system's only high school, Marietta High's fortunes have always been tightly bound to those of the city. During the same period that the black population boomed, a Latino population numbering less than 2 percent in 1980 grew to almost 20 percent by the year 2000—expanding by 600 percent in the decade between 1990 and 2000 alone.[56] By 2012 Marietta High had qualified as a "high-poverty" school for a decade, and the student body was 25 percent Latino, 49 percent black, and 21 percent white.[57] Between 2000 and 2005, in the Marietta City schools, the Latino student population grew by 10 percent, and the number of students on free or reduced-price lunch increased by 25 percent; white enrollment dropped to one-fifth of the system total.[58]

This Southern community's experience of desegregation, integration, and the advance of resegregation is a local journey that mirrors our national struggle over integration's promises and paradoxes. Even among the most equity-minded researchers, those who care deeply about justice for low-income students, resegregation scholarship often inadvertently frames poor, black, or Latino students as the problem: when there are too many of them, a school resegregates, and teacher turnover, low scores, high dropout rates, and wavering community support render it no longer a stable and productive learning environment. In the case of small, deeply rooted districts like Marietta's, which are unlikely to ever join with larger metropolitan systems, addressing resegregation will never be merely a matter of student demographics. In communities like Marietta, which has never been under court order to desegregate and where school boards have rarely fought over districting or racial balance, there is little tradition of public contestation over the state of the schools. What is done is done tacitly, in initiatives like the instituting of elite academic programs intended to draw affluent white families back to the public schools.[59]

Confronting resegregation as a problem of educational justice, not merely a problem of test scores and home sales, will require the reshaping of local public education through community building, servant leadership, and nonschool initiatives that attract and enrich the education of students across class and color. Resegregating suburban systems do not often attempt the kinds of interventions that recast poor students of color as engines of positive educational change, rather than barriers to it.[60] What shape public education reform will take in twenty-first-century Marietta— whether it will be dominated by the goal of bringing back high-income white families or revolutionized by a new integration era—is at the heart of this portrait of a changing city and its flagship high school.

A FUNDAMENTAL INCONGRUITY characterizes Marietta High: it is a one-hundred-year-old high school steeped in the traditions of a small town, even as the very idea of "small town traditions" has been upended by demographic, economic, and cultural change. Marietta is the county seat of Cobb—a prototypical Sunbelt suburb and one of metro Atlanta's largest. Separate from Cobb County's 100,000-student behemoth, Marietta's school system enrolls about 8,000 students, from fourth-generation Blue Devils to youth newly arrived from Guatemala and Mexico. It thereby offers an ideal site to explore the questions critical to contemporary public schooling: What bonds school and community? What threatens that bond? What are the implications for a school system closely and deeply identified with "its" town for citizens who are typically marginalized—poor people of color, immigrants, and the undocumented?

The rootedness of Marietta High in the city and the enduring bond between residents and their school composed the unfamiliar culture I sought to study when I went "into the field." Educated at a private school— Marietta High's rival—I grew up in Cobb, just half an hour from Atlanta, where 40 percent of children lived in poverty, in a county with one of the fastest growing Latino populations in the country. Yet, as a teenager, I could count all the nonwhite kids I knew on one hand, and I didn't have any peers on government assistance.[61] At Marietta High there was violence, homelessness, teachers working second jobs, hungry students barely tided over by school-provided free lunch, and families split up by deportation. These conditions would form the foundations of my inquiry, not because they were foreign to my high school experience, but because they were becoming increasingly familiar to so many Mariettans and so many Americans.

Marietta High moved a few miles from the city center in 2001, but in the preceding decades, the high school was located in the heart of Marietta's oldest community, and many of its students walked to school. The people who lived by the school campus, the ones with cars and front doors decked in Blue Devil paraphernalia, were Mariettans *and* Blue Devils—intertwined identities and intertwined futures.[62]

THIS BOOK is an "ethnographic history."[63] The perspective of my private school education furnished me with a set of initial questions about the "foreign" culture of public education. I spent two years immersed in the community and conducted more than one hundred interviews: eighty interviews with white, black, and Latino graduates across five decades (from the mid-1960s through 2013) and twenty-five interviews with former and current teachers and coaches, school board members, education activists, and city officials. Each semistructured interview was about an hour long (although some were as short as thirty minutes, while others ran to almost three hours), and I recruited interviewees through, for the most part, the "snowball technique" in which one interview led to another. Interviews moved from questions about family and growing up, to reflections on race, class, and community at the high school, and finally to attitudes on education reform and the value of an integrated education. Many of the interviewees recounted deeply personal experiences—or described peers and events candidly—and for this reason, some people chose to take pseudonyms.[64]

The melding of ethnography and oral history in this project allowed me to chart personal histories of desegregation alongside national discourses of race, class, and education over the decades. Graduates revealed the ways, large and small, that they were shaped by high school, from painful racist incidents to moments of powerful understanding across difference—what it was like to be the first Latino class president, how it felt to be crowned the first black Homecoming queen. The testimony of graduates in the pages that follow suggests that race and class difference continue to structure the social and intellectual experience of high school and adulthood despite the fact that colorblindness and diversity rhetoric nearly always precluded conversations about power and structure. Personal reflection is always political, though, and often interviewees grappled aloud with contradictions raised by the high value they placed on their own integrated experiences and their condemnation of state action or collective organizing that could safeguard those experiences for the next generation.

Graduates' reflections were interlaced with deeply ambivalent views on education and difference, reflecting the complex ways institutional commitments shape our identities and choices.[65] One white graduate of the mid-eighties, who had decided against sending his own daughter to Marietta High because of "the influences there," talked affectionately of his lasting interracial friendships: "If you grow up together," he told me, "you have each other's backs." In a similar way, views on public education were usually a fusion of mainstream education reform rhetoric and very personal anxieties about and hopes for the high school, its students, and the community. A black graduate and celebrated football player of the early desegregation era who had educated his children in Marietta's schools disparaged public education and lamented the "million dollars" being "thrown" at failing public schools, suggesting they be privatized. In the next breath, he said he couldn't imagine what students from "the projects"— as he once was—would do without public education.

Indeed, the melding of oral history and ethnographic methods meant that I was often challenged to define my agenda, by everyone from the superintendent of schools—"What is the question you're trying to answer?"—to the high school students I volunteered with—"So, um, why are you here?" Oral history bears a resemblance to "research" as many administrators, politicians, and community members know it: oral history interviews and testimony have an innocuous ubiquity in local museums and cultural centers and at commemorative events. Ethnographic fieldwork, on the other hand, is a more ambiguous enterprise that often renders, as the above queries suggest, the ethnographer and her intentions as local objects of study.[66]

Despite the groundbreaking work of a growing number of researchers, it has taken too long for the scholarly establishment to acknowledge the cost of desegregation to black communities. Thousands of deeply rooted and beloved institutions were closed in the name of money, logistics, physical conditions, or simply at the whims of white leaders. Marietta was no different. Critical to understanding desegregation in Marietta—and its costs—are the histories that highlight the powerful community bonds forged in the fire of Jim Crow and the ambivalence—if not outright resentment and protest—with which black communities met white-orchestrated desegregation.[67] Today, black students and other students of color remain those of whom most is asked and to whom least is delivered, and their experiences have justly garnered scholarly and some popular attention, as the "apartheid" schools of the twenty-first century increasingly echo the profound inequities of the mid-twentieth.[68]

The narrative offered in these pages traces the arc of desegregation, integration, and resegregation at one high school over sixty years, documenting the experiences of graduates of the second, third, fourth, and fifth decades after *Brown* and bringing school desegregation in the 1960s into dialogue with the integration struggles of Latino students of the aughts.[69] These distinct communities of "integrators" have much to tell us about the experience of integration. If desegregation is a Southern high school's coming-of-age story, the story here follows the thread of the narrative out of adolescence and into adulthood. Marietta's journey illuminates what desegregation was like for graduates and what is at stake for future students; it also suggests that "the long integration era" contains within it not only the possibility of resegregation but also that of a new and broader integration movement.[70]

NORTHCUTT STADIUM is the Blue Devil family's ancestral home, and there, as in any family, devotion and unity are entangled with betrayal and loss. And it is Northcutt Stadium to which we turn now, a symbolic cultural anchor in the city and a gathering place where so much of Marietta's story about itself—about race, justice, and desegregation—is rooted. It is where we begin to plumb that story through the experiences of players who came before Jan and Kenny, and who, in and outside school, navigated the hazards and enjoyed the boons of integrated education and set about determining what integration meant for them. As manifestations of our loftiest goals and gravest responsibilities as a democratic nation, public schools are where communities cohere or come apart—where students with faltering English, or no more than a few changes of clothes, or siblings to care for, or a late shift to work every night make good on the notion that an education is a ticket, a ticket for which all Americans must share the cost and in which we all share the bounty.

BLUE DEVIL PRIDE

Marietta Football in the Long Integration Era

"TO BRING BACK the state championship to Marietta High School—that was the summation of—that was great. And that brought not only the high school together . . . [but] the whole community, the whole city together."[1] Aaron Gullatte, a 1968 Marietta High School graduate, looked back on his first and only year at MHS, the year he and a handful of newly integrated black players from all-black Lemon Street High helped MHS secure its first (and, to date, last) state championship. The fall of 1967 was a momentous season, but it wasn't the first state trophy to earn star running back Gullatte's jubilant postgame kiss. Two faded banners still hang in Northcutt Stadium: "Lemon Street Hornets, 1966 State Champions" and "Marietta Blue Devils, 1967 State Champions." They are tattered testimony to how the stories communities tell about themselves—the particular lenses through which they see an ostensibly shared history—have lasting impact on whether an unjust past can be called on to secure equity in the present.

"In every small town, there's good people," Gullatte told me of 1960s Marietta, flipping slowly through an MHS yearbook. Gullatte began high school at all-black Lemon Street; he remembered "the camaraderie, the teachers, the athletes, the student body, just everything. The spirit of the school, it was alive." Both the impact of Lemon Street's closing—the shared grief at, to follow Gullatte's metaphor, the "death" of the school—and black students' quest for representation at MHS that climaxed in the

Homecoming protest of 1969 are illegible and, in the case of the protest, impossible in a desegregation era defined by colorblind camaraderie.[2] As in so many Southern communities, Marietta's all-black high school was closed in the wake of full desegregation. But in Lemon Street's final full year, 1966, the LSH Hornets' state championship win—and the huge integrated crowd it drew—dramatized the high school's profound impact on the life of the city.[3] When Gullatte and the best of the Lemon Street Hornets joined the Blue Devils for the 1967 season and brought triumph to the team, the camaraderie that distinguished Lemon Street for Gullatte and so many of his black peers was called into service by white Marietta, by a cultural moment in need of a redemptive ethos. Colorblind camaraderie was born on the desegregated field and in the packed stands of Northcutt Stadium. In an increasingly segregated and unequal city, the belief that Marietta's integrated team and fan base are registers of the broader community's race relations retains its cultural salience and social power.

Every community needed a way to tell the story of desegregation—both the triumphs and, in Gullatte's words, "the terrible things"—and in some towns, football was not the handmaiden of reconciliation and redemption. The example of the 1957 championship season of Little Rock's Central High Tigers is a sobering one.[4] But in Marietta, the ethos of colorblind camaraderie and its perceived material and cultural victories have continued to serve subsequent generations of Blue Devil players and fans. It has made meaning out of seismic social change—both desegregation and contemporary resegregation—but it has also limited the capacity of those same generations of Blue Devils to reckon more honestly with what desegregation wrought and engage more creatively the challenges of resegregation and structural inequality. Although football fostered a space allegedly free of race and class tension, that color- and class-blindness had little traction off the field, where race and poverty starkly determined the destinies of residents.

In the early-seventies football culture of Marietta High, the game engendered an upending of the social order where power accrued according to toughness, not whiteness and wealth, and where stereotypes about the kids from Baptistown and Louisville—enclaves of poor and middle-class black Mariettans—were turned on their heads and those kids were lionized and carried shoulder high. Coach James "Friday" Richards was one of those kids. His life and career follow the arc of integration—Marietta football got ahold of him and never let go. He spent all but six years of his adult life at

Marietta High; a black graduate of 1972, he returned to coach at MHS in 1979 and served as head coach from 1995 until 2010. As the late Ben Wilkins, who served as championship-winning head coach at Lemon Street and was demoted to the freshman team coach in his move to MHS, embodied for white Mariettans the "smooth transition" of desegregation, Richards embodies the trajectory of integration at MHS.[5]

Because he was a hometown star and Blue Devil icon, Richards's experiences are one means to sort through how class and race operated together at Marietta High and how they were triangulated through the prestige of Blue Devil football from the early seventies up through the aughts. Richards grew up in the projects in Baptistown, a black community that dated to the turn of the century.[6] In a 1903 article about a fight among "gamblers," the *Marietta Daily Journal* warned: "Baptistown is getting a hard name for riotous contact, blind tigers [speakeasies] and gambling. The good negroes of that settlement had better take matters in hand."[7] The neighborhood's reputation had not much improved by 1939, when Marietta was planning the construction of its first (and only the country's second) housing project. Baptistown was described in an editorial as a "hotspot on the police records, on Saturday nights, its crowded streets boil with colored humanity. . . . [Baptistown's] rutted streets lie but a few yards from some of the city's finest homes."[8] In the 1960s when Richards was coming up, Baptistown still had its "brawlers" and, to some degree, its "boiling" streets, but it was home to an entrenched and tight-knit black community.

In 1960s and 1970s Marietta, "the projects" designated an economically mixed, mostly black community. As one black graduate remembered, even when you moved on up into home ownership on a middle-class street (with white residents, in his case) you were only a block or two distant from the apartments where your friends lived.[9] Although the phrase "the black community" is overly general in any context, when black graduates of Richards's generation refer to their community, they are being geographically and culturally specific—the houses and apartments along Montgomery and Avery Streets or Lemon and Cole belonging to folks who grew up near each other and played rec ball together and whose parents all went to high school at Lemon Street and to church at Turner or Zion. At home in the neighborhood and at school, Richards was well liked and well known: he was voted Mr. MHS in 1972, the first black student to win that distinction. He drew fans at Northcutt as the Blue Devils "flashy tailback," in the words of local reporter Horace Crowe, and then even larger crowds playing college ball at University of Florida.[10]

In 1960s Marietta, black and white worlds were separate and yet enmeshed; there was no equality in social or economic life, but there was an interdependence that touched everyone. Richards looks back lovingly on his childhood in Baptistown; he treasured the black community that radiated out from the Lemon Street School, which he attended until sixth grade, and fondly remembers that his mother, who raised him and his siblings on her own, used to sell candied apples out of their apartment.[11] "I thought it was perfect," he said of that community and that time. "But I didn't know any different; everyone around me was poor, so I didn't really worry that we were."

It was not unusual for black families of that period in Marietta to be employed in and connected to the elite white world that bordered the black communities of Louisville and Baptistown. So it was with James Richards, whose grandmother and grandfather had a place right behind that of a socially prominent white family. As a little girl, Richards's mother, Pat, played with their white neighbors' daughter, who was her age. As in many Southern places where segregation was law, Marietta's black and white children who lived near one another strayed outside that law until puberty. When I spoke with the white neighbor, she credited her affectionate friendship with Pat Richards for her own progressive attitudes about race and used the friendship to illustrate how she has always believed that "everybody is equal." Such a "racial learning story"—about how the teller discovered race and its social implications—is, for white people, often a way to credit their own good upbringings and personal openheartedness in the segregated South.[12] The meaning of such a friendship for Pat Richards, who grew up elbow to elbow with white peers who would have access to vaster resources and greater opportunities than she ever would merely because of her color, is harder to guess.

Desegregation in social life stopped at the school doors in the sixties and early seventies at MHS. Richards woke up a kid from the projects, spent the day as star athlete and campus icon, and returned home a kid from the projects, with the neighborhood friends he'd been raised with. Four out of five Richards children attended Marietta High; leading the way was Richards's older brother, a stand-out Blue Devil basketball player, and his sister Martha. The protection and care they afforded him eased his way, but he was not one to lurk in his siblings' shadows. Sometimes broadly grinning, sometimes smirking under the brim of a black hat he paired with his letterman jacket, he appears all over the pages of the 1972 yearbook. But football was at the center of his life and identity, and he and a handful of black students anchored the team during that time. I asked Richards if football fostered friendships across race. He shook his head: "All the kids that came out of the projects with me were my friends already, the ones that I played [football] with, we walked back home to those projects together every day." The fact that Richards had no white friends—despite his membership in the almost all-white Key Club, the mixed pep club, the mostly white football team, and the all-around popularity illustrated by his election as Mr. MHS—demonstrates how class, custom, and prejudice cloud the simplistic clarity of the narrative of a triumphant desegregation era. His recollection that "we walked back home to those projects every day" is not just about the ties that bind childhood friends; it suggests that integration at school, at least in 1972, had limited impact in the social world of Marietta outside its walls.[13] Richards was a leading man in an integrated cast, playing to a segregated house.[14]

The influence and endurance of the ethos of colorblind camaraderie depended on validation by black players and coaches. Beloved by his teachers, coaches, and peers and deemed "the most sought after [tail]back in the South" by the fall of his senior year, Richards rode the tide of desegregation out of Northcutt Stadium and into Division I football—composed of the athletic powerhouses that offer full scholarships and compete in major bowl games.[15] Richards played well at Florida—"an integral part of [their] machine"—but did not last long in the pros.[16] When Richards came home to Marietta in 1979, the Blue Devils were glad to have him back. In continuing the legacy of Coach Ben Wilkins, his mentor, he represented, for white leadership, the successful and nonthreatening incorporation of black Mariettans into the edifice of MHS traditions and culture.

Richards's long tenure encompasses the early desegregation period, full integration, and the turn toward resegregation. Over the decades, Richards observed a widening chasm between the high school's wealthy students and its growing population of low-income students of color. Although Marietta High became a Title I (high-poverty) school in 2002, the percentage of students on free and reduced lunch in 2012–2013 was a little over 55 percent, unlike many Title I high schools in and around Atlanta, which hover in the high 90s.[17] That is to say, MHS has remained reasonably socioeconomically integrated—enrolling homeless students as well as those from moneyed Marietta families. Richards mentioned the presence of sleek, new Mercedes in the student parking lot and then described the dire straits of students he and his wife had taken in over the years—boys, mostly black, whose parents were drug-addicted or incarcerated. A gentle man who speaks with a barely discernable lisp, Richards has more the mien of a kindly grandfather than a hardened coach; he and his wife, also a beloved MHS alum, continued to mentor local youth even when they deemed themselves too old to foster-parent any longer. When Richards was young, being poor had its dangers, but not those it has today—back then, on Lemon Street, being left alone as a high school kid to fend for oneself was not one of them.

Claimed equally by Marietta's black and white power brokers, Richards is a fixture at MHS and in the city, and he has, at least by the accounts of his white friends, relationships across class and color. Hap Smith, a white alum who fondly recalls watching the championship games of both the Hornets and the Blue Devils, called Richards a "best friend" who "will be a pallbearer at my funeral."[18] But the two were not friends in high school—Richards was a freshman the year Hap Smith graduated, and as he remembered, his group of intimate friends included no whites. Coach Richards is a bridge figure; from government housing and a single-parent family to head coach at Marietta High, he represents what many white Mariettans of his generation wish to believe integration meant.

In an era of increasing resegregation and socioeconomic inequality, the creed of colorblindness in Marietta—and its roots in a successful desegregation process—has been nourished by football culture. In football culture, the personal truths of players who cite colorblindness, and whose trajectories have been altered by the desegregated team, coexist alongside the contradictory structural truths that shape social and economic life in Marietta. The game's ritualizing of colorblind camaraderie has always been an ambiguous force in the larger struggle for racial, economic, and educational justice in Marietta.

The accounts of black and white players across the decades attest to the complexities of colorblindness—both as an explanatory device and a lens on personal experience. In the telling of many former Blue Devils, diversity and colorblindness on the team reflected the fact that although racism may persist as a character flaw, individual racists' behaviors and ideas are not reflective of any larger social or structural reality. This contradiction in colorblindness attributes universal explanatory power to individual acts of tolerance while relegating individual racist behaviors to the level of the incidental and anecdotal. How else would front-stage actors reconcile the life of the stage with that of the world beyond it, especially for former players whose social lives remained fundamentally segregated? That is to say, even once they got off stage, after the performance of colorblind camaraderie through the ritual of the game was over, and their post-high-school lives unfurled as almost entirely segregated—professionally, socially, and geographically—ex-players still invoked, decades later, the way the team fostered colorblindness and instilled in them an appreciation for relationships across class and race.

Football had always been an arena for negotiating identity and status, and after desegregation, black players had a stake in that formerly all-white social calculus at MHS. Black and white players experienced, and express, colorblindness differently, as white players were more able to carry football's social capital off the field and less likely to experience a profound disjuncture between the integrated team and the world beyond it. Sonny Birch, a white 1984 graduate and son of an entrenched "Old Marietta" family, claimed that the team was a unit and that every player was judged "not because of his color but because of his actions" on and off the field.[19] The field was home to Birch, who was raised on Blue Devil football: "My dad drove the bus for the football team to all the away games, so I always rode the bus and was always with the football players and the coaches." In the summer, when Birch was a player, the team would have practice twice a day, and he remembered of his black teammates, "they'd come to [my] house during the [mid-day] break, and hang out, and swim and then go back to practice again." Some time after Birch offered up this memory, I asked two 2013 graduates, low-income students of color who had both played football, how race and class mattered on the team: were the more affluent white kids cool and accepted among players of color? "Those kids are our *best* friends," they said with wry smiles that hinted at swimming pools in fancy neighborhoods. In Birch's portrait, a race-less idyll of sorts, boys across class and race were sized up for prowess, dedication, and team loyalty: their clothes, their cars (seldom did kids like Gullatte or Richards have one), and their addresses ceased to matter on the team. Surely the sanctity of "equality" on the field had to eventually permeate relationships off the field?

It was rare even for those white graduates who experienced full desegregation at MHS and insisted that race "never mattered" in social life to have spent the night with a black teammate or really ventured to the Marietta black players called home. Sonny Birch did not date across race. (In a conversation I had with his mother, who coached MHS cheerleading for many years, she explicitly condemned interracial dating because "mixed children" are "set aside.") Nor did he socialize with black students outside of practice, games, and team events. In a sense, the time between the practices was safely liminal; it was not a weekend night, not a place apart, really, from the field and the school. As Birch put it: "At night, we didn't really hang out. It was different areas of the city, so we weren't—we didn't feel unwelcome anywhere, but we just didn't go to where they went and they didn't come to where we went." Birch reflected appreciatively on MHS's racial diversity during his time there, but the relationships of that era seem to have had little impact on his social world in the years since.[20]

White graduates testify that football built bridges across race and class difference, even as they insist that there were no differences to bridge. For Merrell Sperling, a white 1997 graduate who grew up in the care of his divorced mother, Marietta football and its social capital—the networks, affiliations, and relationships that came with it—powerfully shaped his trajectory and sense of self. Football offered social heights of the kind Sonny Birch enjoyed because of his family's name and history in the city, but that would have been otherwise elusive to someone like Sperling, a lower-income student from out of town. Sperling, who still has the build of a defensive tackle, a ruddy face, and a sweet demeanor, described where he grew up as "a mixture [of black and white residents], just kind of a lower socioeconomic" area in southwest Marietta. In the cheerfully appointed classroom where he teaches second grade, Sperling reflected on how football created critical openings for him as a kid who was "not the richest."[21] He recalled appreciatively, "[Football players] fit in with almost everybody—[the] cheerleaders, the preps." He remembered getting flak from white players on other teams when he was the only white defensive player for Marietta, in the same breath asserting that "you're all wearing the same color [on the field]. You wear a helmet. You don't even really know, except for the arm . . . if the guy's white or black."

White alums paradoxically articulated the irrelevance of race on the team by referring to interracial friendships as produced, specifically, by football. Sperling attested: "A lot of my close friends are black guys . . . football had a lot to do with that. Just because you form that bond with those people." Although he came from a racially diverse neighborhood and elementary school, he emphasizes football as a catalyst for his relationships across race. He now coaches Marietta Middle School football, and the city elementary school where he teaches is 84 percent black and Latino and more than two-thirds low income. When I asked him about the demographics of his students in 2012–2013 (25 percent Latino, 25 percent white, 50 percent black or "mixed" was his guess), he counted the diminutive, empty desks with a broad, affectionate smile on his face. Sperling connects the future of the school system directly to the fortunes of the team. He describes the role of Blue Devil football in his life the way evangelical Christians (of which Marietta has many) describe the power of being "saved," attributing much of what he is and does to his years as a Blue Devil.[22] Perhaps providentially, his junior year on the squad, 1995–96, was a stellar season for the Blue Devils, and the last year for a long time that MHS would be a football power in the region. On the subject of the present football program, Sperling asserted that the kids have no "institutional memory," and he hopes to instill the magic of the old days in them: "When you have that M on your helmet . . . it's special. And the kids just have to know how to take ownership in that." Pointing to a picture of his little boy sporting the ubiquitous blue jersey, Sperling talked of sending his two kids through the Marietta system—"I'd love for them . . . to play Marietta football."

In some cases, social power and status established on the team accorded status outside the stadium, as the prestige of "the M" seeped into self-perception, into opportunities, and into one's own destiny.[23] Sperling confided, "Sometimes people even call me Old Marietta," alluding to elite Marietta families—dynasties that fill the ranks of the Touchdown Club (a parent-founded booster club for MHS), the city council, the school board, the newspaper editorial staff, and prestigious law firms. Sperling is not the only person who invoked "Old Marietta," or "OM" in the local shorthand, and does not quite fit the bill; others—who are not wealthy and white or from an "old" family—also staked an ambivalent claim to being "OM."[24] It is an assertion of belonging and self-definition that may not be fully accurate in the eyes of the "real" OMs.[25]

While "OM" is one way that local people gauge and express their place in society, football is a site of identity crafting to negotiate that place. And yet a social identity powerfully shaped by football was also a product of the institutionalizing of integration at sites beyond the field. For some players, football represented a space "separate from the rest of society," a society in which colorblindness did *not* reign.[26] This "separateness" presents a challenge to the consensus memory of desegregation: just how total was Marietta's victory over racial prejudice if football's colorblind world was "separate from the rest of society"?

The very different testimonies of black students who came to football culture from relatively segregated backgrounds versus those who had broadly integrated social lives highlight why some players experienced the stage of football as "separate" from the world beyond it, while for others, life on the field flowed seamlessly into life outside football. In the accounts of black graduates for whom tolerance and acceptance on the team were replicated in the social world beyond the field, the less "separate" football's sphere felt, and the more "real" their stage identities became. Black 1977 graduate and native Baptistowner Jim Dante played two other sports besides football, was an excellent student, and was active in student government. Yet in the late seventies, his balancing of "jock" and "scholar" identities made him illegible to peers who accused him of not "being black" or sticking to "black" activities, as he recalled. Claiming that team sports facilitated his own ability to look past race, he remembered that others lacked that openness: "Lots of people cared about race," he averred, and it was presumably those people who produced the disjuncture for Dante between the team and the rest of his social world.

Football as a "separate" space, as Jim Dante experienced it, undermined colorblindness, revealing it to be applicable only in the particular environment of the team. But an identity as a black scholar-athlete became more legible over the next fifteen years, and seamlessness, not spheres of "separateness," characterized 1993 black graduate Rod Garman's social world. Like Dante, Rod Garman was smart, handsome, and cannon-armed on the field; he had an appeal that seemed to transcend race and racism, in the same way that Richards's appeal defied it twenty years before. Importantly, Garman's class background produced a high school experience that was broadly socially integrated, the experience that Jim Dante desired but never fully realized and that Richards—in the early desegregation era—didn't seek.

Although athletics troublingly remained the central sphere in which black male students at MHS were expected to succeed, other sites of distinction—academics, theatre, band, student government—solidified over the eighties, nineties, and aughts. Black graduates like Garman who benefited from that transformation heralded colorblindness—their own and that of their peers. Garman's experiences, twenty years after Richards ruled the field at Northcutt and fifteen years after Jim Dante graduated, point to the change two decades wrought in graduates' perceptions of the roles of race, class, and football in their lives. Garman grew up in a house his parents owned in a black middle-class neighborhood; both the physical and social geographies of Garman's childhood shaped his path and experiences. In elementary school, he attended an almost all-white Baptist church with a white friend, and in high school he took advanced placement classes populated mostly by white students. All the while, he was a stand-out athlete, beloved by his peers and recognized in turn with superlatives his senior year. "I had all different types of friends," he recalled.[27] Crediting his classes, his church activities, and his team sports, he claimed he was comfortable in any setting—"I was completely at ease with any race," he said. Garman's leadership on the football team must have seemed natural; there was hardly any distinction between his front-stage football role and his life off of the field.

In the testimony of black players such as Richards, Dante, and Garman, it becomes increasingly difficult to credit football with fostering interracial relationships beyond the team; class, upbringing, church and civic participation, and academics created the template for that social life. A banker, who appeared for our interview in the elegant suit he had worn to work, Garman went to college to play ball but had always known he'd go to college regardless. "Graduating from high school was not a major accomplishment," he admitted. Although college injuries precluded a professional football career, he knew there were other promising paths for someone like him. In his narrative, there are no cultural gaps—generated by color or money—for football to bridge.

On the football field, colorblindness is reinforced by the oft-hailed "equalizer" of athletic ability; class, race, and background supposedly dissolve in the heat of a great talent, a strong arm, or sure hands. Among black, white, and Latino graduates I have interviewed, colorblindness is generally perceived as a civic virtue, a legacy of the institutionalizing of integration in the schools. Even for many black interviewees, to admit that racial difference mattered in high school and afterward often seemed as taboo as telling a racist joke or using a racial epithet. For white interviewees, the touted advantages of an integrated education are the erasure of personal prejudice and an experience of diversity that prepares one for the professional world.[28] Yet, "not seeing color," as Garman put it, means that the radical potentialities of addressing difference as structural inequality are neutralized in the public sphere, and in one's self-perception as well.

Scholar Patricia Williams writes, "The words of race are like windows into the most private vulnerable parts of the self."[29] In that sense, Rod Garman was requesting more anonymity in our interview than just a pseudonym, he was also angling at a shift in framework—not wishing to see his name follow a phrase like "black graduate" or "black football star." Like many black and white graduates I've spoken with across the decades, Garman was reluctant to use the words "black," "white," or "race." As poet and scholar Audre Lorde observed, "Too often, we pour the energy needed for recognizing and exploring difference into pretending those differences are insurmountable barriers, *or that they do not exist at all* [emphasis added]. . . . [W]e do not develop tools for using human difference as a springboard for creative change within our lives."[30]

On the field, "difference" is equated with strife and is pressed behind the helmet's grill, the blue "M" the only alliance allowed. And yet despite those limits, new modes of interacting and new friendships were possible on the integrated team. For most black female students of that era, however, such experiences were far more elusive. Football, as a fraternity, a ritual space of masculine bonding, and an operation staffed and run, traditionally and presently, by men, designates only a few specific and narrow roles for girls. In 1967, when Lemon Street High closed and black 1971 graduate Sammie Dean Williams entered Marietta High, it made all the difference in the world that she was black, and a girl.

SAMMIE DEAN WILLIAMS at fifty-eight looked just like Sammie Dean at eighteen—dimples and all—and I told her so. "Oh quit!" she said, pleased. Fiddling a little nervously with her teabag, she drew in her breath: "Now, ask me your questions." Dean grew up playing sports. "I think I would have gotten better if I would have pursued it [in high school]," she told me. "I would have gone out for different sports teams, but when I got to [Marietta High], to me, all of that was gone . . . the majorettes, the cheerleading, the athletic sports."[31] The rich extracurricular life she had envisioned was, she felt, impossible at MHS. Martha Richards had much the same experience: she was a championship track athlete in junior high and a self-professed "tomboy" who loved baseball and basketball. At MHS, she didn't make the girls' basketball team freshman year and felt alienated by how few black students were invited onto the courts and fields in 1966–67. "I don't know why" she said, but it was "much harder for girls than boys" to infiltrate athletics at the high school. That loss, she said, reminiscing on the community-building power of "rec" games and youth leagues back on the Lemon Street of her childhood, was a painful one.

Although studies have shown that black male students of the desegregation era typically had a more difficult time than their female peers in transitioning from all-black junior highs to integrated high schools, at Marietta High, the centrality of football culture meant that the opposite was true for many black female students of that time.[32] For Williams, the double whammy of leaving the Lemon Street community behind and facing the ultracompetitive atmosphere of white-dominated cheerleading, majorettes, and band at Marietta High was paralyzing. Sports, which had been a joyful, central part of school life at Lemon Street, proved just another sphere of "isolation," as Martha Richards put it, at Marietta High. There were not multiple access points to the majorettes or the band as there were for football—those boys not good enough for junior varsity played ninth-grade ball or "B team." An extracurricular culture dominated by a sport she couldn't play, ensconced in groups of all-white girls who intimated her, dissuaded Williams from more reachable goals like girls' basketball. Williams even remembered that she and many of her black peers didn't cheer along with white students at pep rallies—the one seemingly gender- and race-inclusive Blue Devil football space—because "they weren't black cheers, they were white people's cheers." There were no Lemon Street Show Stoppers, that's for sure, whose beautiful flamboyance drew black and white crowds to annual parades. The Marietta band "need[ed]," Williams said, "to get some soul." Throughout her time at MHS, Williams felt that she was "just there for school, and school alone," minus the club meetings, practices, and rehearsals—the ways in which students other than athletes find a role "onstage."

The richness of football culture at Lemon Street, including all-black cheerleaders and dancers of course but also, importantly, a band chock full of black female students, meant that the nearly monolithic whiteness of MHS football culture affected the ability of former Lemon Streeters to adjust and flourish. Terri Arnold, a 1969 MHS graduate, played in the celebrated Lemon Street High marching band (a band that her father, a deacon and activist in the community, helped create when he insisted before the school board that if Marietta High had a band, then Lemon Street should have one too). Playing in the Marietta band was not attractive to Arnold. The band at Lemon Street had been a big family; her father was a "band parent" at Lemon Street, but at Marietta High, the band students, director, and parents were a group of white strangers.

Yet sports did offer a refuge for a handful of black girls in those first years of desegregation. The few black players on the girls' basketball team found in it a welcome release from racial tension in the halls and classrooms and also an inroad to the "in" crowd of football players and cheerleaders. The only black senior to win a superlative in 1970, Lena Bennett Evans-Smith— Most Athletic—was seasoned in the politics of desegregation. She arrived at Marietta High with the small cohort of 1966–67 integrators. One of a hand-picked group of high-achieving black students and white students, Evans-Smith met periodically with the guidance counselor, Edna Lee, to talk about how desegregation was progressing and to address the issues that black students were encountering. She and the other three black students selected by Lee brought up the absence of black history in the curriculum and the lack of black student representation in sports, clubs, and school-wide traditions, the latter of which was central to the protest of 1969. When asked if she recalled the Homecoming protest, she said she only remembered being asked, by a group of black classmates, to boycott the girls' basketball team, on which she was a star player. "Are the black football players boycotting their team?" she asked. Because they were not—of course not—she insisted that neither would she sacrifice her team and her passion to the protest agenda.[33]

The acceptance, even celebration, of black football players in many ways reinforced the marginality experienced by black students who had or sought no place in football culture. For black students who did gain an entrée, such status was not easily surrendered. Basketball was that opening for Evans-Smith and her black teammates. Although girls' basketball attracted crowds of dozens rather than football's thousands, it was a crucial lever for black girls who sought a place for themselves in athletic culture at the high school. Evans-Smith called the desegregation process "very hard," marked by "animosity" and fighting "that first year" (the first year of full desegregation, 1967–68). But she caught her stride on the basketball team, leaving behind the fear and tension of her freshman year. By senior year, she was one of five black players, all of whom, in her telling, were "very good friends" with the white players. If girls' basketball meant bit parts, the team was nonetheless a link to local stars—football players, cheerleaders, and their circles. Still a statuesque beauty forty years later, Evans-Smith won the popularity at MHS that would have been hers at Lemon Street and has a uniquely sunny view of the desegregation era. "I'm proud of Marietta High," she said, for the "smooth sailing" that characterized the period after her freshman year in 1966. For Sammie Dean Williams, quiet among the cheering fans, and Terri Arnold, missing Lemon Street, that kind of belonging was impossible at Marietta. For Arnold, it was anathema— she didn't want an integrated life at Marietta; she wanted her old life back, her home community and high school. Marietta High embodied being "lost" and "not really cared about," and no number of Friday nights cheering on the integrated Blue Devils would change that.[34]

Football culture remained the dominion of white students throughout the early desegregation years. The 1967 team was anchored by several excellent black players, but pep club, band, majorettes, and flag corps—the trappings of football culture—took longer to integrate substantially. Brenda Russaw McCrae managed to integrate the B-team cheerleading squad in 1971 and was captain of an otherwise all-white squad by 1973. She recalled that cheerleading was an important cultural conduit to the social life that fomented around football and its black and white stars. The black cheer-leaders and majorettes of the early seventies were harbingers of change, and black Homecoming queens literally donned the mantle of that new era.

Bedecked in white dresses and (in the contemporary ritual at MHS) escorted by their fathers to signal eligibility, the girls on Homecoming Court participate in a tradition that echoes the sartorial and cultural ways of Southern debutante societies and distinguishes the girls on the court as the community's best young women.[35] In that context, Brenda McCrae's election as Homecoming queen in 1973 signifies a transformation not just of racial politics at the high school, but also of the status of young black women in the broader community. The cape that was draped around McCrae's shoulders was "ancient as gold," as she put it, and perhaps, in some ways, as heavy.[36] Her smile in the yearbook suggests equal parts joy and trepidation. Dreadlocks having long ago banished her high school bob, forty years after her victory, McCrae speculated unsentimentally that she won "because [she] split the vote": black students who voted as a bloc for the single black contender outnumbered the split votes for a host of white nominees. There may be some mathematical sense to McCrae's reasoning, but her high school years were rife with evidence that being black no longer meant being marginal at MHS. The 1967 yearbook, in which black faces are found almost solely in the class picture pages, and the 1972 yearbook, in which a black female student was selected for "Best Looking" and a black male for "Mr. MHS," demonstrate the pace of change at MHS. But the little revolutions of the seventies—as black students formed and joined clubs, won places among Valentine, prom, and Homecoming royalty, and distinguished themselves academically—were slow to grow substantially. White students continued to dominate the socially and academically elite realms at the high school. It was not until the early 2000s that the B-team and varsity cheerleading squads consistently counted more than two black cheerleaders among their ranks, and the honor graduates who proceed first at graduation are always majority white, despite their contemporary minority status in the student body.

Traditionally supported by deeply rooted white families, the football program has both mirrored and shaped the tensions that have arisen as Marietta's student population has become more African American, Latino, and low-income. Football has remained central to changing articulations of Blue Devil community and to the identity Marietta High administrators and many white graduates wish to project. In the intervening years since desegregation, football culture has been transformed from a good old boys club—as many refer to Southern sports, politics, and business dominated by elite whites—to a much wider community that continues to diversify. Along with clubs and football-focused extracurriculars, the fan base looks different, too; girls need not be cheerleaders, majorettes (a tradition whose fringed boots and batons went the way of the dodo), or star athletes to find a place in Blue Devil football culture.

THE EXPERIENCES OF low-income students of color who weren't players but were avid fans suggest that football culture can constitute a site for seeing and understanding race and class difference as integral, rather than inimical, to the Marietta High community. As a transplant from Miami and an isolated, new ninth grader at Marietta High, 2007 graduate Jeannelly Castro had to explain over and over to her new peers that she was not Mexican or "mixed black and white," but Dominican. In Miami, she explained, you were Cuban or Haitian or Nicaraguan, not clumped into one indistinct category like "Hispanic." She soon made sense of Marietta's more whittled down racial lexicon and found her niche at the high school.

As a member of a service club for MHS's young women of color called STARS, she sold concessions on Fridays at football games with other STARS girls. Yet Castro would have gone to the games anyway: "Everybody went . . . it didn't matter what race you were."[37] Although her social group at school was composed almost exclusively of black and Latino classmates—"you cling to what you're comfortable with"—she claimed that she made friends with white students in her classes and activities and that her transition to majority white environments in college and in her job was seamless. That job will soon allow her to move out of her mom's apartment on Franklin Road, a low-income, reputedly high-crime stretch of apartments, but Castro has no interest in leaving Marietta. "Something always brings me back," she confessed, grinning. Like white graduate Sonny Birch's daughter, Megan, a fourth-generation Blue Devil, Castro would like to raise a family in Marietta, send her children to Marietta High, and bring them to Northcutt to watch the Blue Devils play.

Football's rituals and traditions have, from the perspective of some, cultivated a community where students from all backgrounds equally belong. Football as a stage offers a powerful performance of interracial and cross-class unity. Shikera Cook, a 1998 black graduate, grew up in Baptistown and was raised by her mother and grandmother. A shy but poised woman with a dazzling smile, Cook was a struggling student transformed by the local mentoring program in which she now volunteers. Referring to a page of notes she'd brought to our interview, Cook described Marietta High as "family-oriented [and] generational," dedicated to "building legacies" through traditions like the Homecoming parade on the Marietta Square and football games at Northcutt Stadium.[38] After high school, Cook left Marietta for college but returned when she became pregnant in her junior year. Although she eventually got her business degree, she worked as a substitute teacher at her son's elementary school to make ends meet. When asked if her devotion to the Blue Devils endures, she replied in the same charming sing-song as many older white graduates: "I'm blue devil born and blue devil bred, and when I die I'll be blue devil dead."[39]

"It all comes together" at Marietta High, claimed Cook. She attested to the community fostered by tradition, but she also spoke forthrightly about the presence of "haves" and "have-nots" at the high school and the profound impact of "generational" wealth on social mobility. Revealingly, Cook reconciled colorblind camaraderie at the high school with structural inequality through the legacy of Lemon Street—where her grandmother was a student—and its rich traditions and history. Cook's reflections on class and the legacy of Lemon Street shed light on how black Mariettans narrated and contested the city's destruction of its housing projects—projects that played a central role in the cultural and physical geography of black Marietta, as well as the trajectory of the team.

The question of racial justice and the fortunes of the city's poor overlap with the fortunes of the team, which has historically drawn some of its best players from low-income communities in the city, anchored by the projects in Baptistown, Louisville, and Lemon Street.[41] "Those projects bred some good ball players," mused Mayor Steve Tumlin a little wistfully when I asked him about the city's demolition of all its public housing.[40] In the aughts, the city-wide debate over the fate of Marietta's housing projects further revealed football as a field of negotiation over possible futures and never-distant pasts.

Public discussion around "saving" Marietta's projects highlighted two warring visions—in one, low-income black students are integral to tradition and success in football, and in the other, those same students drive a resegregation trend that imperils the high school's reputation and stability. From the perspective of black Mariettans protesting the demolitions, city leaders were dismissive of the deep roots of Fort Hill—the oldest of the projects, dating to 1941—and those of the black Mariettans who lived there: "It's more than a housing project, it's a community," claimed Baptistown native and Lemon Street High alum, James Gober.[42] For other Blue Devil fans and graduates, public housing closures were deemed detrimental to the Blue Devil roster, which by the year 2000 was majority black. And for some, like Coach James Richards, the demolition represented both—a threat to the fortunes of the team and a lack of commitment on the part of the city to its black residents and students.[43]

As Marietta High began to resegregate rapidly in the aughts, the Marietta Housing Authority designated the city's five housing projects for demolition. Although residents were guaranteed subsidized or "Section 8" housing within the city limits if they desired it, more than half ended up outside the city (and districted for Cobb schools instead) in the relocations of 2009 and 2011.[44] Relocations of low-income black families reduced the numbers of low-income black students in Marietta's schools; in that sense, the closings of the projects may have slowed resegregation. But at what cost? Black families who had been in Marietta for generations had histories rooted in the projects and the surrounding neighborhoods, and when the demolition of Fort Hill began in the spring of 2013, protestors and former denizens turned out to register their anger and grief.[45]

AS IN MANY CITIES, redevelopment in Marietta is tied to a history of urban renewal—the process through which municipalities bought up land deemed "blighted," that is, occupied by low-income people of color, and turned those properties into profitable private developments.[46] All but one of the early-desegregation-era black graduates who have spoken in these pages were raised in what locals call "the projects," referring both to Marietta's government housing and the neighborhoods that surrounded those complexes. Today, the black student population at Marietta High is more economically diverse than in the 1970s. Black students are far less likely to come from the neighborhoods of Louisville or Baptistown, but those place names resonate across the years and remain the map on which many older black Mariettans trace memory, struggle, and solidarity.

While students from areas like Baptistown have historically been welcome in the Blue Devil football family and even critical to the team's success, they have also been the students most likely to fall behind academically.[47] One such player was Blue Devil halfback Tavio Hutson, a Fort Hill resident who, with his family, was relocated "in district" when the Housing Authority began moving residents of Fort Hill in 2012. According to the Marietta Housing Authority's director, they took care to ensure that the players who came from Fort Hill would not have to leave MHS. Tavio was a junior at Marietta and a promising athlete; he was also a perilously struggling student. When I talked with Tavio and his mother, they were about to be relocated out of Fort Hill and were looking at apartments in the city that would allow Tavio to continue at MHS. A 1971 black graduate, Oscar Brinson, a key figure in the restive 1968–69 school year at MHS, summed up the social dynamics of his high school years by insisting that if they weren't athletes, black students "weren't noticed" at Marietta High—they could claim no place on the community's primary "stage."[48] For Tavio, such an assessment probably resonates. Distinguishing himself in his remaining time with the Blue Devils could conceivably produce a partial or full college scholarship, and leaving MHS would have jeopardized the tutoring and faculty support that kept his head above water academically and his college hopes alive.

The belief in football as a ticket to college and even more is as much a shibboleth in Marietta as other football towns. Such hopes are palpable in Tavio's and his mother's talk about the future. Sporting just the shadow of a mustache and the soft features of a teenager still several years from adulthood, Tavio was not the strapping fellow I expected. His manner was shy and hesitant, and I strained to hear his voice over the wheezing air conditioner in their apartment. Active at his church, well-liked on the team, and part of several overlapping, integrated social circles, Tavio is "known" at school, he told me. I thought of celebrated running back Aaron Gullatte, who came to MHS before full desegregation, accompanied by unbearably high expectations and white scrutiny. Yet precipices can soften into overlooks on the shifting terrain of memory; Gullatte had smilingly observed in my conversation with him that "athletes are more accepted than the regular student body because athletes have names. Everybody in the stadium knows you; you don't know them, but they know you." The fantasy of social intimacy—that of fans who "know" the players—is critical to colorblind camaraderie at the register of the school community.

Division I football is a dream lived by few Marietta players, like Baptistowner and longtime MHS coach James Richards.[49] That dream and the prestige of the "M"—the intoxicating applause and glare of the lights— can obscure for low-income players like Tavio the financial realities and academic challenges of higher education after the Blue Devils. The distance between a promising tenth-grade starter and a recruited college player can be unbridgeable, and that distance is, too, a space of rupture in the contemporary Blue Devil community. If Tavio hopes to be courted by even a small university, he would have to gain more playing time and more impressive total yardage, and most basically, he must qualify academically. His mother knew it, too: encouraging Tavio to read to his two-year-old sister Jada, she confided that Tavio has "problems . . . reading," and those are not nearly so bad, she said, as the ones he has with math. A world away from the intensive personal attention typical in small International Baccalaureate and Advanced Placement courses, Tavio takes classes with twenty-five or thirty struggling students like himself, instructed by teachers laboring under the burden of relentless testing. Although football at MHS provided him with crucial motivation, it cannot confer a high school diploma or guarantee college admission and a scholarship. But Tavio is thoughtful, conscientious, and focused on the future and, for now at least, a well-loved son in the Blue Devil family. For black students outside the embrace of football, the demolition of Fort Hill had the potential to mean a final exile from Blue Devil territory, where tony live-work-play developments would rise from empty swaths of "historic black Marietta."

By the spring of 2013, Fort Hill, the last project, had indeed been reduced to a bald patch of land. That lot and the other undeveloped parcels formerly home to the projects were managed by the Housing Authority; its leadership was sanguine about the waning of the recession and the arrival of private investors and high-end condominiums. Yet tensions over redevelopment—and unspoken anxieties about resegregation—continued to simmer. They eventually climaxed in a city-wide debate over a sixty-eight-million-dollar redevelopment bond proposed by the mayor. Proponents of the bond promised revivification of Franklin Road and, with it, the city school system.

It fell in part to Ruben Sands, a black 1979 graduate of MHS, to mediate the highly politicized matrix of the football program, school leadership, and city council: in 2012 and 2013, he served as "community liaison" to the Housing Authority (a mayoral appointment). Football's colorblind camaraderie links past and present in both material and metaphorical ways; for Sands, the ethos and its ritualizing through the season's rhythms and team traditions have determined the texture of his daily life from early adolescence to late middle age. Since high school, he has moved lithely across boundaries and between worlds, and he was a wise choice for a local diplomat. As community liaison, he deftly balanced the desires of Marietta's white power brokers and those of the folks he grew up with in Baptistown. In 2016, he became the councilmember representing Ward 5 (Marietta's historically black ward, encompassing Baptistown and the former sites of all the city's projects) upon the suspension of that ward's representative.[50] The Marietta City Council of 2014–2016 had two black members—the most in its history.[51]

Sands shaped a public persona and professional niche from football culture. At a game in the fall of 2012, I spied him arranging equipment on the sidelines; his managerial trot dragged a bit, but he wouldn't be outdone by the bevy of student managers dashing about him. Sands never played on the team, but by the time I met him, he had been a manager for the better part of thirty-five years. When it wasn't football season, he assisted with basketball and baseball—"doing the clock [and] equipment"—but football was his great love.[52] In high school, Blue Devil football defined his social world and his status among his peers. He was raised in the projects in

Baptistown, cheek by jowl with the other kids in his building and the middle-class black families right nearby. The football team was similarly mixed and, in Sands's portrayal, a space of meaningful race and class reconciliation. "I didn't do sports, and I felt like [managing] was a way of contributing—at least you could meet the people and have fun with the upperclassmen." Sands's sense of belonging attests to the Blue Devils' broad definition of "team," at least in his moment in the late seventies. He remembered, "If you was a manager you . . . stood out with the players as well. Once they introduce the players, they normally introduce the managers. . . . You'd go out onto the court with them or onto the field." Delight suffused Sands's face as he mused on Northcutt in football season. MGM could have produced no set as glamorous, as seductive, as the brightly lit football field surrounded by thousands of expectant fans.

Comfortable, open exchange with wealthy white Mariettans and free movement through their social spaces speak to the carnivalesque experience of Marietta football culture for some low-income black students.[53] Sands may not have been a hulking lineman or a fleet-footed receiver totting up blocks and yardage, but he was a Blue Devil, through and through, and still is. He claimed that because of his friendships with the players, even though he grew up in the projects and had very little disposable income of his own, he "hung with . . . the elite people. . . . I got to go to the country club back then and eat lunch with some of the guys, the players that I knew that were upperclassmen [whose] famil[ies] had a little money."

Sands's reflections, perhaps even more than the black players of his era, underscore the contradictions of colorblind camaraderie: "knowing" and "being known" mean both continuing to work two jobs (Sands is employed at a local funeral home and a hospital) and enjoying the power and prestige of serving as a city councilman. If there is redemption in continuity, or structural change possible through a seat at the proverbial table, then perhaps Sands's trajectory—and its dramatic shaping by Blue Devil ball—offers an encouraging metaphor for Marietta's own. And if football endures as uniquely able to bring Mariettans under its banners, then perhaps a different kind of camaraderie is possible through it. "There was still a lot of stuff I could have been doing at my age in my life," Sands told me, "But I feel like there's nothing like Friday night football at Marietta High."

⊀ 2 ⊁

FIFTY YEARS OF "FREEDOM"

School Choice and Structural Inequality
in Marietta City Schools

"AS I LOOK BACK, I see they were just people," Daphne Delk told me, recalling her experience desegregating Marietta High.[1] "They were in a comfort zone and I was scratching around that comfort zone and making it very uncomfortable. To say that they should've went my way would've been selfish in my way of thinking. Because they were just—they were used to what they were used to." As the sole black student at Marietta High School in the 1964–65 school year, Delk endured the isolation and the epithets. It wasn't hostility enough for headlines, like that of other cities, but it hurt no less. On bad days, she took her lunch to her favorite teacher's classroom where the quiet friendliness of his company soothed her nerves, made her less alone in the all-white-but-for-her high school.[2] And yet the "they" to whom Delk referred were not the white students who marginalized her, or the administrators at MHS, or even white leaders in Marietta. "They" are the black Mariettans Delk grew up with: the neighbors who cared for her, the black teachers who sang her praises, the Lemon Street principal whom she had always admired. "They" were the very people for whom Delk felt she was fighting.

As Delk's recollection suggests, her choice to desegregate MHS under what would become the city's "freedom of choice" plan wasn't very free— the cost of the resources she needed and opportunities she craved was losing her community, *any* community, once she left Lemon Street and began her lonely sojourn at MHS. As in other Southern places, in Marietta freedom of choice was born from segregationist resistance to the 1954 Supreme Court decision in *Brown v. Board of Education.* Since the 1990s, in Southern school districts and districts across the country, choice has enjoyed a renaissance as a centerpiece of contemporary free market education reform. In present-day Marietta, although school choice is intended to slow resegregation by drawing affluent white students back into Marietta schools, the cost of "freedom of choice" is the same as it was in the 1960s: educational justice for children of color.

The Life and Afterlife of School Choice in the South

In the first days of April in 1966, almost every household in Marietta, black and white, received a letter with the following message: "Dear Parents: Our community has adopted a school desegregation plan. We will no longer have separate schools for children of different races. . . ."[3] The letter went on to explain that Marietta was adopting a school choice plan: all parents could select a city school for their child, regardless of race.

School choice has a long tenure in desegregation history.[4] In the early desegregation era, governors across the South engaged in "massive resistance" to school desegregation.[5] The Southern architects of private school plans, tuition voucher programs, and freedom of choice were articulating a strategy with limited shelf life in their moment, but crafting a conservative ideology oriented toward future battles over the relationship between individual rights and the collective good—a politics greatly influential in the school reform movements of the 1990s and 2000s.[6]

As early as 1954, Georgia voters ratified a constitutional amendment that gave the General Assembly the power to privatize the schools instead of desegregating them.[7] Such private school plans saw prompt battering in the courts; in Arkansas, for example, a district court ruled against the closure of Central High, famous home of the Little Rock Nine's desegregation efforts.[8] In Virginia, exemplar of massive resistance, tuition vouchers eventually came under fire—because they funneled state monies to white children wishing to attend private schools—but not until after whole districts closed up shop for years.[9] Tuition vouchers for private education were the only option for some white Virginian students in the wake of public school closures in three communities—one of which, Prince Edward County, educated its white students in private schools or "segregation academies" and closed its public schools for five years. Correspondence crisscrossed the South as white leaders contemplated, in vain, how to resist *Brown* by asserting local control over public schools.[10] In 1964, the Supreme Court ruled against tuition vouchers in *Griffin v. School Board of Prince Edward County* for funding private segregated education with public funds.

Freedom of choice was, similarly, a last-ditch attempt at evading *Brown*. Seventy-five percent of school districts in the South adopted freedom of choice plans in the mid-sixties because such plans followed the letter of the law but led to a mere trickle of black students into white schools.[11] Stipulating that individual black and white students could transfer schools at will, freedom of choice plans typically produced no white student desegregators (which would have required enrolling in all-black schools), placing the burden entirely on black students. As far as Southern governors and school boards were concerned, this form of token desegregation secured them federal funding (the 1964 Civil Rights Act included a provision authorizing the stripping of federal funds from segregated schools) while preserving, for the most part, "dual systems"—that is, black and white schools. The choice offered black students by these plans was between isolation in an all-white school or the limited and underresourced curriculum and facilities of their home communities.

In the early sixties, freedom of choice was a ruse, never intended to expand the options of black students, and in 1968, the Supreme Court invalidated it as a desegregation remedy in *Green v. County School Board of New Kent County*. Justice William Brennan opined: "the burden on a school board today is to come forward with a plan that promises realistically to work, and promises realistically to work now."[12] If the ends were not achieved by freedom of choice (and they demonstrably weren't—after three years, 85 percent of black students in New Kent County, Virginia, still attended all-black schools), then the means were not acceptable.[13] Without recourse to vouchers or freedom of choice, and with the major ruling in *Swann v. Charlotte-Mecklenburg Board of Education*, which sanctioned suburb-city busing to achieve desegregation, Southern school districts were compelled to desegregate in earnest.

Marietta's trajectory mirrored that of the Deep South in some, but not all, respects. It too implemented token desegregation through a freedom of choice plan after two years of minimal desegregation between 1964 and 1966.[14] However, the adoption of freedom of choice coincided with the dissolution of an agreement between Marietta and Cobb County. Because of their relatively small black populations, Cobb's and Marietta's black students all attended Marietta's all-black schools.[15] Desegregation brought the departure of the Cobb students, who enrolled in their local, formerly all-white schools. The loss of Cobb's black students left Marietta's all-black institutions with too few pupils to justify the costs of operating. By 1968, with both Lemon Street Elementary and Lemon Street High closed, Marietta had no remaining majority-black institutions. Desegregation was a fait accompli in Marietta, and forms where parents could check what school they wished to enroll their child in gathered dust in the central office. The phrase "freedom of choice" wouldn't return to school politics in Marietta for another forty years.

In the 1990s and 2000s, school choice reentered local and national discourses of education reform, powered by the national enchantment with free market economics.[16] As a strategy to improve struggling schools by forcing them to compete for students, school choice became enshrined in the federal edifice of education reform and in many states' education reform efforts.[17] The choice plans of contemporary education reform are different ideological swords, but no less double-edged, than those wielded by white politicians and school boards to fend off *Brown* in the 1960s. Court decisions of the aughts have enshrined the individual freedom to choose at the cost of integrated schooling, and in some cases, the separation of church and state.[18] It is this value—the value of choice as an end, rather than merely a means—that is at the heart of contemporary choice programs and increasingly dominant in education reform.[19]

Marietta's school choice program, implemented in 2007, is the city's only iteration of free market education policy, although its language courses through system documents. An internal "branding" document discussing Marietta City Schools' "seals, logos, and slogans" identifies Marietta families and students as "customers," school curriculum as "products and services," and the schools system's successes as "the value we deliver over the competition."[20] It follows then that the city schools are a consumer good to be effectively marketed and "managed." Although some scholars equate market-oriented school reform with privatization, Marietta's use of "brand management" language points to the difficult position of the contemporary public school system: trying valiantly to retain its students, it must offer a "competitive" product, even if such terms seem to defy the very ethos of public education—a collective, rather than a consumer, enterprise.[21]

After the failure of a short-lived charter school in the early 2000s and a futile effort to establish one in 2016, Marietta has no charter schools and no voucher program.[22] Tuition voucher programs, another echo from the *Brown* era, saw rising popularity across the country in the aughts.[23] Despite the absence of these other signature free market education innovations, Marietta's leadership has demonstrated deep faith in the gospel of choice to bring affluent Marietta families back into the fold. Through Marietta's school choice policy—often referred to as "open enrollment"—local families have the option of attending any of the seven primary schools in the city, if the school has room. History, geography, and the choice policy have rendered West Side Elementary the far-and-away favorite, and it has become entrenched as the city's only low-poverty, majority-white school that does not have application-based admissions. Its role in the city system illustrates the ambiguous impact of choice. Open enrollment at West Side further concentrates low-income students of color in the other elementaries by drawing higher-income students and their parents away from their own neighborhood schools. Yet, from the perspective of the school board and West Side's white boosters, the school functions as a bulwark against the total resegregation of Marietta's schools by keeping those higher income, mostly white families in the public system.

Marietta families have only one public choice for grades six through eight—the Marietta Sixth Grade Academy followed by Marietta Middle School—but the city's eight elementary schools are themed "choice academies" with open enrollment across Marietta's seven wards.[24] Only one school—a grades three to five magnet, Marietta Center for Advanced Academics (MCAA)—has admissions criteria; the rest are open to any student in the city. The City Schools website exhorts local parents to "choose a space where young minds will grow," but judging by the city's choice program statistics, most parents would choose (were there room and transportation provided) the only school with low poverty and consistently high scores—West Side.[25] West Side Elementary is majority white with more than 80 percent of students meeting or exceeding state standards at the third- and fifth-grade levels and only 31 percent of students eligible for free or reduced-price lunch. The other six elementary schools (excluding the selective magnet school) are at least 60 percent black and Latino with only 10 to 45 percent of students exceeding expectations on the fifth-grade reading assessments. At these schools, at least 50 percent and as many as 90 percent of students are on free or reduced-price meals. (See Tables 2.1a, 2.1b, and 2.2).[26] Marietta's choice plan means that any parent across the city can choose West Side, but that once West Side fills up, parents must wait for their child's name to inch to the top of the waiting list and, additionally, must be able to drive their children to and from school each day.

Table 2.1a. 2010–2011 Enrollment Percentages by Ethnicity

School	Latino	Black	White	Asian
A.L. Burruss	10%	49%	34%	2%
Dunleith	32%	59%	4%	1%
Hickory Hills	44%	41%	12%	1%
Lockheed	42%	48%	6%	2%
Park Street	65%	30%	3%	0%
Sawyer Road	47%	32%	12%	4%
West Side	7%	26%	62%	2%
MCAA	11%	31%	39%	15%

Table 2.1b. 2010–2011 Percentage of Students on Free or Reduced-Price Meals

A.L. Burruss	54%
Dunleith	79%
Hickory Hills	83%
Lockheed	78%
Park Street	90%
Sawyer Road	73%
West Side	31%
MCAA	27%

Table 2.2. 2010–2011 Fifth-Grade Criterion-Referenced Competency Test Reading Scores by School: Percentage That Exceed Expectations

A.L. Burruss	42%
Dunleith	10%
Hickory Hills	39%
Lockheed	19%
Park Street	20%
Sawyer Road	20%
West Side	62%
MCAA	85%

Although choice in Marietta and elsewhere is ostensibly for everyone, low-income students who are bus-reliant are much less likely to apply for a transfer.[27] Just as important as which schools families choose are the schools out of which they transfer. Recent research on choice and "bounded rationality" suggests that some low-income parents may not choose to leave a struggling school because the students, parents, and curriculum at another, ostensibly higher-achieving, school may be alienating or intimidating to parents accustomed to their school and its community.[28] Marietta's choice data show evidence of such a trend: the two schools that are fed by Franklin Road—where Marietta's poorest students are concentrated—also have, over the years, seen the fewest families use choice.[29] One of these two, Park Street, the system's "worst" elementary, sees an average of only three students a year transfer out, versus Burruss, considered the system's second-best school, from which an average of five students leave per year (almost always for West Side).[30] The majority of students using choice each year since 2007 come from Hickory Hills, which twenty years ago enjoyed status equal to that of West Side: Hickory Hills is fed by a historically white area that has seen an influx of Latino families in recent years. The school now has the system's second-highest Latino enrollment (see Table 2.1a).

Although the range of schools to which students choose to transfer is diversifying slightly, the dominance of West Side and Burruss has only been reinforced over the years between 2007 and 2013. In Marietta, choice is raising the profile of favored schools and further damaging the reputation of struggling ones by reifying perceptions about schools into enrollment trends. Employed mainly by white and higher-income families, choice appeals to parents and students who might otherwise leave the system, those who are seen as critical to the academic vitality of the high school. However, the academic success of students of color hangs in the balance.

IN A QUIET ROOM at Marietta City Schools' central office, eight white families watched the associate superintendent, Dayton Hibbs, fill a metal hopper with small numbered balls. After a few moments, a black parent joined the group and then an Indian father and his daughter. Once each ball was dropped in and the corresponding name and number read aloud, the West Side lottery began. There were only two kindergarten spots at West Side and thirty hopeful families (you didn't have to be present at the drawing to secure your spot). Jennifer Fischer, a teacher at MHS with whom I had become friendly, was among the parents. Her youngest child, Brian, was entered in the drawing for West Side. If he got in, her other two children would automatically be admitted with him—a common policy in school districts and an enormous boon for a mother of three. Jenny's kids and the others who had come with their parents were restless, probably wondering how a sunny Friday afternoon had been overtaken by this stultifying errand. Looking around, she offered a little wave to me and a smile to her fellow mothers, also attempting to quiet their fidgeting children and their own nerves. Finally Hibbs began to turn the little wheel of fortune, the balls bouncing around with a metallic jangle, like acorns dropping onto a tin roof. He explained that the first two names drawn would be admitted to West Side, the other 28 would be placed on the waiting list, in the order that they tumbled out of the little wheel. For a long moment, no little ball volunteered itself, and the tense room reverberated with the steady plink-plink of the machine. A numbered ball popped into Hibbs's waiting hand. "M 22!" he called out, "Brian Fischer." "Oh my God!" Jenny shrieked, as she hugged Brian and his bewildered siblings. "It's you, sweetie! It's you!"

Such a scene was impossible just a decade ago, before the destruction of Marietta's housing projects, before the establishment of the school choice policy, before the renaissance of West Side Elementary. In the early 2000s, West Side was fed by both an upper-middle-class white enclave and Baptistown, a historically black community anchored by Lyman Homes, a public housing development. Although many of Marietta's older white alums—the blue-horn-wearing fans who yell themselves hoarse every Friday night—had gone to West Side as kids, they had become less willing to send their own children. Over the decades, West Side had become more than 50 percent black and was no more highly regarded than the city's other six elementaries. During the early 2000s, A.L. Burruss was Marietta's "white elementary." Burruss was not all white; it simply had not yet "tipped"—become majority black and Latino.[31] Still a favored school, Burruss is the star of the choice lottery when West Side has no spots. But how West Side became what parents prayed and lobbied and moved across town for, what they pinned their lottery ball hopes on, is a lesson in race and power—an increasingly urgent lesson, as choice continues to gain cultural and political momentum in districts across the nation.

The Politics and Peril of Choice: The West Side Story

West Side Elementary was not the school Jill Mutimer remembered when she, a white 1984 graduate, and her husband moved back to Marietta from Buckhead, Atlanta's wealthiest community. The Mutimers had a toddler, and they decided to forego their elite neighborhood north of Atlanta where the city's best private schools beckon from lush campuses. The northwest corner of Marietta, where West Side was located and where Jill would eventually run for the school board, was their destination. Built in 1949, West Side Elementary was the alma mater of many elite Mariettans: long before school quality had to have quantities affixed to it, West Side was the city's gem. Mutimer assumed it still was. "I could send my kids to any school I wanted to," she said, naming a well-known Atlanta prep school. "I could send 'em, and I could take 'em," she continued, but "[Marietta] was where I wanted my kids to grow up—it was important to me, it affected my life, it affected who I was—the type of environment, the type of friendships I have. And I wanted that for them."[32] Mutimer was going to make hers a "generational" Blue Devil family and see her children, and ideally her grandchildren, through the city schools. But when Mutimer and her husband moved back, West Side's 2002–2003 student body was only 39 percent white, its test scores were middling, and West Side qualified for Title I funding, the federal aid granted to high-poverty schools. A consultant by trade, Mutimer diagnosed West Side's problem as "perception"—local parents didn't fully trust the school's leadership and rumors had circulated that the teaching staff wasn't what it used to be. Certainly these more specific concerns could have existed inside the larger one: race. "Perception" provided a means of talking about the preferences of local whites (for a majority-white school) without saying so outright. To address the perception problem, Mutimer hosted a large gathering at her house to reintroduce her neighbors to their elementary school and voice questions and concerns to its principal.

Around the same time that Mutimer was recruiting parents in the leafy cul-de-sacs of northwest Marietta, Mary Ansley Southerland, also a white graduate of 1984, transferred her daughter into West Side. Southerland recounted that she and other families were paying high tuition for private school while their city system struggled, and they decided it was time to reinvest in their neighborhood elementary. Southerland recalled, "We recruited [students] . . . working at the kindergarten level [getting] new kids coming in. We banded together, and held hands and jumped in."[33] By 2009, West Side was overenrolled, and white students had jumped back up to 62 percent of the total student body. (See Table 2.3.) No doubt Southerland and Mutimer's activism brought a contingent of white families back into the system, but much was brewing in the school system. Together with the demolition of Lyman Homes and the dispersing of its mostly black students into other schools in 2007, West Side became a "choice academy," opening enrollment to students across the city. The following fall, the system's elementaries were all converted to "choice academies," and open enrollment was instituted across all seven schools; the eighth, the magnet school, remained application-based.[34]

According to 1983 white graduate and former city councilman Johnny Sinclair, who also works as a realtor, these days, parents "go berserk to get their kids into West Side."[35] Although Mutimer contended that West Side today is no better an education than any other elementary, Sinclair said what few will: "race drives the whole thing." West Side, he suggested, may be no better an education than the other elementaries, but it is majority white, the only majority-white school in the city system (in 2010–2011, its friendly competitor, Burruss, was 34 percent white and 49 percent black). In March of 2013, Fort Hill Homes, the last of the city's public housing developments to be demolished, met its end, meaning West Side no longer drew from any concentrated low-income areas. West Side's whiteness serves a critical purpose, one that the city's mayor admitted to me he "wouldn't want to talk about at a meeting of the NAACP."[36] Through its now-sterling reputation and ever-higher test scores, West Side is retaining the mostly white upper-middle-class families who would

Table 2.3. West Side Enrollment Percentages by Ethnicity

	2005–2006	2007–2008	2010–2011
White	34%	54%	61%
Black	51%	32%	26%
Latino	9%	8%	7%
Asian	2%	1%	2%
Multiracial	4%	5%	4%

otherwise flee the system to private or parochial schools. Who chooses West Side, who chooses to leave the system, and who has no choice is the West Side story.

Although it is just one school, West Side's trajectory is the trajectory of choice in Marietta, and the impact of choice on the city schools testifies to what choice critics say will happen anywhere—choice programs will destabilize struggling schools and further marginalize the students who attend them. But choice, rejoins Mutimer and other advocates, is what good education is all about: good education *produces* choices—which college to go to, what job to take, what city to live in—and it is the reigning ideology in school choice circles that *choices* produce good schools. The parents who lobbied to return "the community" to West Side had a choice; most had or would have sent their children to private school—but they chose public education. As Mary Ansley Southerland put it exuberantly, "public education is the underpinning of our city . . . our whole civilization actually!"

How choice proponents in Marietta experienced desegregation, race, and power in high school has a great deal to do with how they frame their contemporary school politics. When white students like Sinclair, Southerland, and Mutimer got to Marietta High in the early eighties, desegregation was a fait accompli. As in many districts around the country, the desegregation victories of the seventies were not yet dissolving into resegregation. Some schools like Marietta High, in cities on the fringes of even bigger cities, had realized the ideal of the then thirty-year-old court decision. Marietta High had essentially achieved racial balance—that is, the percentage of black and white students at the high school reflected the makeup of the city of Marietta.[37] When I asked these white graduates about their social lives at Marietta High, they uniformly testified that "[race] didn't matter." Enjoying the leisure of ignoring race if they wished, these graduates experienced whiteness not as a distinct advantage but as a kind of foil for cultural differences coded as "diversity," and in the eighties at MHS, more difference was socially permitted than ever before. A gay couple attended the prom later in the decade, interracial dating was socially accepted (if somewhat rare), and students had integrated peer groups, teams, classes, clubs, parties, and dances. Black and white graduates took in stride, and perhaps even for granted, that their desegregated lives were the product of a more than century-long, radical struggle for the rights and dignity of marginalized people.

MARIETTA'S FRANKLIN ROAD is the battleground for that struggle today. A mile-long stretch of forlorn apartment complexes and deserted strip malls on the city's eastern edge, the area is currently populated by low-income black and Latino families; the children of Franklin Road make up one-eighth of the entire city school enrollment. Franklin Road is the school system's "disaster," said ever-candid Johnny Sinclair. But it wasn't always. When Jill Mutimer was growing up in the seventies, the area was a magnet for young professionals and middle-class families. By the time Mutimer was in high school, living in an attractive subdivision near the square, Franklin Road had begun its long descent, host to rising numbers of drug deals and carjackings. In the decades since, Franklin Road's entrenched crime and economic distress have become emblematic of Marietta's fall from small town grace and its journey into urbanness. It is a bit hard to imagine Mutimer—carefully coiffed amid the designer furniture of her living room—going to parties on Franklin Road, even thirty years ago. "We all went to the same parties," she said—gatherings at white students' houses off the Square and at the apartment complexes on Franklin. Mutimer used white and black students socializing on Franklin Road to signal that Mariettans of her era didn't experience the starkly racialized geography that today's students do.

When asked if she has lasting friendships with black students from that era, Mutimer said "yes," and then, after thinking for a moment, "not as much." She was a basketball player and had a cohort of black girlfriends on the team, but her enduring friendships are with a white peer group she's had since seventh grade. Mutimer was well liked throughout school and a student leader at MHS, voted "Most Likely to Succeed" her senior year. She remembered that while in high school, she watched how problems at school were resolved. She observed that the power lay not with her teachers or even her principal but rather with the school board. "So you've wanted to be on the school board since you were fifteen?" I asked, astounded. Laughing, she admitted she "filed it away: if you ever really want to do anything you have to get on the school board." She took to the position and served three turns as chair in seven years.

Mutimer's lifestyle, her politics, her education, and her public position embody the promised riches of "choice," but she is not a "suburban warrior," since she keeps her conservative attitudes about national politics separate from local education policy.[38] Instead Mutimer fits the mold of a political type whose power in education politics has never really waned: the

"white moderate." In the late fifties and sixties, these were the Southerners—
very often middle- to upper-class white mothers—who took a pro–public
school instead of a pro-desegregation approach in the wake of resistance to
Brown. They founded organizations like HOPE (Help Our Public
Education) in Georgia, the VCPS (Virginia Committee for Public Schools)
and the CAG (Citizens' Advisory Group) in Charlotte, North Carolina, in
an effort to prevent public school closures and devise, in the case of the
CAG, equitable integration strategies.[39] Many of today's white moderates
in education politics share the aim of their predecessors: to accept racial
change in schools and "save" public education—not because it is right, but
because it is necessary.[40]

Mutimer articulates unpredictable positions: though a self-professed
"Republican, very much so," she holds the traditionally liberal opinion that
vouchers leave behind the most troubled kids and further imperil struggling schools. Unlike some of her white peers, Mutimer is nonjudgmental
about parents of color who don't financially support the Touchdown Club,
MHS's booster organization, or volunteer to work concession stands and
school fundraisers. Mutimer did not refer, as one of her white classmates
did, to "cars, fingernails, jewelry, and smartphones" as a coded assessment
of black parents' values and investment in the school.[41] She offered, instead,
that there are many reasons why low-income parents are "less involved"
than white, upper-class parents. "Life is hard," she said with a little shrug,
and that's no reason to blame the most vulnerable families in the city for
their struggles. But like many Americans and much of white Marietta, she
is not interested in schools as sites of progressive social change. Like her
moderate forbears, she will fight for public schools with no attendant racial
justice agenda. For Mutimer and for white pro–public school parents like
her, schools represent the sedimented social memory and institutionalized
traditions of a time safe from the social, economic, and cultural tumult of
contemporary Marietta.

In response to any questions about demographic change at Marietta
High or the edifice of traditions—attending football games, watching the
Homecoming parade—Mutimer replied: "It's really the same. It really is.
It's the same, it's just different kids." Mutimer's attitude is an important
window on the moderate white movement in Marietta. The actions of the
school board and school leaders demonstrate faith that even though privileged families like the Southerlands and the Mutimers have many choices,
they can be brought back to public schools with West Side's successes, by

the system's high-achieving magnet school, and by the academics of the much-touted International Baccalaureate program available at the high school. By focusing on what the system can offer high-achieving students, school leaders direct attention away from the impact of demographic and economic change in Marietta. When Mutimer was a freshman in the late seventies, she was part of a white, middle-class majority; thirty-five years later, Marietta High was almost 75 percent black and Latino and 58 percent poor.

The reluctance of school system leaders to address resegregation at the register of structural inequality—instead anxiously tracking the percentage of white families like a diminishing balance in a checking account—damages the system's ability to confront the challenges of contemporary change and answer the needs of its new majority. "There are only a small portion of the MHS faithful that are willing to speak out," said 1980 white graduate Mickey King of the school's shifting demographics, when he sought me out for a conversation about the future of Marietta High. King, like Mutimer, is a public schools crusader, but he will quickly tell you how much he believes MHS has changed since he graduated.

His is a values-oriented assessment of how little responsibility his fellow "conservative Mariettans" are taking for the future of their schools—damaged by, in King's view, both the decisions of school leaders and divestment by parents in the lives of their children and the fate of their school system.[42] Having been an outspoken opponent of Marietta Center for Advanced Academics—the science and math magnet for third through fifth graders founded in 2005—he reflected that the quality of the system relied on parents like him resisting both magnet schools and private schools:

> The less and less of us there are the worse and worse it gets for everybody. Conversely if we could just get more . . . [parents] to put their kids in the middle school [and] the high school the better it would be for everybody. But how do you convince parents to do that? They look at the demographic[s] and they say, oh my gosh I don't want my kid to be one of only two white kids in a class of thirty kids [who are all on] free lunch.[43]

King points to MCAA as the culprit when it comes to undermining the system's elementaries: "You pull 250 of your smarter kids out of your seven elementary schools—what does that do to your six other schools?" Finally, he suggests it was the advocacy of parents like him who rescued West Side from what he called "pluralism": according to King, the departure of white Mariettans from West Side would have led school leaders to "backfill" the elementary "with kids from across the district . . . from Franklin Road or wherever, and that changes your school." Rare among white Mariettans, however, is King's insistence that Blue Devil advocates talk plainly about the impact of racial and economic change on the city schools. The adoption of "race-blind" policies such as choice and a shared unwillingness among city and school board leaders to debate openly the issues of race, class, and resegregation shaping public schools forestall a critical examination of what must happen to make educational justice attainable for all of Marietta's students.

Even parents whose families "stretch back three generations or more" in Marietta, like 1992 graduate Chris Poston, are uncertain about the future of the city schools and unsure about entrusting them with their children. West Side is attractive to some of these parents, but in the long term, the maintenance of a majority-white school such as West Side is damaging to Marietta's students at many registers. The existence of a "white school," as several recent graduates of color referred to West Side, consolidates social capital and financial resources and imperils equity at the elementary level, where so much critical groundwork is laid for the city's students.[44] If white moderate support for public education is partly rooted in nostalgia for an MHS that was majority white, that support is conditional upon the success of those white graduates' children in the city schools. Poston is an affluent white alum with a plethora of choices for his children's education; he is "Old Marietta," part of a local elite composed of white families deeply rooted in the city.[45] A developer and home builder, he was hit hard by the recession—"I helped out coaching middle school football when business was so bad"—but he is still a man of means in Marietta, a native son hoping to see his town prosper again. However, he admitted that, if need be, he will leave its public schools for private alternatives.

Private schools in Marietta, like many of those in the rest of the South, are steeped in segregation-era history: rising private school enrollment indexed the intensity of white flight.[46] Contemporary Mariettans have a raft of options in the flourishing of Cobb County's private schools.[47] As Marietta school leaders seek to draw back affluent white residents, they must appeal to a private aesthetic and ethos and offer those families a vision of public education exempt from the tyranny of fairness, a place that looks more like their tree-lined street and less like the moiling, restive city.

West Side Elementary is a family tradition with the Postons: as Poston told me proudly, his mother went there, so did he and his brother, and now his daughter is a second grader. When I asked what made West Side different, Poston replied candidly that it had always been "more affluent" and consequently "less diverse."[48] As he was deciding where to send his daughter, friends had assured him that West Side "felt like a private school." In West Side's promotional video, "What Parents Are Saying about West Side," a blond woman appears first, lauding how West Side is "run like a private school."[49] Compared with the dour façade of Park Street or the utilitarian design of Lockheed, both majority-minority schools on the east side of town, West Side looks like a private school too. But marketing West Side as "like a private school" will not attract families who are committed to public education as a community value, but rather families who see West Side as a financially and individually strategic choice for them and for their children.

Choice as a dominating ideal in the school system and in our culture naturalizes the prioritizing of the individual over the group, the family's interests over those of the community.[50] To put one's own child first isn't simply acceptable but, from the perspective of the parents I spoke with, it is a moral obligation. What, then, of the community? This conundrum registered on Chris Poston's face when I asked what he would do if he got a letter informing him that his daughter had been redistricted to Lockheed Elementary. Before him were the seductions of higher test scores and fancier facilities versus his memories of learning something ineffable about community and brotherhood just by playing on a team full of kids different from him. He shook his head. "Hard to say." He went on: "If every white person said, 'I'm pulling my kids out,' well, you just made the problem worse! You can't complain about it and add to the problem." Despite damage to the system or personal investment in the community, if his child weren't getting the best he could give her, Poston admits he would already be halfway to the nearest private school. But as with Southerland and Mutimer, nostalgia is powerfully motivating for Poston—he played Blue Devil football and he takes his children to the games. He envisions them, ten years down the road, as Blue Devil athletes, Homecoming queens, and class presidents. He has a sense that the city schools—and the city itself—need die-hards like him, but his faith has conditions, and he won't relinquish his choices.

For Mariettans, choice extends beyond open enrollment or private academies—just beyond their doorsteps lie the Cobb County public schools (Marietta is Cobb's county seat). The system is ten times bigger than Marietta's and boasts some high-achieving schools, but it is a point of pride with Marietta's rather old-fashioned leadership that the city and county school systems will never merge. Bobby Ryan, a 1992 white graduate, enrolled his daughters in elementary school in "the county," as Mariettans rather disdainfully deem Cobb. Of the renaissance of the Marietta schools, he is not convinced: "I've had a lot of friends come to me and say, 'We're trying to get people to come back to Marietta.'"[51] They enumerated West Side's accolades—"I'm sure it's doing great," he conceded—and they reminded him that he was a Blue Devil and his kids should be too. But Ryan doubted that all the vocal Blue Devil supporters with children at West Side would stay through middle and high school. Ryan recently moved to the wealthy eastern corner of Cobb County, but in his former neighborhood in Mableton, a similar tactic was used. Upper-income Mableton residents encouraged him to stay and enroll in their district's elementary school, but he claimed the poor performance of the high school is no secret and he wasn't about to buy a house just to move again when his daughters started high school.[52]

The politics of the neighborhood are critical to a long view of the politics of school choice. In 1970 Marietta, when black citizens made up only 14 percent of the population, black and white citizens lived shoulder to shoulder, with little geographic segregation, but entrenched social segregation.[53] Freedom of choice in the sixties was a strategy that relied, if perversely, upon the cohesion of neighborhoods and communities: white communities would close ranks to intimidate potential desegregators, and black students would find it difficult to leave the security of their streets and schools for the hostility of all-white institutions. Such assumptions had some traction in the Marietta of the 1960s, but consistent with other Southern places where whites solidly outnumbered blacks, desegregation in Marietta did not produce the major cultural and geographic dislocations of school closures followed by white flight. When substantial desegregation came to Marietta in the late sixties, white Marietta did not, by and large, de-camp to the suburbs or to private schools; rather, the city's white population grew between 1960 and 1970, and the number of high school students in private and parochial schools dropped.[54]

It was this era of a racially and socioeconomically mixed "downtown" in which white graduate Bobby Ryan was raised. He grew up in the heart of town on Church Street, one of the north-south arteries that bounded

Baptistown, where Daphne Delk's family lived. A fixed star in the cosmos of his childhood was Joe's Store—a liquor joint and gathering place in the heart of Baptistown, where Ryan would meet his friends for bike rides and where his father would drop off the Baptistowners after ninth-grade football practice. As Ryan tells it, his parents offered rides and routinely made dinner for teammates and neighborhood kids whose parents worked or weren't in the picture. He recalled that there were several spaces that produced friendships—sports, classes, and of course, the neighborhood. Broad discursive and political shifts, and his own path out of Marietta, shaped how Bobby Ryan remembers and revises his old neighborhood. His ambivalence about his race- and class-diverse upbringing illuminates the complexity of an ideology and politics focused on individual choice instead of community cohesion.

Ryan thrived at Marietta: he was a good athlete, class president, and a friend to folks across "cliques," as he recalled. But when he and his wife were shopping a couple of years ago for a house in Cobb County—and for a neighborhood in a good school district—despite the entreaties of old friends who were Marietta boosters, Marietta was not a contender. "Being brutally honest with you . . . I would never put my kids into that school system. I've got two girls. I actually think it'd be different if I had boys." Citing safety and parental involvement, he said, "It has nothing to do with race; it has more to do with . . . community support." As exemplars of the "support" he's talking about, he mentioned the three highest-scoring, lowest-poverty schools in Cobb County, none of which are more than 15 percent black or Latino. All three schools are about the size of Marietta High, with similar academic and extracurricular offerings, but they are high-income bastions of the suburban dream of thirty years ago. In East Cobb, kids don't get around on bikes anymore, and they don't hang out at liquor stores. In Ryan's story are embedded discourses of racial innocence, of urban coming-of-age, and of social mobility. Palpable in his memories are the materials for a progress narrative, which places Ryan's contemporary choices for his children's education at the end of a trajectory away from his middle-class home, where there wasn't enough money to send all the siblings to college or enough anxiety about living in an economically and racially diverse neighborhood.

"I was playing in the projects growing up," Ryan said, chuckling, "I just didn't know any better." Free play, social improvisation, and uncontrolled space in his children's social orbits are alarming to parents like Ryan; the freedom of his childhood bike rides around Baptistown and up to the Marietta Square is translated into a dire threat in the lives of his own kids. The diversity of his friendships, in terms of both class and race, would represent "a safety problem," as he put it, for his girls. Now, he interprets his insouciance at having his bike stolen or his cleats swiped as naiveté ("I thought that was just how the world worked!"). He should have recognized, he realizes now, the bad elements of Baptistown for what they were, instead of moving blithely through surroundings with too few race and class boundaries. A sales executive with the proverbial corner office, Ryan seems a far cry from the kid who hung out at Joe's Store and rode bikes with black and white children from across the class spectrum, who forgave petty theft and pretty much took the world as it was, imperfect but gloriously wide.

In describing those years, Ryan at first used the name Baptistown, then "the projects," and then toward the end of our conversation, "the ghetto." As Ryan has changed, so too have local and national discourses of race, class, and neighborhood. He was raised during the backlash against progressive legislation of the 1960s that expanded welfare substantially to families of color who needed it. By the 1980s, "welfare queens" and Willie Horton were entrenched in the national lexicon as symbols of the parasitism and criminality of black poor people.[55] With Clinton's 1996 vow to "end welfare as we know it," being a poor person of color came to merit not government aid but "work-fare"—diminished support that required landing jobs that, had they existed, would have kept applicants off assistance in the first place.[56] An even clearer illustration of the distance between the Marietta of Ryan's childhood and that of today is the city's contemporary war on public housing (in 2013, the last of five public housing developments, dating to the forties, was demolished and its residents relocated). Today the Housing Authority argues that residents must be moved out of public housing in order to "benefit" from the example of "folks that have good jobs" in the mainstream, to quote former Marietta Housing Authority director Ray Buday.[57]

In the 1960s and 1970s, the projects in Baptistown were part of its economically eclectic community; the people who lived in them were not labeled as drug users, parasites of the state, or chronically unemployed, as they are now. But the brick and mortar of Baptistown's government housing are gone, as is, it seems, the time in Marietta when public housing and its ethos of shared care giving and open doors were not anathema but intrinsic to the social vitality of the whole neighborhood. As on Franklin Road, a once economically diverse area, the mix of working-, middle-, and upper-middle class has all but disappeared in downtown Marietta, and white graduates' memories of that era are volunteered from, in the cases of Mutimer, Ryan, and Poston, racially and economically homogenous workplaces, neighborhoods, and peer groups.

Although the "neighborhood school" is a resurgent value in public education (allowing as it does residentially segregated districts to resist school desegregation in the name of neighborhood and community unity), viewing and judging schools as service providers is increasingly common, not only among education reformers but also among parents. For Ryan, the efficiency of that enterprise and his and other parents' satisfaction can be gauged by (what else?) test scores. I interviewed Ryan at work, at the offices of ApolloMD, which does "clinical outsourcing" by contracting out services such as anesthesia and radiology to participating hospitals or "buyers." ApolloMD advertises that its "physicians are paid according to the patients that they see and procedures they perform. With physicians highly motivated to move patients through the department, the midlevel providers and other staff members embrace this new 'culture of productivity,' leading to improvements in both efficiency and patient satisfaction."[58]

Like health care, schools are increasingly subject to free market logic, and like judging a physician on the speed at which he "moves patients through," judging a school solely by its scores reduces the complex human relationships—the community—to a set of numbers. Test scores, as researchers have demonstrated, are a product of much beyond the school's control—family and friends play a role, for example—but test scores stand in for—and in turn become a referendum on—the quality of school instruction and curriculum. Test scores aren't just the province of sites like the Georgia Department of Education, but are used in real estate and home buying to tout certain districts over others and to lure parents who have the resources to follow high scores to their host schools. The long-term impact is greater and faster resegregation.[59] Test scores impact the dynamics of school choice, and social capital strongly influences test scores.[60] Social capital—the relationships, affiliations, and behaviors that build community—points to a whole host of factors outside the school, but it also encompasses the impact of who you go to school with, and where, and whether it feels like a community.

This language of outcomes is not solely the province of white parents of means. It is a colorblind, structure-blind ideology that black parents of means subscribe to as well, as the school politics of Ryan's classmate and childhood friend, Rod Garman, demonstrate. Rod Garman, a black graduate of 1993 who appeared in the guise of football star in Chapter 1, has no compunction about leaving Marietta and never looking back. Homecoming king, top student, and respected leader, Garman managed the magic trick of being neither nerd, nor jock, nor prep while being all three at once. The one affiliation that tripped him up briefly was "black." Garman spent his elementary years in a mostly white Catholic school and at West Side. By the time high school rolled around, he was accustomed to being accused of "talking white": he took all advanced classes, went to a mostly white church, and socialized with white peers. Ryan and Garman knew each other at West Side; Ryan commented that Garman caught some flak for his grades, his friends, and his elocution. Asked if he felt torn between identifying with black and white peers, Garman replied, "I was never torn. I didn't care. I experienced it [some teasing from black peers] but not enough to change who I was because that's who I was—who I am."

About school choice and private education, Garman said unequivocally, "I think you should have the choice if you have the means." Garman's declaration invites the question: what if you don't? Garman graduated from MHS with a football scholarship to University of Georgia but ended up a banker. He and his wife live in Atlanta, and his daughter is enrolled in a private Christian school, although, as he pointed out, his local public elementary school in Buckhead is excellent. About choosing private education over public, and about the diversity offered by a school like Marietta High, he said, "I have a daughter and I want her to have the best education; that's what it comes down to. I can answer your question in several ways, but the truth comes out when I [consider] my child." It wasn't that he didn't appreciate Marietta—he had been adored there—but "it wasn't the same anymore." When I pressed him, he said, "it's not as [racially] balanced." Garman noted the relevance of race to school quality and parental perceptions, but not to his own high school experience or his life since. Garman's own trajectory is proof for him that opportunity and advantage are individual and not affected by structural inequality in the school or outside it.

What community and race mean to Garman may have something to do with what they meant for his mother, whose values and beliefs were fired in segregation's kiln. Garman's mother graduated from Lemon Street High in 1959, valedictorian of her class, no less. In that time, one's own destiny and that of "the race" were inextricable—race men and race women defined the battle, and it was, to echo Jill Mutimer, a battle over perception. How whites perceived the behavior, abilities, and contributions of black citizens was central to the struggle not just for equal rights, but decent treatment. Respectability was the watchword of many middle-class black Americans of the early and mid-twentieth century.[61] Representing one's community and one's race well was paramount: that duty is visible in the folded hands, white dresses, and hopeful bow ties of all-black Lemon Street High's first graduating classes.[62] Ms. Garman was raised in that tradition, a devout Christian who imprinted Garman and his sister with "character, not color" mantras and insisted that high achievement and dedication to one's community were what the family name required, what representing the Garmans meant. And Rod Garman reflected that if he ever felt any pressure in his many incarnations as a celebrated athlete, student, and leader, it was "to always represent my family [and] my mom."

Aaron Gullatte, a black athlete twenty years Garman's senior and a star of the first integrated MHS football team, said much the same thing. A 1968 graduate of MHS, Gullatte, too, had come from Lemon Street, and even after it was closed, he was charged with being, and felt himself to be, an emissary of its ethics and its traditions. But Rod Garman's sense of community, of representing something larger than himself, did not bind him to Marietta—where his mother and sister still live—or to a view of community as more than the sum of individual bonds forged with longtime neighbors and kin. Perhaps his knowledge of his mother's history—in which the high school she loved was demolished and her community irrevocably altered—may have taught him something about fending for oneself. From his mother's losses, Garman may have gleaned the importance of advancing the interests of your children and protecting their hard-won privileges, instead of holding too tightly to the sanctity of the community and being wedded to the health of the whole.

Success in Spite of Choice: Latino Graduates of MHS

In twenty-first-century Marietta, that "whole" is increasingly composed of Latino students, who, without a spate of choices at their disposal, have a strong stake in the public schools. Marietta's "choice academies" do not fare well under the scrutiny of these students—especially those who attended the system's struggling, high-poverty elementary schools. Diana Rios was born in Mexico but has been in Marietta since she was five. She went to Lockheed Elementary (never a well-reputed school and by 2013 considered one of the system's worst) and came up through Marietta Middle School and entered the elite International Baccalaureate (IB) program in high school. (See Table 2.4.) She has long contemplated the impact of white, high-income interests on Marietta schools. Although high-income families bring much needed resources, they also want public education on their terms—that is, tailored around the interests of their children rather than those of a diverse group of students. She reflected on how social capital and academic experiences at the elementary level affect opportunity later on: "When you look at it, most of the IB students that graduated last year came from Burruss or West Side, and from Lockheed I think it was just me . . . so you can really see it when you look at it that way. . . . I guess you could argue that the elementary school where you start off . . . says what kind of student you're gonna be in high school."[63]

Even back at Lockheed, Diana's parents impressed upon her the importance of excelling in school. As a ninth grader at MHS, she knew the IB program might be her only shot at college if her family didn't get their green cards. And they didn't, not until right before she graduated. Diana

Table 2.4. 2012 MHS IB Students by Elementary School Attended

A.L. Burruss	111
Dunleith	35
Hickory Hills	46
Lockheed	57
Park Street	31
Sawyer Road	40
West Side	67
MCAA	167

Data drawn from "Marietta High School Diploma Program, November 2012," a presentation to the Marietta City Schools Board. Presentations available to the public through www.marietta-city.org, accessed February 16, 2013. These 2012 data lend insight into the status of Marietta's elementary schools in the early 2000s, when the 2012 IB juniors and seniors were in elementary school; in another generation, by the class of 2020, contemporary trends like West Side's ascendency and Lockheed's decline will be visible in the IB enrollment data.

carried the anxiety of her family's immigration status—the pressing "uncertainty" as she said—all the way through school, knowing that limbo could remain her family's reality indefinitely. When they heard from their lawyer that the whole family was being granted residency, she said they had "everybody over" (much of the extended Rios family lives in Marietta, near Diana's parents) and they wept and celebrated a new life free from fear. Diana's feelings of belonging in Marietta were made tangible in her "papers" and those of her parents and siblings. Families like Diana's are increasingly the warp and weft of Marietta; they live on the "wrong side" of the square as one of Diana's classmates put it (speaking of his own family), in a world that feels five hundred instead of five miles from West Side. They are typically districted for the lowest-performing, highest-poverty schools in the system, which do not, as Diana pointed out, produce many IB or Advanced Placement students. We talked about what the achievements of West Side mean in the context of the struggles of Park Street and Lockheed. Diana acknowledged the furor any redistricting would cause, noting, "people want their students to go to the best school but you always have to think, what's best for everyone?"

The "everyone" to whom Diana refers continues to shift and grow. In 2005, the school system absorbed hundreds of Katrina evacuees along with record numbers of Latino students. The population swell caused overcrowding followed by deeply contentious redistricting, for which the school board had to bring in a mediator. To parents' dissatisfaction with their assigned schools, the introduction of school choice in 2007 was a politically canny solution—now all families can ostensibly select whatever city school they wish. Although the superintendent professes surprise at West Side's popularity, and school leaders suggest that school choice "spillover" from West Side and Burruss will bring similar status to the other elementaries, disappointed parents of the choice lottery seem disenchanted at the idea of enrolling at their third or fourth choice.[64]

The question of how to support every kind of student—MHS's burden as the system's only high school—drove the long days of former Superintendent Emily Lembeck, a take-no-prisoners type who, even skeptics agree, is a smart woman who did a hard job well. Lembeck brought "freedom of choice" to the Marietta schools, along with the innovation of the "charter system" whereby city schools are exempted from certain state mandates. Under her leadership, the system has seen some success narrowing the achievement gap between low- and high-income students and has been included on national lists of top high schools.[65]

In an effort to engage parents across the city, especially Latino parents, Lembeck's office instituted "community conversations" and "coffee talks." One at Lockheed Elementary, where Diana went, drew a crowd of about nine—no parents, a handful of teachers, the principal, and one rather conspicuous ethnographer. Lockheed is 90 percent black and Latino with 78 percent of students on free or reduced-price lunch. Its test scores are the second worst in the system, and as of the 2012 school year, it had the city's highest transience rate—34 percent—meaning more than one-third of the students who started the year at Lockheed did not finish it there.[66] The event was held in the library, where projects on Frederick Douglass and Mary Todd Lincoln lining the walls announced the fifth grade's Civil War unit. Lembeck talked openly about the struggles of a "high-mobility" system like Marietta City, and she offered an anecdote—clearly familiar to the faculty there—about a second grader in Marietta who enrolled in five schools in one year. Marietta High's enrollment is up—a good sign if it is due to satisfaction with the system. But, Lembeck admitted, the spike is more likely attributable to the hardships of the recession bringing more families to live with relatives on Franklin Road, which will likely increase transience and which school leaders see as a major barrier to enrollment stability and academic achievement at schools like Lockheed.

Lembeck's earnest compliments for the faculty of Lockheed and cheerful reciting of the school's test score improvements reminded me of the words of Valarie Wilson, president of the Georgia School Boards Association, commenting on 2012 controversies over charter school funding. She insisted that a school is as good as the community behind it—"with community support, any—*every*—school can turn around."[67] That is what Diana Rios would like to see: not that all the struggling Lockheed students be shuttled to West Side, but rather that West Side's monopoly on prestige and support be challenged by community investment in the Lockheeds of the system.

Diana and the other three Latino students in her IB diploma class came up through Marietta's lowest-scoring, highest-poverty schools, entered the IB program—in some cases against stark odds—and have flaunted stereotypes (especially among their peers, claims Diana) about the tenacity, permanence, and commitment of Latino families and students.[68] Their stories are about, in some ways, the absence of choice. As undocumented immigrants, they had to negotiate the cultural and spatial geographies of inclusion and exclusion in Marietta, knowing they represented, in the eyes of school leadership, a "problem" demographic, to whom certain critical resources, privileges, and paths would remain out of reach. Reflecting on resegregation at MHS, Diana offered, "Just like I think it's bad for a school to be mostly white people, I think it's bad for it to be mostly minority for the same reason [that diversity is enriching]." She continued, "We'd have a lot less IB and AP students [if white enrollment foundered]. I feel bad saying it, but it's the truth. So there has to be that kind of balanced ratio, you know?" Diana's belief that white students will continue to dominate advanced classes, a common one among recent graduates regardless of race, illustrates how academic tracking reinforces ideas about the relationship between class, color, and achievement. Unlike too many students of color who choose not to attempt AP or IB courses, Diana was undeterred by how few IB students looked like her, talked like her, and came from her part of town. West Side teems with dedicated parents, tireless advocates for their children, but some students like Diana do their own advocating, working creatively and fruitfully with the resources they've got and cultivating a progressive vision for the future of the system.

Among recent Latino grads, the ethos of the community versus that of the individual is a particularly vexed question. Some Latino Blue Devils see themselves as Mariettans, as part of that "family," despite the political and structural forces that alienate them. Lauren Garcia, who came to the United States from Brazil when she was six, went to Park Street Elementary and then to Pine Forest before it was transformed into MCAA, the magnet academy for third to fifth graders.[69] Lauren's little brother attends the magnet school; her other three siblings attend Park Street. Because of her own experience and that of her siblings, she is intimate with how choice functions for families on the east side of town, in the apartment buildings at the school district's borders. On the subject of redistricting and eliminating choice, Lauren becomes animated: "I think it'd be really interesting and really cool . . . if you were to start implementing the diversity from such a young age."[70] About Park Street, she commented, "Of course [parents] are still going to [choose an elementary school] based on who goes there. Hardly anyone is gonna go to Park Street for that reason." Insisting that it was a nurturing place, she praised her teachers at Park Street, whom she said she still knows and connects with through her brothers. Lauren could not at first think of a thing she would change about Marietta schools. She was president of her class three years running—a popular, charismatic, campus leader who was always urging her Latino peers to run for student council, apply for the IB program, and even just go to football games. But when we talked about choice in the elementaries, she reversed herself a bit. On the point of abolishing the choice system and redistricting schools for better racial balance, Lauren affirmed, "that's one thing Marietta could do."

Under the current school system leadership, and in the context of a national love affair with free market–oriented education reform, such a disavowal of choice is unthinkable. Of two minds about markets and community, Chris Poston first asserted that as far as resegregation is concerned, "most things will correct themselves." Yet, at the end of our conversation, he said a little plaintively, "I want the whole thing to work good because I want Marietta to be good. [We need to] continue to have people who are not just trying to get what's best for them and . . . their kid's . . . school, they're trying to get what's best for the city." Contemplating what's best for the city, I think of Diana and Lauren and of their IB classmate Amy Rocha. All three first-generation Latin American immigrants who came from the system's lowest-achieving, poorest elementaries, they achieved at the highest levels, despite the anxieties of undocumented life in the United States and the challenges of inhabiting dual worlds at home and at school.

Choice has yet another resonance for these students. Diana's immigration status as a nonresident narrowed her options into a tiny pinhole of possibilities compared to her IB classmates: apply to Mexican universities and be unable to return to see her parents, apply to state universities with little hope of acceptance and none at all for financial aid, or try her luck at private universities and a scholarship. She was admitted to Kennesaw State University before she got her green card, so she deferred. When she starts classes at Kennesaw, she'll do so as a Georgia resident and she'll enjoy the tuition benefits of that status. From her perch at the top of her senior class, Kennesaw State was not what Diana had dreamed of, but, as she said with a smile, "there's always graduate school."

For similar reasons, Lauren Garcia ended up at a private university in Kentucky, where she was offered three scholarships that amounted to a full ride and where admissions officers were not interested in her immigration profile. Amy Rocha, who goes as far back as elementary school with Lauren Garcia, is enrolled at a prestigious Canadian university where she was warned that she would not be able to re-enter the United States and her still-undocumented parents would never be permitted to visit her. Certainly, Amy, Diana, and Lauren created avenues for themselves through dedication to their studies and their community (Lauren was involved in student government, and Amy was the editor of the school newspaper, the *Pitchfork*), but those avenues were much more narrow and demanding than those of their nonimmigrant, high-income peers. Although they claimed resources and made crucial allies in the administration at Marietta High, what advantages they might have reaped at West Side, through its parent network of lawyers, politicians, and local elites, is a troubling unknown.

Choice has long been and continues to be a powerful force in the politics of American public schools. As education analyst Andrew Rotherham put it, "choice is like gravity, it's irresistible."[71] Even without a voucher program or a network of charter schools, Marietta is being shaped dramatically by choice and its proponents. School system leaders are betting on choice— that through it, the system will gain more through retaining affluent families than it loses by closing the circuit of social capital at the elementary level and excluding students who need those advantages the most. Among these leaders and among Marietta's public school advocates, a more fundamental calibration is needed: the assumption that high-income white families are the lifeblood of public schools is dangerously myopic. It was, after all, Daphne Delk who first felt the drums of *Brown* thrumming and quietly carried its revolution into Marietta High.

Loss and Legacy

"I was purposed," Delk said of her role at Marietta High, and she observed that many of her Lemon Street High School peers "weren't there yet." She said frankly, "My purpose was—if I could make it through and open the doors for others . . . it would allow them to get some things that would give them a life that would take them far beyond the boundaries of where they were living—inside of a black world." Reflecting on the Marietta of her youth with a little smile, she said, "It was sort of pristine," a place "right out of a book." During her childhood in the 1950s, Delk lived in Baptistown, in a single-family home, which was separated from the government housing— the projects—by a fence. Except for fences like the one behind Delk's house, middle-class and poor families lived side by side: in a small community like Marietta in the Jim Crow era, when all black newcomers were steered to the same few streets, there was little opportunity for black residents of means to spread out.

Delk described herself as "different" as a child, as a dreamer and "someone whose big question in life was why—why can't I?" She informed her mother who, like more than half of employed black women in 1960s Marietta, worked as a "domestic" for a white family that she wanted to go to Marietta High.[72] She didn't need to be told that unlike at Lemon Street High, at Marietta High there were foreign language classes, a well-appointed gym and theatre, and plenty of up-to-date textbooks. Treville Grady, Delk's classmate, spoke up—she would join Delk. Treville's mother, Katherine Grady, was a hairdresser and—as hairdressers and barbers often did in small communities—she played the role of expert and advisor on all manner of community matters: she thought the girls should go through with it. The school board requested that the two write and submit a letter to the Board of Education justifying their fitness to attend MHS and describing their motives for transferring. Admitting the two girls was consistent with what the board hoped they could get away with—a freedom of choice plan. For Delk, jumping through this arbitrary hoop was only one of many exercises in justifying herself and her quest, which would be trying both for her and for the Lemon Street community.

Freedom of choice was the beginning of the end for Lemon Street High and the other two schools in the black community.[73] Principal Marion J. Woods, a beloved, respected leader, "wasn't very happy," as Delk remembered, at her and Grady's petition to transfer. "Why are you doing this?" he had asked her. Seldom did the administration of all-black schools survive desegregation with their authority intact; if they were not fired, black principals were demoted to assistant principals in newly merged administrations at white schools. Woods perhaps foresaw that in Marietta, like elsewhere, desegregation would proceed according to the demands of the white school board and city leaders, not the hopes of black educators and families. Woods had worked hard to equalize the black and white systems and produce institutions like Lemon Street Elementary, which had been transformed from a "firetrap" with outhouses to a modern facility with bathrooms and heat in 1950.[74]

The hardships of segregated education on black communities demanded enormous resourcefulness and strong community bonds, which frayed in the tension of the white-directed desegregation processes.[75] Before Delk's admission at MHS was final, Woods had left Lemon Street to be principal at Wright Street, an all-black elementary school in the city, opened in 1962 when Lemon Street Elementary reached its capacity. In 1967, when Wright Street integrated fully, Woods retired from teaching. Unlike Woods's successor at Lemon Street High who transitioned to assistant principal of

Marietta High, Woods only worked in the all-black schools of Marietta. Having served the community as an educator and principal since 1929, he witnessed profound change in those forty years; perhaps he retired with a sense of optimism. But he may have known all along—as his reaction to Delk's plan suggests—that the legacy he had built at Lemon Street and then Wright Street would not survive desegregation. By the mid-seventies, white leaders had closed all three schools in the black communities— Lemon Street High, Lemon Street Elementary, and Wright Street Elementary.[76] But in the fall of 1964, all that was yet to come, and Delk was sixteen, poised to make Marietta history, listening to the warnings of her frightened peers: "You're gonna be killed!" "Well, you know, it's not about me," she had retorted.

Delk felt that her choice represented the nascent freedom of all her peers. Yet, as a high-achieving student with dreams of college, raised in a two-parent, two-income home, Delk already had choices some of her classmates never would. She talks about desegregation in terms of personal goals, work, and success. She claimed that she determined and shaped her environment and her own life, rather than the other way around. Despite her contention to the contrary, in many ways, "it" was about her. Although the politics of desegregation across the South was dominated by white supremacist governments and politicians, the trajectory of desegregation in Marietta and many other communities was constituted by the actions of a handful of black community leaders, teachers, parents, and, of course, students like Delk, who weighed desegregation's boon—feeling a part of a vastly powerful change—against its burden—feeling very much alone. Just two weeks into their tenth-grade year, Treville Grady let Delk know she'd have to withdraw.[77] Delk was "heartbroken" at the abandonment by her comrade in arms. She and Grady "had a pact" to desegregate MHS and graduate together. Despite the setback, Delk was undeterred. That first year at Marietta High, Delk had little choice about where to sit in the cafeteria—alone—or what extracurricular activities to do—none were permitted her. On desegregation's ship, she was both first mate, charged with power and special orders, and a stowaway, alone and unprotected, bound for unknown places.

To ask students like Delk what "desegregation" meant for them underscores the perversion of *Brown* by freedom of choice: their schools were not desegregated at all. These black adolescents were isolated in all-white environments, an experience antithetical to the spirit and purpose of

Brown. The fact that Delk was prohibited from participating in extracurricular activities her first year at MHS and then continued to keep a careful distance from the social life of the school—she didn't go to the prom or other events—was a comfort to the administration and helped smooth the process for those after her who had more latitude, in both large and small ways. She made friends eventually and was widely liked for her sense of humor. When she graduated in 1967, she was recognized by her senior class with an award, "Girl of the Year."

Daphne is far more than just "Girl of the Year" in the annals of Marietta's history—she is an icon of individual achievement and personal courage. She called segregationists on their bluff and turned the game against them. Yet the rub of white supremacy was that the game could never be turned. Freedom of choice obscured structural inequality's impact on black students and segregation's cultural impact on black and white communities by suggesting that all the students had to do was simply choose—equal resources, good facilities, and academic opportunities were there for the taking. Delk's experience of desegregating Marietta High through freedom of choice points to its contradictions beyond the shunning she endured in venturing out of "a black world."

Freedom of choice brought greater freedom in terms of expanded academic opportunities for black students, and yet it diminished freedom in the form of shuttered black schools and demoted black leadership. It wrenched away, in the name of *Brown,* what many black citizens had worked so hard to build. Choice has always been an ambiguous force in Marietta. Freedom of choice plans marked the demise of Jim Crow in Marietta's schools while also condemning to obsolescence rich traditions and institutions in black communities. The choice plan of the aughts was the school system's first tacit acknowledgement that resegregation had come to Marietta and must be faced, but the price of white students returning is equity for students of color who have no other choice but to stay. Creating a hierarchy of competing schools through the choice program means that some schools "win"—the most experienced teachers, the high-level grants, the most talented students, and the greatest community support—while other schools "lose" at all those registers. Correspondingly, the students at these challenged schools often lose as well, or face unfair disadvantages, as the graduates' stories here attest. Yet, in the rationale of free market education reform, it is not structural injustice that hobbles the trajectories of these students, it is their failure—and that of their parents—to *choose* wisely. If anything, choice is more dangerous now than in the 1960s, cloaked as it is in the universal language of markets, competition, and, of course, freedom.

While freedom of choice was a tool for protecting white "rights" and desires, courageous students like Delk seized the opportunity it offered and made way for seismic social change. In the mid-sixties, Marietta's freedom of choice plan was a tremor before a much larger convulsion. Similarly, today's choice system and the zeal with which the school leadership promotes it reveal anxiety about social transformation—*re*segregation rather than desegregation—and attempts to stave it off. Marietta's choice policy will inaugurate a reinvestment in the school system by whites or demonstrate the necessity of a reinvention of it without them.

The truth that plagues "choice" is this: because it turns on the actions of the individual, it appears to be disconnected from the destinies of others. In this sense, school choice is a fantasy in which the freedoms of a privileged few masquerade as "market forces," in which choice is supposed to improve all schools, not just the West Sides of the world.[78] Markets are not natural or organic; they are a reflection of the people who compose them—their backgrounds, behaviors, and desires; consumption is cultural. In that sense, free markets aren't free at all, but rather are fundamentally produced by historical and contemporary laws, court decisions, policies, and politics that further empower the privileged.[79] Choice in Marietta is good evidence that nonstructural, individually oriented approaches do not address structural problems. The invisible hand did not create education inequality in Marietta—it is the product of entrenched discriminatory practices and racist structures—nor will the invisible hand correct it.

Waving goodbye to Delk after our interview, I watched her walk to her car, and suddenly she was a tenth grader again with a satchel clutched against her side, making her way through the halls at MHS, a teenager ahead, and even a little outside, of her time. Of this generation, it is students like Diana, Amy, and Lauren who wear Delk's mantle and will define Marietta High's legacy. Although they'll have far more choices for their children than their parents did for them, public schools must hope for the support of graduates like those three. They pushed relentlessly from the margins into the elite echelons of social and academic life at MHS and experienced in their community both the vicissitudes and the great promise of this enduringly difficult and inspiring experiment in American democracy—public education.

☀ 3 ☀

SOME KINDS OF BLUE

Tracking at Marietta High

"HELLISH," SAID 2001 graduate Tiffany Turner, "that would be the best word."[1] Describing her experience as one of only a few black students enrolled in an elite academic program, the International Baccalaureate (IB), during its pilot years at Marietta High School, Tiffany recalled facing vicious, unveiled racism among her classmates. "I was called a nigger no less than four times, by four different people," she attested, with no intervention from teachers who overheard the slur. Marietta's white students, free in many things, were free with their words, and Tiffany bore the brunt of their anger at her incursions into the inner sanctum of advanced classes. In a history class sophomore year, a white student told her he wished black people were still enslaved. "You wish I was a slave?" She asked him incredulously. "Yes," he replied. During her junior year, a white classmate hurled an epithet at her during a conversation about the correct answer on a quiz. Near the end of high school, after four years of ignoring individual racist acts and ingrained institutional ones, she finally made herself heard in a letter to the local newspaper. From her childhood in Marietta in the mid-eighties to her young adulthood in the late nineties, Tiffany bore witness to, and in moments crossed through the flames of, the remaking of Marietta and its high school.

Tracking: An American Tradition

There is perhaps no greater betrayal of the legacy of *Brown v. Board of Education* than educational disfranchisement of black students in order to make desegregation more palatable for whites through academic tracking. White students and students of color alike are wronged by intensifying stratification inside the "desegregated" public school. From third-generation white Mariettans to recently arrived Latino students, graduates consistently observe that tracked classes shaped their friendships and social networks and hence their self-perception and academic goals. Tracking or "ability grouping" is far more than a matter of different curriculum and instruction; tracks have identities that shape and are shaped by the students who populate them, creating distinctions that further stratify social life and reinforce damaging narratives regarding race, class, and achievement.[2] Tracked academics offer another lens on the institutionalizing of integration in Marietta: the creed of colorblindness naturalizes the stratification produced by tracking, positing, as did one student we'll meet in these pages, that there is no black, white, or Latino at MHS—there is only "having brains" or not.

At Marietta High, entrenched barriers, prejudices, and assumptions were amplified in the 1990s by the adoption of the elite IB program, which bore the marks of tracking, but perhaps the promise of something different, too. As with Blue Devil football culture, the possibilities of more expansive modes of inclusion exist in the IB program, but reinventing integrated education at the site of the IB will require dedicated and bold investment at the levels of students, teachers, and parents. A remade IB program could, if guided by the critiques, dreams, and demands of students of color both in and outside it, help to inaugurate a new integration era at MHS.

IB programs, Advanced Placement (AP) and Honors classes, and vocational or "technical" courses are all forms of ability-based grouping, a practice that dates back to the nineteenth century when educators and reformers sought ways to prepare students both academically and vocationally.[3] As the enrollments of public schools skyrocketed with the passage of child labor and compulsory education laws, schools saturated with immigrant students were overwhelmed by the problems of social and economic inequality intrinsic to this heterogeneous population. The school reformers of the era equated public education with civic education.[4] American education, believed many Progressive Era school reformers, should endow students with civic virtue, a respect for democracy, and an American identity. But Polish, Italian, and German students had different needs and cultural touchstones; Jewish and Catholic families desired the right to shape their nonsecular education; and Native American and African American children were excluded from and exploited through, respectively, the national project of public education. By the mid-twentieth century, many of these European groups—both northern and southern—were nonwhite no longer, and the injuries of ability grouping were borne, in great part, by black and "brown" students.[5]

The Civil Rights Era, and with it the Black Power, Red Power, and Chicano Rights Movements, all targeted the unequal education offered to students of color—an injustice made manifest in special education, vocational education, and remedial courses filled with these students, usually without regard for their talents, interests, or academic abilities. In the 1980s, tracking came under fire, and its critics began a national movement to "de-track." They decried tracking as a mechanism that bestowed further advantages on already privileged, high-achieving students and condemned low-income minority students to the academic dregs. Above all, claimed critics, tracking promoted segregation—a regression to the unequal opportunities of the pre-*Brown* era.[6] Tracking is a "tradition" in education that successive twentieth-century reform movements manipulated but kept fundamentally intact.[7]

In the post-*Brown* era at Marietta High, there was no lipstick on the pig of race-based tracking. "Basic," "business,"—encompassing the vocational courses that would later have their own track—and "college prep" constituted the possible paths for students.[8] The predominance of black students in basic courses and white students in college prep courses is obvious from just a glance at the yearbooks of that era. In Marietta High's class of 1974, for example, of sixty-five black graduates, only six were college prep. (Perhaps not coincidentally, by 1988, although these tracks still existed in practice at MHS, they were no longer immortalized in yearbooks with the italicized phrase *basic course, business,* or *college prep* next to each senior's name.) Marietta High, like many public schools across the country, maintains the vestiges of that system through its array of AP, IB, college prep, and vocational courses; now, college prep courses at MHS loosely equate with "basic" and vocational with "business." Until the adoption of the IB program, AP classes, which do not require applications or teacher recommendations, were the realm of high achievers at MHS, but with the IB and its culture of cohort solidarity came a powerfully and nominally race-blind mechanism for arranging, separating, and privileging students.

The heterogeneity of contemporary schools is a primary justification for tracking, just as it was one hundred years ago. The de-tracking movement instigated statewide efforts to de-track middle and high schools in Massachusetts and California, but ultimately, the movement had a greater impact on discourse and public perception than it did on actual practices in schools and policies advocated by school boards.[9] The dilemmas that de-tracking seeks to address today are not new, and the means by which citizens circumvent or opt out—through home schooling, private education, and gifted programs—of the democratizing agenda of public education are many. Even as the work of many scholars and reformers has rendered "tracking" a bad word in education policy, programs such as the IB became and still remain central to local efforts to staunch white flight through cultivating a space of privilege and distinction for "gifted" students. In Marietta, as elsewhere in our resegregating nation, gifted tracks constitute a last redoubt of high-income (mostly) white students in public schools.

Like magnet schools in the desegregation era and since, the International Baccalaureate program was adopted by Marietta High in order to retain or lure back white families who would have chosen private education or less racially heterogeneous public schools. And like school choice, the IB program reveals the ambiguous consequences of race- and class-neutral school reform in a city system fundamentally shaped by those very factors. In the years since its adoption in 1995, the IB has been a lens on the tensions of community at the high school. As Tiffany's experiences suggest, the adoption of the IB program exacerbated the phenomenon that has nearly always accompanied tracking—the "school within a school" dynamic, known to social scientists as "second-generation segregation."[10]

At Marietta, the IB has improved the high school's reputation in ways that merely adding more AP classes could not and, arguably, made it better equipped to support its eclectic population. MHS has many immigrant students—as much as a fourth of the student body in recent years—for whom English is not the language spoken at home, and the program emphasizes the importance of cross-cultural understanding and literacy through its foreign language requirements and focus on "international-mindedness." Although the IB program has never had more than half a dozen Latino students in a single diploma class, it has provided a critical springboard for those high-achieving undocumented students whose performance in the program earned them full rides at international or private universities. Recent IB Latino students know they have beat the odds and that most of their peers, especially the undocumented, won't get scholarships or even pursue higher education. At this register, and many others, the IB program raises important questions of community.

Despite the advantages of its curriculum, the IB is not, currently, a mechanism for schoolwide integration; that much is clear. The substantial in-school segregation fostered by the application-only IB program and the funneling of resources toward its mostly white, elite diploma classes negate the positive effects of luring these high-achieving students back into resegregating schools. IB does, however, help answer a question that is critical to integration studies: how can public schools be environments in which students build community through difference, challenging the racism and classism reinforced by what they see on TV, read on the Internet, and hear in their own families and peer groups? Consistent with the findings of desegregation scholars, seldom do I hear from graduates that their social circles retain the diversity they had in high school. And often even by high school, graduates who had friends of all sorts in elementary and middle school have tacked back toward their own.[11] Many graduates deem sports and academics the most critical spheres for cultivating diverse friendships; white 2006 graduate Hope Gross and black 2012 graduate Allison Goins both testified that when other demands pushed sports out of their schedules, that sphere of interaction with a mix of students disappeared. Both Goins and Gross left their Marietta Middle School peer groups, which were race and class diverse, for the IB program in high school. In doing so, their worlds contracted yet again. But the important catch, the exception to this contraction, is the IB program itself, a site of potentially powerful community building—were it to be radically expanded.

The International Baccalaureate program, claim its supporters, cultivates global citizenship and community engagement among its students, but these concepts ring hollow in the context of the kind of tracking that the IB reinforces. Tracked academics reserve for a small number of usually white, privileged students the great instruction, skills, and experiences that should be central to every high school education. In its ethos, the IB fosters the goal of building community through difference, but in its implementation, it hobbles that process. Thinking of the IB program as both an effective opening up and "internationalizing" of American curricula and a reinforcement of race- and class-based elitism is key to understanding how such programs further entrench a superficial school integration that demands deepening and expanding.

Although the program draws excellent students from across the city and county, the ability grouping of these students through an application-only program strengthens local beliefs that a "regular" education at the high school is for "regular" (read: minority, low-income) students, while a superior education is reserved for high-income, mostly white students. The stories here illuminate the fallacy of that assumption, documenting the benefits, both in social and intellectual capital, accrued by low-income IB graduates of color. Although the International Baccalaureate Organization (IBO) offers both primary years and middle years programs, the most popular incarnation of the IB is a six-course diploma program for eleventh and twelfth graders that includes both a substantial writing and community service graduation component. It is the diploma program with which this discussion is concerned. Some of these IB graduates reflect on how the special opportunities they enjoyed reverberate, negatively affecting educational equity for struggling students at the high school. In the testimonies of graduates of color, the IB program appears to model modes of critical inquiry and cultural understanding that are crucial in a racially and socioeconomically diverse institution, yet its exclusivity reinforces both the attitudes about and structural realities of race and class that have so long ordered public education in the United States. The reflections of MHS students across the academic spectrum—those in English to Speakers of Other Languages (ESOL), AP, "college prep," and "tech prep" coursework—offer key insights into the impact of tracking on their trajectories and the possibility of an inclusive intellectual community in tracked education.

The Jim Crow Present

In the early eighties, Tiffany Turner's family moved to Lee's Crossing, one of Marietta's oldest and, back then, toniest neighborhoods. They had been turned away from Laurel Springs, where black homebuyers were met with a host of reasons for rejection—except, of course, the color of their skin. Having learned their lesson, the Turners bought the house in Lee's Crossing sight unseen—that is, they were the sight, and they remained unseen. They were welcomed with a chilly silence and, a couple of years later, a burning cross in the front yard. This would have been about 1986, in Marietta, Georgia: the father, a police officer; the mother, a housewife; the children, four smart, polite youngsters without a single neighborhood playmate. For Tiffany, a charred spot in the grass is the truth of Marietta, the revelation of a present corrupted by a not yet confronted past.

Through her elementary years, Tiffany and her siblings were shuttled by her mother from one private church school to another, until they landed in the Marietta system at A.L. Burruss Elementary. In fifth grade she and her brothers, alone among their all-white classmates, forged some fragile friendships. At Marietta Middle School, where a stream of mostly white Burruss kids joined the roiling waters of Marietta's more racially diverse elementaries, came a new discomfort: that of being "not black enough." Tiffany was intellectual and eloquent; she recalled that her way of speaking, her white A.L. Burruss friends, and her middle-class family were alienating to her black classmates in middle school. By high school, she was fluent in exclusion and worried "the whole world" was like Marietta, in which she felt she "had no place."

When Tiffany was at Marietta High, the student body was 46 percent black, 38 percent white, and 11 percent Latino; the IB program—students in grades nine to twelve taking pre-IB and IB classes—was approximately 74 percent white.[12] Tiffany progressed through the IB program with a few black classmates, all of whom, in her memory, also encountered the thinly veiled hostility and sometimes overt racism that so marred her years at MHS. Remembering her bitterness at what racist white students cost her, she said, "I really felt like I had lost the only thing I really loved, which was school." She closeted her rage in those years and was seen as a "happy . . . popular" student, a fixture at football games and voted onto the Homecoming Court. In the final issue of the 2001 *Pitchfork* student newspaper, she is pictured beaming under a headline announcing the twin state championships of the boys' and girls' track teams, on which she was a discus thrower.[13] In the "shout-outs" section of that final issue, her few inches of space are dedicated with the usual exuberance to her good friends and to their coded jokes and affections. Tiffany was never perceived to be nursing the resentments of the marginalized because she was at the center of school life—not on the margins at all. But she was indeed angry, angry and increasingly hopeless as a "culture of silence," as she put it, made it taboo to talk about anything—justice, bigotry, history, and MHS's divided community—that she felt mattered.

Tiffany's black IB classmate, Christina Thornton, testified to the culture that Tiffany described. "Marietta was going through a big change racially," she said, and "white people felt threatened" and attempted to protect "the status quo." Marietta was indeed a different city in 2000 than just a decade earlier. Economic growth in Cobb County and black migration into metro Atlanta boomed; new black residents streamed in from Atlanta, across Georgia, and across the South. By 2000 the black population of Marietta, at 29.5 percent, was the highest it had ever been, higher than in 1930 before the Second Great Migration.[14] At Marietta High, black and white students navigated this changed geography, for themselves and often as proxies for their parents, bearing an animus much older than they were. Christina endured racist name-calling and hostility from white peers, but the "silence" part of the "culture of silence," as Tiffany called it, was unfamiliar to Christina. On Senior Field Day, Christina overhead a white parent, whom I'll call Susan, say of Marietta High's black students, "You give them an inch, they'll take a mile."[15] When Christina told Susan that her comments were inappropriate and unkind, Susan was affronted and took her indignation to the principal. Calling Christina in about the incident, the principal asked her if she had indeed accused the parent of being racist. "I said she made racist comments," she replied calmly. One afternoon in World Civilizations, Susan's daughter insulted Christina and voiced surprise that "an n-word"—as Christina told it, avoiding the slur—knew so much about the topic at hand. After class, Christina took her aside with some advice, "You worry about what you know, and I'll worry about what I know." Behavior like Susan's and her daughter's was rare, claimed Christina—open racism, if seldom addressed, was frowned upon at the high school. Most white MHS families were "better at concealing" their prejudice, observed Christina.

By her own account, Tiffany's reaction to racism at school was very different from her friend's. Christina "knew how to use her voice," recalled Tiffany, "Everybody knew she was pissed off . . . and knew exactly what she felt." But that was never Tiffany's way—"I would never go off on them [racist classmates]—I would just be hurt inside." In extracurricular activities like color guard, track, and the student newspaper, she took some refuge. And it was the track team, to which she was recruited to be a discus thrower, that brought her into Coach Ken Sprague's orbit. A white father of two racially mixed children (one of whom was also on the faculty), Sprague was uniquely sensitive to the challenges faced by many of MHS's black students. Resented by some of his colleagues for his outspoken criticisms of the high school, Sprague, a math teacher and weight-lifting coach, mentored Tiffany. He saw what she saw and was pained by what pained her, lending "validity," she said, to her experiences and perspective that no one else ever had. It was not just the racist students she encountered individually, but, to her and Sprague's mind, the edifice of white supremacist views and values that shaped the institution. They both felt that, in Tiffany's words, "there was just no expectation for black students to succeed," and unless they were Friday-night football stars or crowd-drawing point guards, they were "worthless" to the city school system.

Not just black students, but students of color in general were not faring well as desegregation turned to resegregation in the late nineties at MHS, when the school graduated the first classes of the IB program and saw rising Latino and declining white enrollments. During Tiffany's senior year, 2000–2001, there were eighty-three black dropouts and thirty Latino dropouts.[16] There were almost as many black dropouts as graduates (102 black students graduated in 2001), and there were more than four times as many Latino dropouts as Latino graduates (there were seven graduates; Table 3.1).[17]

These dismal statistics were not solely Marietta's shame: in 2001, Latino students in Georgia had the lowest graduation rate in the country: two out of three in the class of 1998 did not graduate.[18] At MHS, only 64 percent of the freshmen Tiffany entered with graduated with her, 4 percentage points below an already sagging national average graduation rate in 2001.[19] In 2001, 70 percent of the students who were "retained" (not promoted to the next grade) were black.[20] As Marietta High became more African American

Table 3.1. MHS Dropouts by Race/Ethnicity in 2000–2002 and Class of 2001 Graduates by Race/Ethnicity

	Grades 9–12 Dropouts in 2000–2002	Graduates in Class of 2001
Black°	83	102
White	23	117
Latino	30	7

°Black also encompasses students identifying as "mixed race."

and Latino, the achievement gap between these students and their white peers announced itself in no uncertain terms. Sprague was immersed in the bleak world of these inequities through his tutoring of black students for the SAT and work with black athletes in his remedial math courses. In the early 2000s, Sprague lobbied unsuccessfully for the SAT to be administered to all students (as of 2012, almost a fourth of seniors did not take the SAT) in the conviction that the test was an important tool for anyone who might be considering college in the future; he argued that MHS was attempting to protect its reputation and bolster its test scores at the expense of students of color.[21] There is nothing shocking about Ken Sprague's and Tiffany Turner's indignation; it is only shocking they were so alone in it. Neither had a more privileged viewpoint or clearer lens on the dynamics of race and class at the high school than any other student or teacher; they simply refused to look away.

A circuitous path had led Ken Sprague, now is in his sixties, from his hometown of Cincinnati to Marietta High, where he taught math from 1999 to 2010. From a hard-luck upbringing and education in a "99 percent black high school," Sprague moved to Los Angeles as a young man, plenty ready to flee Ohio.[22] In 1970, Sprague bought Gold's Gym, which was foundering, and turned it into an iconic brand. He sold the chain and "retired" to Oregon in 1979, where he began taking courses in secondary education (he is now certified to teach four subjects and capable, he claimed, of teaching "anything but foreign languages"). In the late nineties, he and his second wife followed his son, Ken Jr., to Marietta, Georgia, where Junior had taken a teaching job at MHS. Sprague joined the faculty himself a short time later. Newly immersed in the "cultural norms" of the South, as he called them, he was appalled at the educational injustice he perceived at Marietta High and made his faculty position a bully pulpit for his views.[23] His Gold's fortune made job security at MHS unimportant to him, and "maybe because they know I'm litigious," he said with a mischievous smile, the school board and communications director never sought to silence the whistle-blowing math teacher.[24]

Through a decade of school board showdowns and denunciations of the leadership and priorities of the high school, one constant endured: Sprague's conviction that MHS did not value black students, especially black males. In 2004, he opined in the *Marietta Daily Journal:* "Roughly 90 percent of black children entering [the] high school spend much or all of their day in virtual dumping grounds. All of the problems of public

education, and all children persona non grata in the IB classroom, are concentrated in the non-IB classroom. The injustice of the non-IB classroom
is striking." And then again in 2010, he decried the lack of progress: "This
year's [the] 10th anniversary of the International Baccalaureate Program,
roughly 1 percent of black males entering ninth grade ultimately earn an
IB Diploma; 99 percent don't."

In Tiffany's era, there was one black male in all her IB classes. Although
he left the program and did not graduate with an IB diploma, he won a full
scholarship to University of Georgia (UGA) and earned his Bachelor of
Arts (BA) degree in two years. (Tiffany observed that judging from the
white students she knew who were excited about UGA—among them the
boy nostalgic for slavery and the girl who spewed racial epithets—her black
classmate could probably only bear two years there.) Tiffany clearly differ-
entiated her black peers in the IB program from the black students who
were protected, as she saw it, by "staying together and taking all the same
classes." To these same students who had rejected her, claiming she wasn't
"black enough," she wanted to retort, "I feel like I'm the blackest one here.
I'm one of the only kids who has to deal with angry white people every
day. . . . I'm in the middle of a . . . pretty hostile environment." Halfway
through high school, Tiffany began to see more success on MHS's track
team, but that "front stage" in an integrated group only seemed to throw
into relief the isolation she suffered in her broader social world. Tiffany's
experience of alienation from her black peers strongly buoys the findings of
Susan Yonezawa and her colleagues that black students may "ostracize"
peers in higher tracks.[25] The "pull of the peer group," writes Yonezawa
and colleagues, and "major institutional and culturally constructed obstacles" often deter black students and produce "leveled aspirations"—that is,
the conviction that one doesn't belong on an advanced track, among
advanced students.[26]

The language and attitudes so reminiscent of Jim Crow were not the
only aspects of schooling in Marietta that heralded a difficult journey for
black students. Sometimes the writing was, quite literally, on the wall. Up
until the 2001–2002 school year, when MHS students took up residence in
the gleaming new complex across town, the high school's home was still a
mid-forties edifice in downtown Marietta.[27] In the main building, on
the door of the ladies room, were words that had been painted over
repeatedly—a phrase that seemed to resist decades of efforts to efface it:
"Whites Only." When Tiffany was a student, it had been thirty-five years

since MHS was integrated and Jim Crow banished. The bathroom door was next to the auditorium, and it is logical that even at a whites-only institution, the bathrooms next to space used for public events would bear the signage of segregation. Over the years, coats of paint were haphazardly brushed across the words. But such a past cannot be painted over; paint will only, as Tiffany recalled, produce "peeling layers." Rather, the layers must be sanded away, down to the words themselves, down to their truth, and then removed. That this process—an honest reckoning with racial injustice and the history of segregation—never happened at Marietta High has shaped the school and community's transition into the new era of a white minority.

At the apex of Tiffany's senior year was prom, and it was annually documented by a four-page color photograph spread in the *Marietta Daily Journal* on the following Sunday. As Tiffany told me, "I was a senior, and I was so excited about the newspaper coverage. I just knew I was gonna be in there . . . and I picked up the newspaper, and I went through, and I think there were close to one hundred pictures from our senior and junior class[es] at Marietta High School. And there wasn't one black student in any of those pictures. Not one. I just cried." She was astonished at the marginalizing of such a great number of her peers and, for a moment, disarmed by their sudden invisibility: "[Is] my school not really as mixed as I think? Are there not . . . many black people? No, I'm not insane." In pained frustration, Tiffany dashed off a Letter to the Editor, which was part well-reasoned plea and part fearless indictment: "The pictures in the *Marietta Daily Journal* could fool a person into believing that we are still a segregated school system. . . . I am an African-American Marietta High student whose voice was not heard. I am positive that at least one picture could have been included of a minority. In the future, I am sure that it will be greatly appreciated if extra precautions are taken to ensure that our entire student body is fairly represented."[28]

Without notifying her, the paper published it two weeks after the dance. In describing to me the community reactions to the letter, Tiffany started to cry—"it was awful"—no black students voiced support for her position, and white students openly derided it. Black teachers did, however, find moments to take her aside and applaud her courage. The happiness of her graduation from MHS—which she'd so anticipated—was tainted by the aftermath of the letter. She was stared at, whispered about, and, at Senior Day, bullied and insulted by the mother of the student who had, two years before, called her a nigger. On that same day—one of supposedly happy commemoration of the class's accomplishments—the boy who had suggested that black people be reenslaved taunted Tiffany's younger brother until he punched him. "I didn't really know how to verbalize anger" in high school, Tiffany reflected. The letter—an effort to do just that—had caused her such strife. "Would you take it back if you could?" I asked her. "Oh my god, no," she said, "I'm very proud of myself."

Betraying *Brown* to Staunch Resegregation: The Paradoxes of the IB

As Tiffany is quick to point out, the white IB students of her era were not all the unashamed racists she described. One of them I knew quite well—I remember when he left the private school we'd both grown up in. A funny, irreverent boy, he was a lyrical writer and a hapless romantic. His futile pursuit of my glamorous, dismissive best friend inspired our English teacher, who forced us through *Great Expectations*, to nickname him Pip. Despite his amorous miscalculations, he was thriving at our school, appreciated by the teachers and admired by his friends. But he left because his district high school had just adopted the International Baccalaureate program, a development we whispered about in our ignorance as if it were a rival faction's impending coup d'état. And in a way, it was. The IB program at Marietta High, just down the road from the private school I attended, would surreptitiously drain several of the best students from our classes. In the mid- and late 1990s, the International Baccalaureate program was making gains not just in Georgia schools, but across the United States.

Founded in 1968 in Switzerland by a group of secondary school teachers, the IBO aimed to provide an internationally oriented curriculum and diploma program that would be recognized by universities worldwide, creating common standards by which to judge the graduates of a public school in Brazil, a private school in Texas, and a prep academy in France. Although this creation of a common rubric was an important goal of the founders, historians and proponents of the program contend that more essential to the mission of IB is the "global dream" that animates it and what author Paul Tarc calls the "transnational social movement" cultivated by the IBO.[29] In 4,583 schools in 150 countries across the world, the program boasts more than 1.3 million students. (Of those 4,583 schools, 1,751 are in the United States, and 75 are in Georgia.[30])

There is a whiff of the miraculous in Marietta High's adopting of the IB program, more specifically, in Mariettans' embrace of it. Not only was the IB established at Marietta High without any local resistance, despite its cost, but it was the fourth school in Georgia to adopt the program, although Atlanta and its environs are host to much more progressive districts.[31] In 1994 and 1995, the *Marietta Daily Journal* ran a series of articles touting the IB and calling adoption of the program "a huge step into the ranks of the elite" and "the kind of educational reform that parents have been asking for."[32] A lone voice dissented—that of white 1980 MHS graduate and MHS parent—Mickey King. A frequent letter writer, King condemned the lack of outspoken conservatives on the school board. Decrying Marietta's nonpartisan school board elections, he argued that they had led to the instituting of the IB program and the expectation that all talented students would take part in what he deemed the "left-wing radical[ism]" of IB's "political indoctrination package."[33]

Considering Marietta's and Cobb County's recent history, it is hard to imagine a place less in need of conservative representation. In 2002, Cobb County Schools placed "evolution is a theory, not a fact" stickers in more than 30,000 biology textbooks. When parents sued, a four-year legal fight erupted, costing the district $250,000 and ending in a settlement and a great deal of adhesive-dissolving soap.[34] In 2010, the *Marietta Daily Journal* editors (and many readers) inveighed against the university system of Georgia chancellor for not taking a stand against the Development, Relief, and Education for Alien Minors (DREAM) Act and purported "criminals" like undocumented (honors) student Jessica Colotl. Colotl was jailed and almost deported while attempting to finish her bachelor's degree at nearby Kennesaw State University.[35] In this political climate, the IB was marketed, and accepted, as an undeniable victory for the high school and a mark of its prestige in the metro area. Among parents and community members, there was very little debate about the IB, which King bemoaned: "Why are we—conservative Marietta citizens—allowing this to happen?"[36]

The IB program is a United Nations–endorsed curriculum that emphasizes a global, rather than strictly national, perspective on world history and politics. The global scope of the IB's curriculum and its organizational ethos deserve, as King exhorted, a closer look. The former director's description of IB students as "global citizens" helps illuminate the organizational mission: "A global citizen is one who seeks out a range of views and perspectives when solving problems. He or she does not 'tolerate' or 'accept' cultural difference or viewpoints, since these words implicitly place the speaker at the centre of what is acceptable and right. Global citizens proactively seek out those who have backgrounds that are different from their own, examine ideas that challenge their own and then enjoy the complexity."[37]

Rather than passively acquired, knowledge in the IB classroom is forged in debate and in the exploration of multiple perspectives. One of three core requirements, the "Theory of Knowledge" course elaborates how the program seeks to encourage rigorous analysis not just of specific subject matter but of the very act of learning: "Theory of knowledge encourages critical thinking about knowledge itself and aims to help young people make sense of what they encounter. Its core content focuses on questions such as the following: What counts as knowledge? . . . Who owns knowledge? . . . What are the implications of having, or not having, knowledge?"[38] Courses such as social and cultural anthropology and global politics further embody this rather profound departure from what theorist Paulo Freire called the "banking" model of educating students, "in which the students are depositories and the teacher is depositor."[39] There is much in the IB's approach that would render it an ideal means of exploring local issues of social justice, educational equity, and populations of color, if, that is, populations of color were well represented in the program.

"It was brought into existence in Marietta to stop white flight," avowed Ken Sprague, who assessed the IB program as yet another disfranchisement of Marietta's black students. I pressed him on whether there wasn't some good in slowing down the resegregation of MHS. "There was never any equality in representation [in Marietta City Schools]" replied Sprague. "It was 'We serve the white students, then we look at the rest.'" In a trend consistent with Title I (high-poverty) schools of Marietta's size and demographics, the IB program does indeed serve mostly high-income white students, who make up less than a quarter of the school population. And not only does it require money in annual fees that could be spent on intensifying support for failing students, but it requires the restructuring of the school day to accommodate a very small number of full IB students. IB classes necessitate block scheduling, which means that, for example, students have biology every other day, for ninety minutes, instead of daily classes of forty to fifty minutes each. Some argue that this arrangement further challenges struggling students.[40] Perhaps most important is the reality that bringing more white students to MHS, only to segregate them into an exclusive program with the best teachers, intensifies the plight of low-income students of color. It may hail from Geneva, but the IB program at Marietta is a product of an American past and present in which structural inequality mediates students' social and academic experiences.

Much like Blue Devil players and fans describing colorblindness in football culture, recent graduates paradoxically testify to and dismiss the salience of race and class in their tracked academic and social experiences. Onyeka Aniemeka, a Nigerian student who graduated partial IB in 2012, described social life at Marietta as shaped by socioeconomics.[41] How "rich or poor you were" affected where you socialized and with whom. It mattered if "you could afford to go to concerts all the time" or only "hang out [here]," said Onyeka, gesturing with a giggle to the Wendy's dining room where we were nursing our Frosties.[42] Beyond money, what most defined student life was "how smart you are," explained Onyeka. She went on: "The segregation [at MHS] isn't based on race, it's based on your brains . . . either you're an IB student or a college prep student at Marietta. And teachers will treat you that way too." Even though Onyeka brought up socioeconomic class, as few graduates do, she divorced class from "brains," which is about, in Onyeka's terms, possessing innate intelligence and valuing academic achievement. Although Onyeka noted that power structures and city politics outside the school walls shape opportunities within them, she placed the responsibility to achieve squarely on the students themselves. Her roommate Bella—a 2012 Filipina grad of MHS who went full IB—offered a perspective on her and Onyeka's "foreignness." They both immigrated to the United States as children, and, as Bella asserted, "[because] we're foreign . . . we appreciate opportunity more." They agreed that the company they kept was determined by who "cared about school," as Onyeka put it, and those students, they reflected, were usually high-income Asian or white students who composed the majority of their IB classes.

The notion that segregation at MHS is produced by the individual alchemy of "brains" and "values" instead of tracking's reflection of structural racism and poverty is not a new perception among students and recent graduates. An article researched at MHS in the late nineties focused on black students who were "early leavers" enrolled in the school's alternative diploma program. The students observed that teachers and school administrators who disproportionately targeted black students for disciplinary action or remedial coursework were not ever discriminating or acting on their prejudices but rather "differentiating between 'high achievers' and 'low achievers' and 'teacher's pets' versus 'troublemakers.'"[43]

Segregation based "on brains" similarly theorizes a set of behaviors that compose social relations at the high school. In the interpretation of contemporary students, these behaviors—failing classes, making good grades, being selected for honors, being suspended from school—are strictly those of individual students and teachers in the context of specific relationships. Tracking reinforces this notion that intelligence and achievement, on their own, structure relationships and community at school, without recognizing the impact of the discourse and resources of an unequal society on who is and is not perceived as "having brains."

The separateness that smarts entail at the high school is intrinsic to MHS's publicizing of the program. Marietta High's webpage for the IB program actually highlights the achievement gap between IB and non-IB students: Marietta High IB students score, on average, 300 points higher on the SAT and 6 points higher on the ACT (a 36-point scale) than non-IB students do.[44] Foregrounding these data to represent the program sends a strong message to parents that, if enrolled in IB classes, their children will be among students with scores like theirs and, implicitly, families, values, and backgrounds like theirs. Marietta's IB program sanctifies this segregation and lends it the aura of truth through the incontrovertible "proof" of SAT and ACT numbers, AP and IB exams passed, and college scholarships earned. Through its supposed "segregation by brains"—stratifying students into those deserving of an excellent education and those not—the IB in many ways reproduces barriers it is supposed to be breaching. Segregation by brains is the rallying cry among proponents of gifted education. Bright students, in this argument, not only deserve but *need* the best courses, teachers, and resources in order to have their superior potential accessed and enhanced. Works such as the 2004 report "A Nation Deceived: How Schools Hold Back America's Brightest Students" and the 2005 book *Genius Denied: How to Stop Wasting Our Brightest Young Minds* mark a backlash against what the authors call America's "lowest-common-denominator culture," which prioritizes the needs of low-achieving students to the "educational neglect" of the gifted.[45] Suggesting, as these texts do, that gifted children face hurdles in public school to the same extent as their struggling peers seems misguided—who is more likely to have an advocate in public schools, a gifted child or a failing student? Yet, the point is well taken that tracks are "politically and socially significant spaces" for low- and high-achieving students alike.

It is critically important to document the impact of tracking on struggling students, but it is also essential to consider what happens to high-achieving students in tracked high schools. Such students are led by discourses that permeate their schools and communities to believe that they are intrinsically better and should be kept separate from those "below" them. In a 1963 essay, James Baldwin described racism as not just dehumanizing and wounding for black Americans, but for whites, too, who because of it suffer "an inability to renew themselves at the fountain of their own lives" and to "see themselves as they are."[46] Tracking has deep and damaging implications for its chosen, as well.

For full IB students, as the freshman, sophomore, and junior years progress, the passageway between IB and non-IB becomes increasingly narrow, and for some, closes altogether. A rowdy panorama shrinks to a portrait of, in 2012, forty-seven stole-bedecked seniors. Mickey King's daughter, Savannah, a 2010 graduate, refused this route. Savannah's choices suggest that a stellar education can be had outside the IB program and that pushing excelling students into it intensifies academic stratification at MHS. One of the few STAR students—a statewide recognition—in the last ten years who wasn't an IB graduate, Savannah King took the path her father advised, which was, essentially, one of her own devising.[47]

One is astonished by the number of educational options enjoyed by privileged students who have transportation and a stay-at-home parent in a metro area like Atlanta's. As a child, Savannah was homeschooled, attended a private, Christian, hybrid school, and went to her local public schools, which were in Marietta.[48] She remembered that her self-motivation— beginning her day's assignments every morning before her mother awoke— produced plentiful free time, which she used playing sports and going on field trips with other homeschooled or hybrid-schooled kids. In middle school, she attended Marietta Middle and continued to flourish academically, but she said she was surprised that she was encouraged to fill out her schedule—urged by her teachers to choose "all advanced classes"—without even speaking with her parents.[49] To borrow a line from the fiscal showdowns of recent years, just as a budget is a "moral document," so too is a course schedule. The queries behind the class titles are: What are you here to learn and from whom, and with whom, and *why?* Some graduates processed such questions unconsciously, but Savannah made an intellectual exercise of them as she proceeded through her school years.

By high school, Savannah had embraced the importance of tailoring her path at school to her own desires and curiosity, not those of the institution: she played soccer and was a cheerleader (recent squads have been about fifty-fifty white and black), which she said would probably have been diffi-cult if not impossible with full IB coursework. She remarked of the IB math and literature classes she took (she did not take IB world history, often targeted by critics of the program's "ideology") that she never felt that she was being "indoctrinated." On the point of her little sister's educa-tion, Savannah lobbied her parents for Marietta High instead of the small, private school she'd been attending. Her parents worried that in reg-ular classes, her sister would be distracted by the "behavior problems" of that "peer group," as Savannah said, where the quality of instruction is eroded by the demands on the teachers to be "disciplinarians." Savannah remarked that though her sister might not excel in AP or IB courses, it was "the academic discourse" that would make the difference. "Maybe she will struggle," admitted Savannah, "but she'll benefit from the questions and commentary . . . [of students] who facilitate a good discussion."

In Savannah's advocacy of high-level classes for her sister lies a persua-sive de-tracking argument: a slower student benefits, she asserted, from astute peers and compelling curriculum and exerts no negative impact on the intellectual community. Savannah herself is a testament to de-tracking in the sense that she resisted institutional categorization. She credited the high school with shaping her socially and intellectually. Raised in a conser-vative Christian family and educated in her primary years in small groups of like-minded white students, she praised Marietta High as being full of folks she'd "never be around . . . any other way," which "forced" her to "develop socially and interact with people different from" her. Whether such "forced" interaction challenges prejudices and builds community is a question to which we'll return.

At Marietta High, the tracking of high-achieving white students may be detrimental to community, but the tracking of struggling students of color threatens community *and* the success of the student. Tracking is exacer-bated by policies that do nothing to support, and arguably do much to undermine, the achievement of minority students. Athletics, which gradu-ates testify facilitates their friendships across race and class, also has undue influence on the academic trajectories of many students of color. Even as Marietta's football fortunes continue to wither and very few seniors win college scholarships to play, the program endures as a central cultural touchstone. Although the high school leadership emphasizes that suc-cessful credit recovery programs, intended for students who have failed core classes and cannot be promoted, and expanded afterschool tutoring are testament to their commitment to academics above all else, football consumes twenty after-school hours a week and does not demand that players pass all their classes. A student will remain eligible for football even if he is not going to be promoted to the next grade level—an advantage for the coach of a talented player, but likely not for the player himself.[50] The fact that most public high schools have such requirements, and hence most high schools hobble struggling student athletes with low expectations in the classroom and high expectations on the field, doesn't exonerate Marietta High.

Student athletes receive tutoring support, should they want it, but the goal of such academic intervention seems to be maintenance rather than excellence. Caleb Cox, a 2009 black graduate who enrolled at Kentucky Christian University on a football scholarship, recalled that he was tutored for the SAT by a black peer (the daughter of beloved coach James Richards) who took advanced courses all the way through high school. He recalled being impressed that the classes she took at MHS were "college stuff."[51] Another friend taking AP and IB classes told Caleb he had been exhorted to perform well on the end-of-year tests to buoy the school's overall results. "Well, they didn't say [anything like that] to us in college prep," he'd admitted to his friend. Without critiquing these categories and distinctions, Caleb testified to their existence. Like ethereal music emanating from a hidden source, the classes that high-level students took were a classroom away, yet of another world entirely.

Classes in high school can be, as they were for Caleb, merely what happened between basketball and football and track practices, and can even come to resemble them, as he recalled with a chuckle: "Me and my football buddies, when we had classes together, it was a party in [there]!" But engaging courses with compelling curriculum—Caleb remembered having a couple of those too—can also be a fulcrum in community formation. Students who "have to sit next to each other" and "work together on projects," as 2005 graduate Ashley Ashton put it, are challenged and even changed by the experience of hearing another perspective—what Savannah King called higher level "discourse" and what 2005 graduate Elizabeth Daigle deemed "rigorous debate encouraged by excellent teachers."[52] Tracked academics reinstantiate divisions that students already carry with them—notions about their own abilities and those of their peers, and about their place in the world—that should and can be challenged by the intellectual community possible at a racially and socioeconomically diverse school.

"Come to MHS in the morning, before classes start, or at lunch," urged two recent grads. I had asked about "self-segregation," a term referring to those divisions students carry with them, and a troublingly popular phrase—like "reverse racism"—that seeks to name a phenomenon entirely outside the structural and historical context that produced it.[53] Whatever one calls it, the racial topography at MHS immediately strikes the visitor: white, Latino, and black groups of students take up habitual positions in the brief windows of the school day unstructured by classes and practices. As if they had been directed by signs or corralled by ropes, their arrangement has an aura of permanence: at the foot of the atrium's central staircase stand the black students; around the staircase's upper perimeter are Latino students; and at the front of the atrium are the white students. Megan Birch, a 2012 graduate, elaborated on the raced spaces beyond the main building, pointing out that the attractive senior courtyard is actually populated by IB students and other white students like herself, while non-IB black students ("a rougher crowd," in Megan's words) claim a concrete landing nearby.[54]

In the main atrium the IB students have their own cohort (near the clump of white students), but within that group, the class and race lines that structure student life everywhere but the athletic fields dissolve a bit. The Columbians, African Americans, Mexicans, Asians, and "Anglos," as recent IB graduate Cesar Verde puts it, find themselves on the same team, spending whole days together, enjoying the privileges and bearing the academic stresses of the program. It matters that you're "full IB"—that you toil together on essays, service projects, mock debates, and long exams; that you go to events together, give presentations together, and sometimes even travel together. Your solidarity is taken for granted in the IB program. For some IB students the privileges of gifted programs are all they've ever known, and perhaps it may go unnoticed that they were specially chosen. But, for others, entering the social and political space of the IB is an experience of self-making, a rearranging of the social world and one's place in it.

Cesar Verde, a 2012 graduate, was an anomaly among IB students. He began Marietta High as a college prep student, emerging from an eighth-grade year in the ESOL program. Most nonnative English speakers in

Marietta's schools pass through ESOL en route to college prep curriculum, in varying doses, but only a very small number move into the IB program and AP classes, as Cesar did. As a boy, he and his siblings accompanied his mother from Mexico to the United States to join their father, but around fourth grade, they moved back to Mexico where his mother was trying to retain her teaching job. He spent his formative middle school years in his hometown of Guanajuato, and when the family returned to Marietta (where his father had secured citizenship for everyone through the amnesty provision of the 1986 Immigration Reform and Control Act), he was placed in ESOL. Transitioning from the middle to the high school, the other Latino students were still Cesar's peer group; he stood with them in the mornings before school, where they congregated across the staircase from "the Anglos." When Cesar enrolled in pre-IB classes and then was accepted into the IB program (he was referred by a Colombian friend in the program, rather than urged by a teacher or his parents), the terrain shifted, and he found himself mingling with the Anglos before school, where most of his IB classmates gathered. Contact with his ESOL classmates dwindled to a cursory greeting in the hall, and what Cesar called "a weird distancing" developed between him and his old friends and his old life.[55]

Color and caste at MHS map onto the geography of the city in predictable ways: Verde made the same migration outside of school, in the city, as he did moving across the atrium at Marietta High, toward the other side of the staircase. West Marietta, where the stately old high school—now Marietta Middle School—looms among historic homes and where the Homecoming parade winds through streets every fall, is what Verde defined as "the community of Marietta." In that part of town, the Marietta Square's coffee shop and pizza parlor became Cesar's haunts, as they were for his white IB friends. He recently urged his parents to buy a home there (where house prices hover between $200,000 and $400,000), although an injury that put his father out of work and the pay of his mother's job in retail render such a move unlikely. Cesar imagined his younger brother enjoying rituals that he came to late and as an outsider: biking to the square for the Fourth of July celebration and joining the crowds who line the streets for the Homecoming festivities. If the family moved to West Marietta, his brother would become invested in the "real traditions," as Cesar put it.

The IB student community exists both apart from and inextricably in the world of "Old Marietta" where whiteness is a prerequisite and family money is taken for granted. But even as the IB is in some ways anchored in the hierarchy of the city and its Old Marietta ranks, IB cohorts are increasingly dotted with students with no real tie to Marietta, who spent whole stretches of their academic lives in other cities or countries entirely. The program's diversity is one of its greatest assets, but that diversity is still a far cry from substantial. As Cesar's memories suggest, it is difficult, if not impossible, to exist in two worlds at once—that of the Latino student community (whose families live east of the square, in apartments close to the expressway) and that of the upper-income Mariettans in the program, who are mostly white students whom Cesar codes as "the community of Marietta."

Although Cesar shaped himself into an IB success story, his achievements remain rare among Latino graduates. Despite the fact that Latino students compose an annually increasing proportion of the student body, and black students have held steady at half of the population, MHS leadership was seemingly unprepared for the challenges of its new era. Test scores stagnated or dropped between 2000 and 2012, and the achievement gap between white students and students of color grew, as did that between high- and low-income students. The culture of the current era of education reform—that of the 2002 No Child Left Behind Law (NCLB)—is a culture of what some deem public humiliation and punishment. Under NCLB, graduation rates and test scores determined whether a school would be labeled failing, put on a "watch list," designated a "focus school" needing special attention (as MHS was in 2012), or, after successive years without improvement, closed altogether. One can't say for sure whether increased attention to black and Latino achievement at the high school is cynical, altruistic, or some combination of the two, but the 2012 SAT scores demonstrate what MHS is up against. (See Tables 3.2 and 3.3.[56]) The data should also be read with an eye to the fact that of 350 2012 graduating seniors, 268 took the SAT; that is, 23 percent of the graduating class did not take the test at all. Presumably, all mean scores are higher than they would be if all students, not just those encouraged to take it or expecting to go to college, had been required to take the SAT.

Slowly, the system has implemented changes: greater after-school support (for which the district now pays participating teachers), more focused outreach to minority—especially Latino—parents, and better monitoring by coaches of athletes' grades (spearheaded by former head football coach, Scott Burton). However, recent changes to the calculation of the graduation rate spell a major setback for Marietta High, both in terms of public perception and a very real need to track the students who leave MHS before

Table 3.2. MHS Mean SAT Critical Reading Scores in 2008, 2010, and 2012
         by Race/Ethnicity

	2008	2010	2012
Latino	488	449	444
Black	441	452	457
White	535	562	539

Table 3.3. MHS Mean SAT Critical Reading Score by Family Income

Family Income	Mean Critical Reading Score
Less than $40,000	467
Between $100,000–$120,000	490
More than $200,000	600

graduation. According to the 2011–2012 guidelines, MHS must take into account the attrition of the entire four-year cohort, instead of simply calculating what percentage of seniors starting the school year ended up graduating, with adjustment for "official" dropouts.[57] It appears that graduation rates suddenly plummeted in 2011 because the new calculation includes students who withdrew during or after ninth grade. Not all of these students dropped out; some simply enrolled elsewhere, but because the high school didn't keep records on those students, their withdrawal decimates the "cohort" graduation rate. The "cohort method" is a public relations disaster for high schools, like MHS, just now adopting it. The difference in graduation rates produced using the previous "leaver" method and the "cohort" method—applied to the class of 2011—is stark. (See Table 3.4.)

The new cohort calculation method shows Marietta, and many other schools throughout the country, to be in dire straits. Increased attention and pressure on struggling public schools have fostered a mania of blaming, most of which is focused on school leaders and faculty and their failure to produce higher test scores, larger graduating classes, and smaller achievement gaps. Most of what students encounter outside school walls is not in the control of the teachers, administrators, and school board. Greater income disparity across the country accelerated by high unemployment, an anemic welfare state, and the denial of basic services to a large immigrant population all shape the lives of students who can't simply leave their

Table 3.4. Impact on Graduation Rate of Cohort Calculation Method

	2009	2010	2011 ("Cohort" Calculation Year)
Latino	68%	74%	39%
Black	81%	77%	54%
White	92%	91%	82%

troubles at the school doors. "The problems in public schools," one local educator said to me, are not Marietta's problems, nor those of the state of Georgia, but rather "America's problems."

Although Marietta High is doing better than some of its mediocre peers in supporting poor and minority students and in creating paths to prepare them for work and higher education, one obvious, if challenging, opportunity remains. Distinct from a host of factors over which MHS has no control, the IB is an area where administrators, teachers, and parents could collaborate to expand the program's reach to students whose lives it could change. As for how such reform is instituted and catalyzed in a school, Onyeka Aniemeka observed that the buck didn't stop with teachers and principals. "[The role of the IB] is just so political," said Onyeka, "it paints a good picture for the school. [Administrators and teachers] want to keep the IB kids happy, to keep the school happy, to keep the board happy." Marietta's all-white school board is not risk-taking.[58] A vise-like grip on the status quo, in the face of intensifying resegregation, characterizes the board's efforts to enhance the school system's reputation and draw high-income families back. This ethos has produced unwavering support of the IB program on the school board and absolutely no momentum to restructure the program toward ameliorating the striated social and academic environment at the high school. However, in the absence of institutional change, students themselves at times transgress, blur, and question tracking's categories so they don't feel so permanent and so powerful.

LaKenna Andrews, a black 2005 graduate, was not a great student; by the standards of the city schools, she was solidly below average. For above-average adolescents, there are options: in middle school in Marietta, students can be tested for entry into the accelerated STEM (Science, Technology, Engineering, and Math) magnet program or the MILE (Marietta Independent Learning Experiences) program. These possibilities for "gifted" students could also accurately be described as those available to children whose parents are savvy about which tests matter and why or parents who protest a lower track for their child. A dizzying list of acronyms on the city system's website describes the ten different annual assessments for middle and high school students.[59] These scores are used to categorize and place students internally and to assess the school for benchmarks like AYP (adequate yearly progress—which was phased out in 2012 with changes to NCLB).[60] Because of her scores on the assessment tests in middle school, LaKenna was placed in the high school's lowest track: "I had no idea I was in tech prep [instead of college prep] in ninth grade."[61] LaKenna recalled "tech prep" as remedial core classes, like math, in combination with vocational electives. In middle school, she recalled, "I didn't care what score I got [and so] I guess I was [placed] on a team that was challenged on certain things. It didn't matter to me back then; I didn't know what we were taking the test for. If I had [known], then I would have tried a little more." LaKenna's lack of interest in and talent for test-taking was translated as a lack of interest in her courses and in her future, which wasn't the case at all.

LaKenna's sense of powerlessness in discovering that middle school test scores "would just pretty much be your future" was somewhat mitigated by the help of a compassionate guidance counselor, who moved her out of tech prep when a classroom assistant noted that she seemed unchallenged by the material. After transitioning into college prep, she never felt that she received anything less in the quality of her classes and teachers than did advanced and IB students. She did observe, however, that since "tech prep [students typically] ended up going to the same schools [as college prep students], it's really stupid [to have such a track]. . . . Being in tech prep [signified that students were] only good enough to go to technical school or trade school when we were obviously better than that." The stigma of the tech prep track as LaKenna experienced it suggests that the track was eroding student confidence instead of creating opportunities for those with nontraditional talents. Fortunately, consistent with national trends in vocational education, there is no longer a tech prep track or diploma at MHS, and tech prep classes have been repackaged as the "Career Pathways" program, part of a 2006 federal overhaul of vocational education.[62]

Making a successful transition from high school into the workplace via a two-year college or associate's degree is increasingly elusive in an era when jobs are few—or at least those that do not require higher education in areas like science and engineering.[63] Dr. Tim Brown, director of vocational education at Marietta High, says that one of the major hurdles in his work is altering the perception that everyone needs a BA from a four-year college. "That is so, so wrong," he said. He gave the example of HVAC (heating, ventilation, and air conditioning), a field that needs no college degree but for which training is offered by Marietta High in partnership with the area technical colleges. HVAC, in Brown's thinking, should be far more popular than it is, but "white-collar" tracks such as health care and accounting are ascendant in career and technical education nationally, instead of "blue-collar" work in areas like heating and cooling or auto repair, which Brown thinks offer more reliable and concrete work opportunities.[64] Many of the white-collar tracks—architecture, early childhood education, finance—require a bachelor's or even a master's degree in order to be parlayed into jobs.

The paltry enrollment of many of MHS's "career pathways" suggests that college prep students who could benefit from focused career education are not participating in the program.[65] Only 12 percent of seniors in the 2012 class completed a career pathway and were poised to begin "postsecondary education" in their field (the Career, Technical, and Agricultural Education [CTAE] office does not have data on which students actually did). Most of those were Junior Reserve Officer Training Corps (JROTC) grads, that is, students who will enter the military after graduation in exchange for an eventual full or partial college scholarship. Brown articulated the goals of the program as allowing students to test and hone their interests and showing students that although all the pathways require further preparation after high school, not all rewarding work requires a college degree. Yet the program's white-collar career focus doesn't seem to reflect that ethos, and students of color, particularly, are falling into the gap between the rhetoric and reality of Career Pathways.

In tenth grade, LaKenna pursued a "healthcare sciences occupation" but lost interest and didn't complete the program at MHS or try to pursue further education in that field. Throughout high school, she was intent on going to college and is on her third try at a BA. She began at Fort Valley State, a historically black university in southern Georgia and a popular choice among black Marietta grads.[66] Accumulating debt all the while, LaKenna has been caught uncomfortably between the desire to get a degree and the need to find a full-time job that can pay for it. After I turned off the recorder, we talked about a trip she took to Kenya with her grandparents, who were missionaries to a village. She mused about what mission work means and how it operates in the particular context of the small community like the one she visited. "I'd like to do something like that someday, go to Africa and do that kind of work" she said, smiling brightly.

In 2014, Marietta piloted the IB Career Curriculum (IBCC), which combines two IB-level core courses with a career pathway such as graphic design, early childhood education, or programming. What might such a program have nourished in LaKenna, a below-average student with above-average curiosity, who had traveled outside the United States and pondered the impact of mission work in poor communities? Having clambered up from tech prep into college prep, the IB program probably didn't seem within the realm of possibility when she was a high school junior. It remains to be seen whether the career certificate option will fundamentally alter the culture of IB, expanding and diversifying its ranks, or if IBCC will instead function to protect the IB diploma program from meaningful desegregation. In the meantime, the "regular students" variously interpret and act on what such a label means and portends for them.

When white 2001 graduate Claire Duffie—my friend whom "Pip" pined after—transferred to Marietta High, she joined the ranks of the "regular" students. Although she took pre-IB classes in ninth grade, she made the switch to college prep as soon as she could. Most of her white peer group stuck with the program or took a host of AP classes, so her academic cohort was "the Latino kids and a lot of black students," as she said.[67] Her teachers, she recalled, were more likely to be "babysitting" and "dealing with behavior issues," leaving her free to indulge in her passion for theatre— monologue writing, scene blocking, and set designing—since there was little reason, in her mind, to pay attention. She claimed she could imagine how a more driven student would be infuriated by the pace, the distractions, and the atmosphere of her regular classes, but she wasn't that student. At our private school, she recalled, her daydreaming made her the target of our demanding math teacher's censorious lectures and our English teacher's worried attention. She grinned remembering the English teacher: "If she could have sat next to me in every test and explained the meaning of each and every question as we approached them, I think she would have. . . . She wanted me to feel like I was a valuable part of the classroom." She went on, "You don't get that" attention and guidance at Marietta High, "not because [the teachers] don't care, but because they really don't have time." Some teachers do "have time"—those teaching small IB classes of students enthusiastic about the subject matter—but Claire's college prep teachers, who were managing big classes of often boisterous students, didn't have time for the quiet daydreamer with a script tucked into her algebra book.

Like LaKenna, Claire graduated from Marietta with mediocre grades, ill-equipped for a four-year college. She went for a semester to a university a few hours south of Atlanta; twelve years later, she was without a BA (unlike LaKenna, however, she has no debt—thanks to the support of her affluent parents). When we talked, she was working as a waitress and "thinking about going back to finish school." Her experiences make clear the parallel between private education and the IB program—ideal teacher-to-student ratios; close relationships among students, faculty, and parents; stimulating courses; and all the extra support one could imagine. In the IB program, like at the private high school I attended with its 100 percent graduation rate, there are no cracks to slip through.

Contemplating the Master's Tools: Curriculum, Community, and What the IB Could Be

With the IB comes, paradoxically, the tools for analysis that lead some graduates to criticize the program for its elitism and homogeneity, but those critics have as their peers some evangelists as well. Tianna Quiller, a black graduate of 2012, told me how she endured a multi-bus commute to school and back once she moved out of district, so that she could stay at Marietta in the IB program. Tianna, the daughter of a lesbian mother whose long-term relationship ended when Tianna was in high school, struggled to maintain the pace and rigor demanded by the program, but she prevailed and graduated with an IB diploma. "It was great, just great," Tianna said of MHS through homesick tears, as she sat in her dorm room at Mississippi State, missing Marietta.

Between 2008 and 2012, Tianna's high school years, when the recession was ravaging cities and families, the homeless student population in Marietta increased 65 percent.[68] Tianna told me that she and her mother had had a very difficult time while she was in high school, but I didn't press her beyond that admission. A year later, however, I saw her photograph on the front page of the local paper—standing behind a podium, a mid-sentence smile gathering on her lips. She had been chosen as one of four Americans to address the International Baccalaureate's annual conference. Of course she had been, I thought, a charismatic student with a compelling story. But I didn't know the half of it. The headline read: "Marietta High School Alum Shares Story of Success Despite Homelessness."[69] Tianna had moved out of district, that much was true, but she moved because her mother lost her job, and they could no longer afford an apartment. She spent her senior year in extended-stay motels and left school each day unsure of where she would spend the night. Ashamed, she didn't tell her friends or teachers, and only when she missed her final exams did she finally admit to the IB program's coordinator that she had been living out of a duffel bag. Then I understood Tianna's tearful professions of love and loyalty, her Blue Devil ardor that really no one else I'd spoken to had matched. If you don't have a home, then the home of high school has an entirely different resonance, as does the home of a small, tight-knit program like IB.

Lauren Garcia, a recent IB graduate who moved from Brazil to the United States in first grade, praised the program for the opportunities it provided her as an undocumented student. Being with "the best of the best," as she said, and receiving intense "one-on-one attention" was a great asset and equipped her to win the scholarships that pay for the private university where she enrolled.[70] But Lauren also reflected on the way that the opportunities enjoyed by IB students are a lens on those not available to struggling students. "Because we get . . . special attention," she offered, "some of the attention that should be given to other students isn't given to them. In IB you also get a lot more encouragement than you would if you were just a regular student [and] I think that's one of the biggest downfalls. . . . I think everyone deserves equal encouragement, especially the academically [struggling students]."

A sense that that treatment and attention enjoyed by IB students are more than a matter of particularly committed IB teachers simmers in the perspective of some former members of the diploma class of 2010. Will Dean, a black graduate, took all pre-IB and IB courses through his junior year. For more time to study, he sacrificed his great love, baseball, only to eventually drop a class that disqualified him from full IB. An impeccably polite, soft-spoken young man, Will was at first hesitant to render judgment on the program, but, in stops and starts, he unfolded his perspective:

> Sometimes I would see the IB program as a way to separate white students from minority students, to create a barrier. Marietta was a

predominantly white school and Marietta is very—they love tradition. Sometimes it could be hard to accept that you have a greater population of minority students there [hesitating] . . . please—in no way am I picking on anybody! That was just my take on what the IB program was there [for] and once again, no one has told me this, it's just what I've seen. So do I feel like whites were given more advantages than black students? I won't say that, exactly, but I do feel that there was a lot of love . . . placed into the students in the IB program, versus AP students or the rest of the population. So more of the scholarships for graduates were going to students in the IB program. . . . [I]t kind of makes sense because that program is quote unquote more rigorous than what was given to the rest of the population, but why couldn't the IB program be—why couldn't more blacks or Latinos be given the opportunities to participate or be helped to participate in IB or the higher level classes at Marietta? That was just my take on why IB was set up.[71]

Will framed his interpretation carefully: he subtly euphemized the city's sometimes regressive politics (Mariettans "love tradition") and eschewed placing blame on "whites." Yet, he suggested, the racial homogeneity of the program is not accidental, and struggling students of color could also benefit from being "given the opportunities" of an IB education.

Partial IB students like Will can offer analysis from that no man's land between the rarified world of full IB and the hoi polloi of college prep. Black 2009 graduate Camille Hill, also partial IB, dropped the full IB load in order to participate in the Youth Apprentice Program (YAP), which allows seniors to work part time. Like Will, she had intended to pursue the IB diploma, and when she started pre-IB classes in ninth grade, she discovered a social landscape reconfigured by tracking. "It was very daunting," she admitted.[72] "I remember my first [IB] class coming in; I was like, 'Oh I'm the only [black] person here—where is everybody else?' I guess I didn't really realize that it . . . [wouldn't be] the same [classmates from middle school]. [IB] was a completely different atmosphere and I realized [then that] everybody wasn't in the same level, education-wise."

Of course, no two students experience tracking and its dynamics exactly the same way, and some students of color were less struck by the demographics of their classes: a 2010 full IB graduate, Ryan Henderson, reflected that the IB program was "pretty diverse," a dearth of Latino students but "enough" black students.[73] (Henderson is the child of a white mother and black father.) He estimated that in his classes of full and partial IB students, black students made up "about 30 percent, probably." Although there were demonstrably more black and Latino students in Ryan's era than at the program's inception in the mid-nineties (of forty-seven IB candidates in 2012, thirty-one, or 67 percent, were white), majority-white IB cohorts are troubling in a 72 percent black and Latino institution.[74]

It was plainly world shaking for the white students of the mid- and late nineties to acknowledge not only that black students were a permanent presence in "their" advanced classes, but also that, in many cases, they were their intellectual superiors. Priscilla Graves, a black English teacher who worked at MHS from 1995 to 2004, recalled that it was "frustrating" to see high-achieving black students assailed by racism and social alienation.[75] She observed of the high school, "It had been one way for so long; the mindsets hadn't caught up with the transitions being made." I asked Tiffany Turner if she thought Mariettans' "mindsets" had evolved in the years since she graduated in 2001. Had anything changed for black students at MHS? She doesn't go back much, she confessed with a wry laugh, but from the experiences of her younger brother at MHS, she judged that: "[Black students] have a different mentality of what it means [to be high-achieving]—they don't expect to be not the smartest kid in the school. [Black parents] don't necessarily encourage their children to only succeed in athletics. It's a different breed of black people—and white people—it's different. Even now, my brother, he graduated in 2005 or 2006 and even his class, it seemed a lot different. He hung out with more of the white students—it's different. It is easier."

Demographics shifted at the high school between 2001 and 2012 (from 11 percent to 22 percent Latino and from 38 percent to 24 percent white), and IB enrollment shifted with them. Tiffany observed that "statistically speaking" there must be more high-achieving black students at MHS than in her time. A good thing, she imagined, since when she was there, "it was decidedly uncool [for black students] to be smart." In 2012, there were, in fact, not a great deal more black students than when Tiffany graduated— an increase of 4 percent with little change in the overall high school enrollment numbers.[76] However, as Tiffany guessed, more black students are participating in the IB program. She recalled the presence of three other black students in her IB classes and, at her graduation, one full IB black graduate. In 2012, 293 students of color enrolled in IB classes, up from 235 in 2008. (See Table 3.5.) This total includes ninth and tenth graders who were taking a "pre-diploma course" or "pre-IB" classes. Distribution of IB students across grade levels is important because the attrition among students of color as they move toward eleventh- and twelfth-grade IB coursework is high. For example, in 2010, 83 of 169 ninth graders (49 percent) who were enrolled in pre-diploma classes were students of color.[77] That same year, 49 of 142 twelfth graders (35 percent) who were enrolled in IB classes were black, Latino, or Asian.

Once seniors of color have labored through that year's IB coursework, the hurdles remaining to graduating "full IB" are substantial—a barrage of IB exams, costing up to $700, and a demanding final essay requirement.[78] Most of the IB seniors of color in 2010 did not complete all requirements for the IB diploma (there were seven nonwhite diploma graduates in the class of thirty in 2010). Although the attrition of nonwhite IB students is a distressing trend (and not one mentioned in the "Key Areas for Improvement" in Marietta's 2012 IB Review), the climbing percentages of black and Latino students in IB classes signal a degree of positive change since the late nineties. Still a kind of fortress, IB has seen more nonwhite students finding ways in and, like Lauren Garcia did for Cesar Verde, marking out a path for their peers to follow. (Table 3.5 shows demographic change in the IB program from 2002 to 2010.[79])

In the decade or so since Tiffany graduated, not only have white students become the minority at MHS, but influxes of Latino students have affected both the composition of the IB program and the way those students reflect on paeans to diversity. Brazilian-born 2011 graduate Amy Rocha suggested that the IB community uniquely fostered the exploration of difference over the appreciation of diversity. As she related with exasperation, "Students [outside the IB program] can't talk about politics with me, they can't give

Table 3.5. MHS IB Participation Percentages by Race/Ethnicity

	2002°	2006	2008	2010
White	74%	61%	59%	55%
Black	N/A	25%	27%	28%
Latino	N/A	6%	5%	9%
Asian	N/A	5%	4%	5%
Other	N/A	3%	5%	3%

°Data disaggregated by ethnicity were not available (N/A) for 2002.

me insights on their culture because honestly they don't think about those things. So I find myself valuing diversity so much more . . . [when] people are bringing good things into my life rather than just making the crowd look colorful."[80] Amy's reflections resonate with educator Marie-Therese Maurette who laid the theoretical groundwork for the IB program in the late 1940s and had this to say of "international education": "It does not happen by chance, by some kind of mysterious osmosis. It is not caught; it is taught. Rubbing shoulders . . . helps . . . but it is certainly not enough."[81]

Amy's dismissal of "diversity"—a value and a virtue often paired with colorblindness in the reflections of many graduates—points to her perceptions of the shortcomings of integration as experienced by students outside the IB program. Offering a distressing appraisal of the "diversity" at MHS outside IB's bounds, Amy told me: "There's such a large immigrant community in Marietta, and such a large majority of them don't go through IB and don't care about their studies and go to school and get in trouble and by sixteen they're pregnant." She continued, "The Latinos are a clan. You don't see any intermingling. Only with a very few outgoing individuals. And most of them are speaking Spanish more than they're speaking English." Of eighty 2011 Latino grads (a distressing 39.1 percent graduation rate), fewer than 5 percent graduated full IB.[82] The disappointment and frustration evident in Amy's assessment reflect that of education researchers across the country.

For Latino graduates I've spoken with, the impact of racial, income, and ethnic diversity at the high school and the impact of tracking are connected. Although Amy skewers the superficial "diversity" that she says many students tout, that diversity is notable to students in college prep classes that "don't have many Caucasians," as 2013 Guatemalan-born graduate Benjamin Derra put it.[83] Bridget Reyes, a 2013 graduate whose family hails from Mexico, couched her observations in different terms than Amy Rocha, but she also placed little inherent value in diversity.[84] Yet Benjamin and Bridget both identify the IB program as uniquely diverse, compared to the homogeneity Benjamin said characterized his college prep curriculum, and, they noted, IB students seem more "open-minded" about difference.

In Bridget's and Benjamin's analysis, the term "diversity" is revealed as a code for a contentious past and a tenuous present in black–white relations, relations in which they have little at stake. As Bridget put it: "I don't think diversity matters that much, I guess you could say." She went on: "I think as long as you're doing good in school and you're involved, then you're fine.

Whether it's a sport or a club then, I think you're fine. 'Cause I don't have that many white or black friends, and all I hang with is Latinos. But I think I did fine!" Benjamin echoed, "I don't think any [students] notice [diversity at the high school]. . . . I don't think it makes much difference." In stark contrast to most of my interviews with their black and white peers, Benjamin and Bridget pay no lip service to the demographic makeup of the high school as shaping their experiences, achievement, or worldview. Both Bridget and Benjamin testified to the exalted place of the IB students and the resentment it fosters: Benjamin recalled that the full IB students had been booed at graduation practice. Maybe it was a just "a joke," he suggested, but he didn't really think so.

The scorn that some college prep students have for the IB program sometimes has its foundations in scorn for their own curriculum. In reflecting on how "easy" her college prep classes were, Bridget claimed that college prep students are done a disservice by that curriculum and by the "low expectations." She went on: "When I talk to [other students] about education, they see the gap [between college prep and IB] and it's really huge. . . . I think IB gets the better teachers; they get higher expectations, but they also get the resources they need because they have such high expectations. I think if CP [college prep] had higher expectations and teachers believed CP was as good as IB, CP would be much better and we'd learn a lot." Both "involved" students who are college-bound and who went to football games and gathered at the square for community events, Benjamin and Bridget are not dismissive of diversity because they are unengaged in their community. They are dismissive of it as a category of experience for the privileged—for example, the handful of Latino IB students who have classes, field trips, and projects with black, Asian, and white students.

When it comes to advanced academics, Latino students are dramatically less likely than their white peers to be identified for entry into gifted tracks or to enroll in advanced math and science courses, which research shows are strong indicators for academic success over the long term.[85] Some students not only don't enroll in such courses, but are barely aware of their existence—as AP and IB are typically the province of students who have long had their academic skills validated and praised by their teachers and parents. One Latino student who was supposed to graduate in 2013 but instead had to enter the credit recovery program told me he "didn't know" if he had taken any AP courses—"Does that mean 'advanced'?" he asked me guilelessly. His comment suggests that not only did he take solely college prep courses, but that "CP" for him was a closed circuit in which he didn't socialize with anyone enrolled in advanced classes. In observing the academic and cultural chasm between the majority of Latino students at MHS and the handful of Latino IB students like her, Amy Rocha was also indexing the marginalizing of Latino students in public high schools across the country, even those high schools with curriculum and teachers who could make a dramatic difference.

Prompted by program demographics at schools like Marietta High, the International Baccalaureate Organization has focused on expanding its numbers of "underrepresented" diploma students. A recent report suggests that, perhaps shockingly, Marietta's 2012 diploma class demonstrates better inclusion than many of its IB peers. (See Table 3.6.) The IBO reported in 2007 that a scant 9 percent of IB high schools in the United States had twenty or more "minority candidates."[86] Marietta is at the cusp of that 9 percent, with at least ten Latino and black IB diploma candidates in 2010, 2011, and 2012. In light of national data, Marietta is faring better than most IB schools in terms of recruiting and retaining "underrepresented" candidates. However, applauding Marietta's IB program for these numbers allows one to hold the high school to an unacceptably low standard. The enhanced intellectual experience of IB graduates seems indubitable, and the benefits of the IB's sophisticated and challenging curriculum do so as well. Just

Table 3.6. International Baccalaureate (IB) Enrollment Percentages by Race/Ethnicity

	USA IB 2011	MHS IB 2011	MHS IB 2012
White	56%	53%	47%
Black	7%	27%	28%
Latino	9%	12%	18%
Asian	15%	6%	6%
Other	13%	2%	1%

Data drawn from "Marietta High School Diploma Program, November 2012," a presentation to the Marietta City Schools Board. Presentations are available to the public through www.marietta-city.org. This table depicts overall enrollment in IB classes, including even students who take only one IB class. Contrastingly, in 2012, the group of seniors taking all IB courses—called the diploma class—was far less diverse than this data would lead one to believe. The diploma class of 2012 was approximately 67 percent white, 17 percent black, and 13 percent Latino.

because race and class structure opportunity doesn't mean opportunities should be eliminated because they reproduce that structure.

Many de-tracking proponents do not support the elimination of challenging classes, but rather, the elimination of traditional institutional barriers, such as recommendations and applications. The IB program at Marietta High requires an application, grade reports, and standardized test scores for the previous year and, for students transferring into the system, four teacher recommendations. Components such as a traditional essay or even just a parental signature could present major hurdles for students the IB categorizes as "underrepresented." Another IBO report on the "diploma gap" (assessing why the program is not reaching "high-need" underrepresented students) depicts a diagram of a filter. Of the high-need students at the dozen or so schools studied, only 21 percent are prepared (that is, at or above grade level) for the IB program. Of those, fewer than one in four are offered entrance into the program and choose to participate. "This low rate," concludes the report, "stems from school and student perceptions that IB is an elite program for a small number of high-achieving students, rather than a high-quality curriculum to be made widely accessible."[87]

The IBO report emphasizes that, at many schools, and Marietta High is among them, the program is treated as an advanced course of study exclusively for gifted students. Contrary to this portrayal in subscribing high schools, the IBO insists that the "instructional system . . . is both feasible for students of average skill proficiency, and transformative for minority and low-income, i.e., 'under-represented,' students."[88] One interviewed teacher testified, "We have students who are number one in their class and number two-hundred in their class in the IB."[89] An MHS teacher with both IB and non-IB students similarly noted, "It is not [the students] who are going to score the highest on an intelligence test" who succeed in the diploma program, but rather those with a "work ethic."[90] To encourage underrepresented students to attempt the program, some school districts have intensified recruitment and support efforts and modified or eliminated application requirements. The results they've achieved offer a way forward for other districts willing to move away from solely courting high-income families and toward addressing the needs of low-income ones.

In the mid-2000s, the Arlington School District in Virginia began to address its achievement gap through enrolling more minority and low-income students in AP and IB classes using "rigorous recruitment and support procedures."[91] Not only did the high schools in the district eliminate prerequisites for high-level classes, but they also carefully coordinated their efforts with district parents—to ease doubt that opening up high-level classes would mean lower standards—and teachers, who would shoulder the challenge of teaching these more heterogeneous groups. "Cohort groups" for struggling students requiring greater one-on-one teacher support and summer sessions at nearby George Washington University were critical to lending students new to high-level courses the hand they needed. By 2008, 73 percent of Arlington School District students were taking IB and AP classes, with substantial gains particularly in the enrollment and success of black, Latino, and low-income students in advanced classes. A similar de-tracking effort in the Rockville Centre School District in New York to increase passing rates on the state regents exam yielded even more striking results.

Through heterogeneous grouping that began with abolishing low-track math and science classes, extended into mixed group pre-IB classes in English and social studies, and resulted in completely de-tracked course-work for the entire 2003 graduating class, 82 percent of the black and Latino Rockville seniors passed the regents exam that year, up from 32 percent in 1996. The careful cultivation of parental, educator, and administrator investment was critical to the de-tracking successes in Arlington and Rockville. Because of the commitment of resources, the demands on teachers, and the dubiousness of high-income, white parents, de-tracking is an enormous undertaking for a school district. Further, if de-tracking is not executed energetically and conscientiously, it has, research suggests, minimal success with the low-tracked students it targets.[92]

Although researchers disagree about why, research shows that parents who are vocal about tracking—that is, mostly affluent parents who meet with teachers, go to community forums, and even contact their school board members—are emphatically committed to preserving it.[93] School district leaders would need determined gumption for reforming the IB application process (or abolishing it) and funding support programs for low-income minority students in pre-IB and IB courses.[94] At stake are not just the rigorous courses, the array of support mechanisms and privileges, or the veritable guarantee of instruction from the school's best teachers, but also the ultimate goal of acceptance into and scholarships for college. After years in the trenches of their classes, low-income students of color should be allowed an equal shot at attaining state aid for college.

For better or for worse in Georgia, the merit-based HOPE scholarship has defined state policy on aid for higher education. HOPE supports high-achieving students (those with grade point averages [GPAs] above a 3.7) with a full ride and those with a GPA between 3.0 and 3.7 with ascending amounts of financial aid. In 1993, Georgia "led the way" nationally with merit-based rather than need-based scholarships; now in a dozen other states, a majority of state aid is merit-based. The ZIP codes from which recipients come reflect the predictably middle- and upper-middle-class status of their families.[95] The University of Georgia, the state's flagship university, enrolls the majority of HOPE recipients. At Marietta High, acceptance to UGA is 83 percent for IB grads versus 7 percent for non-IB grads.[96] That so few non-IB Marietta students are able to attend UGA on HOPE is worrisome. The students who most need the scholarship are not the ones being accepted, a dynamic exacerbated by the increased GPA requirements but one that could shift substantially with the expansion of the IB program.[97]

Altering the IB program—loosening its requirements and expanding its community—would stoke controversy in Marietta and instigate a difficult but necessary battle. The IB program, not unlike Blue Devil football, is a sacred cow in Marietta. The 2012 graduates Bella Dima and Onyeka Aniemeka named, without prompting, IB and football as the "most important" programs at the school. "The school is centered on IB and football," said Onyeka. Bella called IB a "privileged" group that is put first, quite literally: "You even walk first at graduation," she recalled. Their testimonies reinforce a common perception that the two programs are the school's priorities, consuming resources and attention disproportionate to the number of students in them. But a great deal is at stake for MHS's image in the football and IB programs.

Marietta City Schools' leadership is indeed deeply concerned with how Mariettans perceive, talk, and write about the school—more so, some say, than with education quality and *equality*. Both critics and supporters refer to Marietta's "PR campaigns" around school choice, the magnet elementary, and the IB program. The school system's communications director—its "brand manager"—is vigilant in mediating public conversation and perception of Marietta's schools. What, then, does the school's image have to do with its quality? As school leaders I've spoken with have insisted, the way that people see MHS affects the resources it can obtain, levels of parental support, and attractiveness of the system to high-quality teachers—that is to say, the quality of the education it offers.[98] Discussing the school system with the local graduates and parents who dismiss the school as "bad" and "struggling," I have often found these critics have little familiarity with its current programs, facilities, or staff. The pervasive notion in public discourse that "public education is failing" affects individual school systems like Marietta's profoundly.

The battle against a behemoth of such discursive power—failing public schools—is inextricable from the daily struggle by teachers, parents, schools leaders, and students themselves to make schools effective, fair, and supported. A Google search of "failing public schools" yields 13 million results; a similar search on Amazon produces almost one thousand titles. If these are courts of public opinion, the verdict is in. Bemoaning this trend, reformer and education historian Diane Ravitch counters that "Our public schools educate 90 percent of the population, and we should give the public schools some of the credit for our nation's accomplishments as the largest economy and the greatest engine of technological innovation in the world." She continues, "The negative rhetoric that now comes from . . . every media outlet . . . [is] demoralizing teachers and causing many excellent teachers to leave the profession."[99] In places—usually Southern states—where teachers cannot collectively bargain, where merit pay is tied to test scores, and where salaries are actually dropping, teachers are driven out of the profession by material hardships that accompany the afore-described political culture and legislative agenda that undermine public education and scapegoat educators.[100]

When an article I wrote lauding the high school's diversity was published in the local paper, a teacher whom I'd interviewed e-mailed me: "Thank you! We really needed that!" She later said again how nice it was to hear the system praised instead of pilloried. Indeed, the high school labors against a barrage of doubts, insults, and accusations in the public sphere; parents take issue with numbers they can access online or at data-aggregating sites like "SchoolDigger" and "GreatSchools," which assign ratings and stars to featured schools. Test scores, achievement benchmarks, and demographic data are a source of energetic public dialogue, but the lack of opportunities for low-income students of color gets very little airing in Marietta, as do the continuing impact of structural racism and the need for real commitment to improving the higher education and job prospects of the city's black and Latino students.

Integrated academics are critical to cultivating educational justice; "integrated schools" segregated by tracking reflect a definition of integration that, like the creed of colorblindness enshrined by a racial harmony narrative, will never produce equity for low-income students of color. The community-expanding dynamics of Blue Devil fandom are latent in the IB program, but at present, colorblindness coalesces into a refusal to acknowledge that poor students of color are structurally disfranchised and unlikely to reap the benefits of the IB program—regardless of their work ethic, their brains, or their motivation. At Marietta, an effort to expand IB by loosening application requirements and opening classes fully would likely be contentious, but already the school and its leadership are recalibrating, knowing that MHS cannot be, in the twenty-first century, the place it was just twenty years before. As the income gap continues to widen, as the children of the past decade's immigration waves progress through middle and high school, and as the number of affluent whites continues to shrink, Marietta will decide whether IB and AP students will be a blossoming community or a nearly extinct breed of sought-after "highest" achievers.

THE NEW INTEGRATORS

Latino Students

IT IS A TUESDAY afternoon, and Kendra and I are bent over our journals. Well, Kendra is bent over her journal—covered in the graffiti of idle moments in civics or biology class—and I am flipping through my field notebook for a blank page. A mentor with YELLS, a service and leadership club for students of color at Marietta High, Kendra is waiting for the bus to bring the elementary school students, one of whom is Dominica, her mentee. All semester, Kendra has been plotting how to get Dominica into poetry and out of trouble. The mentees are third and fourth graders: Latino and black children who all live on Franklin Road, the depressed strip of apartments and hollowed-out shopping plazas where the club's service activities are focused and where its members meet each week. Kendra glances over at my notebook—"Why aren't you writing? C'mon!" I explain that I haven't written poetry in a long time, and I don't know where to start. "You can start *anywhere*," Kendra says pushing her journal onto my lap, open to a poem about following your dreams that she had begun in lunch that day. "You can start here," she said gesturing around us.

On Franklin Road

For hot afternoons and sleepless nights:
  *Ramada, Quick Trip, Fast Trip Convenience Store, Fast Tax, Fast
  Emissions, Fast Tire Check, Franklin Auto Repair, Econolodge, Coin*

Laundry, Yes Mobile, Pay Your Bills Here Payment Center, 24 Hour
Rapid Refunds, Marietta Wing Mart, Franklin Liquor Store, Latin
Music and Video Rental

Crossing Franklin between clumps of cars, two boys toting skateboards
and little girl pushing a doll stroller; sneaking a smoke on their break,
willing the day to cool off, a teenage couple entwined under an awning;
looking into the blank blue between power lines and street lights, a kid
leaning on a cop car, waiting for the cuffs

For fluent hands, for bright combs and elastics, for home-cooking,
for home:

Martha's Pastelería, Mi Rancho II, Comida Hondureña, Iveth's Beauty
Supply and Hair Braiding, Delia's Dominican Hair Salon ("cortes,
cejas, hombres, mujeres, niños") Supermercado Iguala Meat and Fish,
Tienda Dollari Mas, El Guate Taqueria, Cinnamon Ridge, Castlebrook,
the Crossings at Wood Station, Nuestros Niños Pediatrics, First Step
Learning Center (Now Enrolling)

White lights and paper lanterns strung in a twinkling cursive, laughter
spilling down the staircase from the *mercado* up top; backpacks trun-
dling off the bus and dispersing like bright droplets across the complex
parking lot; a glow flooding the asphalt around the after-school center,
parents and children trickling in for coffee and a sugar cookie at the
evening community meeting

For the distance between what's hoped for and what is:

Cherokee purple and beefsteak tomatoes, crooked neck squash, summer
squash, roquette arugula, picklebush cucumber, serrano, habanero,
sweet yellow, cayenne peppers, chocolate mint, lemon balm, purple
basil, French oregano, English peas, sugar snaps, napa cabbage,
rainbow chard, cornflowers, sunflowers, butterfly bush

Plots bordered by split-face blocks, pansies spilling out of their cores,
newly planted seedlings seeking out the sun; students weeding, toting,
harvesting, the smell of earth and renegade mint plants rising up
around them; snatches of Spanish and English weaving through the
staked tomatoes; children each with a palmful of seeds, and a patch of
ground, ready to see what will bloom

Not far from where Kendra and I sat, in a spot overlooking the community garden in the courtyard of Liberty Pointe Apartments, is the leasing

office where Daniella Sanchez spends her days. Bilingual, charismatic, and patient, Daniella is terrific at her job managing Liberty Pointe—one of those rare "good" jobs in tough economic times: kind coworkers, reasonable hours, and decent benefits. When we met, she was smartly dressed and sporting delicate gold jewelry; the two tattoos peeking out from under her sleeve were the only hint that she was not to the manner born. In fact, to what Daniella was born is at the heart of her story. Her experiences as an undocumented student on the economic margins in Marietta are a testament to the powerful determination of such students who face a system in which persecution is a matter of course.

Without papers, Daniella and her mother came to the United States from Mexico City in 2003. They settled in Cobb County, near, but not in, the city of Marietta. An excellent student of English, Daniella was moved in and out of Cobb's transitional academy for international students in just a few months, ready to be integrated into the school system at large.[1] After a short stint at a Cobb County high school, Daniella was anxious to move on again: boisterous, violent students ran the show, intimidating the resource officers and fostering a tense, uncomfortable atmosphere. She found that Marietta High was nothing like that. "It was very nice!" she recalled. "Everyone was doing awesome."[2] After enrolling, Daniella joined Marietta High's JROTC (Junior Reserve Officer Training Corps) program and loved it. As she gathered from her peers, JROTC would pay for college. From there, she would go to medical school and train to be an obstetrician-gynecologist. "I had A's, A's, A's," she said, recalling how motivated she'd been in the middle of high school to earn a high grade point average and excel in JROTC. "But of course," she told me with a sheepish smile, "there was a boy." After Daniella got pregnant, she attempted to stay in school—to change nothing, to let no one know—but word got around to her teachers, and eventually she confessed to a guidance counselor, who was sympathetic, offering to get her a doctor's appointment and investigate child care options. I "should have done better," thought Daniella, but things could still turn out. She could still go to college, still serve in the Navy, still have the life that living in the United States promised a smart, hard-working student.

Cobb County authorities, armed with the power of both federal provisions and state law to identify and detain the undocumented, were ready for Daniella's family and the thousands like them. Two months before Daniella gave birth, her mother was pulled over by county police for a minor traffic offense. It landed Ms. Sanchez in jail because she had been driving without a license. For the undocumented, citizenship is mostly about the many "papers" the paperless lack: work permits, business and home loans, Medicare and Medicaid, Section 8 vouchers, food stamps, Pell grants, state scholarships, unemployment, retirement, workers' compensation. . . . Needless to say, when asked to "show her papers," Ms. Sanchez had none. A five-thousand-dollar bond was posted, but Daniella was told that even if she and her sister devastated their savings and paid it, their mother would still be transferred to ICE (Immigration and Customs Enforcement) and deported. The daughters did not attempt to get a lawyer, and like 94 percent of detained immigrants without legal representation, Ms. Sanchez was deported.[3]

The "deportation machine" tore another family asunder.[4] Left alone with their children—Daniella's baby and her sister's kids—in a house they couldn't pay for without their mother's income, Daniella and her older sister were forced back to the trailer park where they'd lived upon first arriving in Georgia. Daniella had to leave Marietta High; she was once again districted for Cobb County schools. She, her sister, and their children struggled to stay afloat in Cobb, and Daniella forged ahead toward graduation from her new high school. It was precarious and difficult, but they were doing it, until, that is, the next encounter with Cobb's law enforcement. "My sister," said Daniella with a sad smile, "she was very good with me—but not so good with the police." A cocaine user, a lover of dance clubs, an instigator of fights, and a reckless driver, Daniella's sister eventually got into real trouble. Even though she gave a false name—associated fortuitously with a documented immigrant—and her correct address to an arresting officer ("A correct address with a fake name?" exclaimed Daniella. "Who would do that?"), she was, astonishingly, released on bail. After running her fingerprints the next day, however, police eventually identified her as an undocumented immigrant with a previous charge. Around 1:00 a.m. a couple of nights later, officers came to the trailer park, looking for the Sanchez's unit. The last time Daniella saw her sister, she was disappearing around the back of their trailer, with "her keys and her stuff," as Cobb County police rapped on neighbors' doors seeking her.

What is the recourse for a teenager whose family members are fugitives of a state intent on leaving her with nothing and no one? At seventeen, Daniella was alone with her baby. Out of options, she confided in the social worker who ran the class for teen mothers in which she was enrolled at her new high school.[5] "I told her, 'I'm about to lose my home, and I have a kid, and I don't have no family.'" With the help of that social worker, a volunteer with the teen mothers' program, and a sympathetic immigration officer, Daniella obtained a work authorization. Soon after graduating, she got her "first real job" working in the leasing office of an apartment complex ("They needed someone bilingual!") and eventually an even better job at Liberty Pointe. Although Franklin Road is known for drug activity, violence, and its ramshackle complexes, each perpetually "under new management," Daniella calls it home and wants to make it safer. She encourages her residents, even the undocumented ones, to call the police if they are victims of a crime or even notice a suspicious-seeming neighbor. However, "a lot of people don't feel safe" because of "the racism against Hispanics," explained Daniella, and "the new law [HB 87]," which empowers local police to investigate the status of and detain immigrants suspected of being undocumented during routine procedures like traffic stops.[6]

Not "feeling safe" in the immigrant community is less about the fear of a mugging or car theft than the knowledge that a missing tail light may mean the end of life in the land of opportunity. Daniella's tale is unusual only in its ending—the stability that she crafted out of chaos. The repercussions of her mother's ordeal demonstrate that each deportation not only deeply damages the life of the deportee but also rends the web of work, childrearing, spousal support, and elder care in immigrant families and communities. Instead of civic responsibility, rights, and belonging, citizenship in the twenty-first-century United States has been defined by the threat of deportation.[7] Immigration enforcement like that which ensnared Daniella's mother severs the ties of "communal belonging"—to family, workplace, church, and neighborhood—and forcefully precludes "the integration of the criminalized alien as [a] legal subject" who is welcome and protected in his or her community.[8] Instead of opportunity, America has become the land of loss, loneliness, and "rightlessness."[9] And instead of a bridge to the future for immigrant students, high school has been rendered an island from which the bustling and beautiful mainland is ever receding. Daniella Sanchez learned about all that—watching what was hoped for slip away and carrying the loneliness, heavy as a sleeping child in her arms. Along with her own tenacity, serendipitous encounters with kind adults may have saved Daniella's life. However, her experiences point to the structural truth that for many immigrant students in Marietta and across the United States, the nightmare of being deported remains more real than the dream of becoming an OB-GYN.

The Daniellas of Marietta's schools have sought solid ground to stand on but have found little institutional support for their struggles. Like its high-poverty peers across the country, Marietta High School (MHS) is a shock absorber of rising inequality in the city: it faces increasing expectations of and demands on teachers, students, and school leadership as well as plummeting levels of state and federal funding.[10] In the aughts, MHS has seen ever higher enrollments of low-income Latino students and falling numbers of affluent students and has teetered on the edge of racial and socioeconomic resegregation.[11] There is, for the most part, no burgeoning malice toward or conspiracy against poor and undocumented students at the high school; on the contrary, MHS is staffed by committed teachers and administrators who want all students to flourish. However, the education reform agenda in Marietta is a neoliberal one, and the programs promoted by the school board are not designed to open doors for poor students of color or students without documents.

Market-oriented education reform—embodied in federal policies and flourishing across the country in local districts—does not prioritize the struggles of marginalized students or the formulation of creative and progressive policies that might bring them greater justice and opportunity. Education reform policies like the Bush administration's No Child Left Behind Act and President Obama's Race to the Top—which set aside funds for struggling districts to hire for-profit companies and corporate consultants and which emphasized the use of school choice and charter school alternatives—have their parallel in neoliberal economic policies of deregulation, privatization, and contraction of the social safety net.[12]

Just as the dominance of free market economic policy has altered how we understand "the role of government and the relationship between the individual and society," so too has market-oriented education reform changed the relationship between child and school and between school and community.[13] Students like Daniella—the undocumented, the low-income, the marginalized—are stranded by reform agendas in which they will never be "equally privileged" actors in the market, nor will they be viewed as potentially competitive "products" of the school system in the global marketplace. Assessed through the plethora of scores that typically define student performance, the majority of Latino students and poor students cannot measure up to the affluent, savvy students and families for whom market-based education policy represents a further expansion of their "freedom."[14]

Marietta's reforms are undertaken with good-intentioned faith in the free market: the system itself struggles to remain "competitive" in an era where faith in and support for public education is eroding. Marietta City Schools are a system, like other resegregating urban districts, where school reform has been guided by the goal of luring back affluent families and high-achieving children.[15] However, the instituting of the International Baccalaureate (IB) program for academically advanced students, the embracing of school choice, and the founding of a selective science and technology academy—a public, application-only elementary that competes with local private schools—have not measurably slowed resegregation.[16] Instead, these programs and policies have intensified the economic and racial isolation of Marietta's poor students at the level of the classroom and the school.[17] As Marietta's Latino student population grew from 17 percent to 30 percent in the decade between 2001 and 2011, such reforms did little to offer those struggling students greater opportunity.[18]

Education reform in Marietta does not seem a landscape in which parity for poor and undocumented students is possible, much less an integration movement that prioritizes those very children. Yet, in the struggles and accomplishments of Latino students at Marietta High, a new era of integration, instead of one of intensifying resegregation, is nonetheless becoming possible and real. Latino students are the "new integrators." Through community building on Franklin Road and school-based activism at MHS, Latino students resist local discourses of citizenship and transience that reinforce their status as a "barrier" to higher achievement in a market-oriented schooling model. Latino students' efforts to bring Marietta's undocumented and poor families of color into the schools' fold are critical to a new vision for education in Marietta.

The decades between the mid-sixties integration of Marietta High and the early aughts, when Latino students began to enroll in significant numbers, have remade Marietta economically and culturally. By 2020, a city that was majority white in 1990 will likely be more than a quarter Latino and a third black, and barring major policy changes, more than 20 percent of the city's inhabitants will be poor.[19] Although the 1986 Immigration Reform and Control Act's amnesty provision has helped to root a documented middle class of Latino families in Marietta, with positive consequences for their second-generation children, it remains the case that Latino students are most likely to come from poor families and, in Marietta, least likely to finish high school.[20]

Since the mid-2000s, the research and recommendations of desegregation scholars have been focused on the growing numbers of Latino students in American schools, both documented and not, and their growing
isolation.[21] In 2011, the graduation rate for Latino students in Georgia was
less than 60 percent.[22] In Marietta, the straits are direr: over the last ten
years, graduation rates for Latino students at MHS have inched upward,
but they are still far below those of white, black, and Asian students. In
2010–2011, all states were required to institute a new and much more rigorous graduation rate calculation method.[23] By the new calculation, only 39
percent of Latinos in MHS's 2011 class graduated.[24] Free market education
reform has neither drawn upper-middle-class families back nor made the
system better for the students who remain. "Once we picked [ourselves up]
off the floor," said the superintendent of seeing the new rates, and stopped
"thinking of every excuse, [we asked] 'What do we have to do?'"[25] The students of this discussion answered that question in powerful ways and
formed a new vision for education and community in the process. Marietta's
contemporary challenges aren't the first time the school has been racked
with the transformations of a new population and a new era, transformations for which school leaders had few answers. The past offers some
instructive parallels.

In negotiating the choppy waters of change, Latino students integrating
Marietta High have faced some of the same challenges as the black students of the mid-sixties. Many of the same arenas of interaction—the field,
the classroom, clubs, and the community at large—are the sites where
black students, and now Latino students, make the transition from members of the student body to its leaders and activists. The second-class citizenship endured by black citizens (and by Mexican Americans in places
like Texas and California) during the Jim Crow era has some resonances
with the "underclass" to which undocumented youth are being relegated.[26]
Yet after the *Brown v. Board* decision in 1954, the exclusion of black children from white schools and any group, team, or affiliation thereof had no
legal foundations. During the desegregation era at MHS, law no longer
enshrined the divides between black and white students.

Conversely, contemporary immigration law delineates sharp distinctions, not based in skin color, but based on a difference you can't usually
see: "legal" and "illegal." "They [feel] they are not supposed to talk about
[not having papers]," 2011 MHS alumna Amy Rocha, who is herself undocumented, told me. "They are just . . . shadows." In Rocha's interpretation,

the undocumented student's difference is paradoxical; it is invisible and yet it makes them invisible, too, at least to the administrators and teachers whose support those students most need. For the undocumented students at Marietta High—and the principal estimates that they make up 90 percent of the Latino student population—citizenship finds its social salience in the quotidian details of studenthood: who drives to school and who can't, who takes an internship and who doesn't even apply.[27] And it finds its political salience in the discourse of transience.

Transience discourse lends what scholar Patricia J. Williams calls a "hypervisibility" to undocumented students—not to their individual struggles—but to their impact as a demographic on Marietta's schools.[28] Although Williams discusses the quality of "hypervisibility" in relation to contemporary black Americans, it can be fittingly applied to the experience of being a hypervisible and yet marginalized person without papers. Williams writes, "How, or whether, [they] are seen depends on a dynamic of display that ricochets between hypervisibility and oblivion." The "hypervisibility and oblivion" of undocumented immigrants in Georgia magnifies their supposedly negative impact on Georgia's communities, schools, and economy while obscuring their rights and struggles as parents, workers, and students. The discourse of transience, what could be called an "obsessive indulgence," to quote Williams again, among school board members and local politicians, draws on and reproduces those dynamics of political hypervisibility and social invisibility. Transience discourse frames undocumented students and their families, who are often on the move due to economic necessity, as impediments to the stability and good repute of both the high school and the city.

Many of the low-income Latino students I interviewed lived, at one time or another, on Franklin Road. On Franklin, a population of five thousand overwhelmingly black and Latino residents make their homes in low-rent apartment complexes on Marietta's east side. Since the early 2000s, when Franklin Road's businesses and residences began their decline and crime took hold, the students of the corridor were identified as "the problem"— responsible for declining achievement and graduation rates in Marietta's schools.[29] A number of redevelopment proposals were floated during the aughts, along with a major bond to buy up properties along the Franklin Road corridor. Common to all proposals was the hope of sending Franklin's transient students elsewhere, a move that would, in the words of the 2013 school board chair, "transform the school system [since] a lot of our highest-needs and transient students come from the Franklin Road area." Although "transient" denotes a person or group of people who are not permanent denizens of a place, the term's discursive power in Marietta is in the framing of Franklin Roaders as marginal to the city and detrimental to its schools. Community building on Franklin constitutes a frontier of integration in the efforts of students and residents to refuse the stark separation of the city's troubled corridor from the community of its schools.

Today, the job of the school—to transform the country's children into engaged, educated, and employable citizens—has not fundamentally changed, but popular support for the institutions that shape the polity has disintegrated profoundly. The charter school and school choice movements have jeopardized support, both financial and popular, for public schools, which are still doing the lion's share of educating the country's most vulnerable children.[30] There are places where market-oriented reforms such as school choice have been welcomed by local parents and where charter schools have proven to be powerful sustenance for local communities, but by and large, the most disadvantaged children are not accessing the best of these innovations.[31] Public schools in the twenty-first century are the embattled heirs of their nineteenth- and twentieth-century ancestor institutions—schools that produced educated men from the illiterate newly emancipated and American citizens from the polyglot hybridity of an immigrant nation.[32] Injustice and discrimination have pervaded the history of American education, but so too have the democratic principles that, ostensibly, join Americans together as Americans. In this discussion, memories of desegregation, the threat of resegregation, the persistence of tracking, and the adoption of choice are given greater context and deeper power by the idea that public education in a neoliberal era represents the making or unmaking of that imperiled promise of "justice for all."

Mexico in Marietta: Global Neoliberalism in a Local Place

"By the reckoning of the U.S. Census Bureau, the United States has become one of the largest Latin American nations in the world," wrote cultural critic and scholar Richard Rodriguez in 2002.[33] As recently as 1980, Marietta, Georgia, had only a 1.2 percent Latino population; ten years later, it had grown by only 2 percent.[34] However, by the year 2000, Marietta's Latino population had shot to 17 percent, consistent with metro area and statewide trends. Atlanta's Latino population boom during that period was the greatest of the twenty largest metro areas in the United States, and Georgia saw a 300 percent increase in its Latino population between 1990 and 2000.[35] As of the year 2000, there were more than 435,000 documented Latinos living in Georgia, but estimates including undocumented individuals are as high as 800,000.[36] By 2010, there were almost one million Georgians identifying as "persons of Latino or Hispanic origin."[37]

In many ways, notions of a better life and more opportunity in the United States, the impetus for so many immigrants bound for *El Norte*, are born of a Mexico leached of opportunity by neoliberal policies championed by the United States.[38] Not by chance did Marietta's population come to be more than a fifth Latino, 65 percent of whom are from Mexico, according to the 2010 census. Those decades have reshaped Marietta's demographic and political contours, but a changed Marietta has its roots, in part, in a changed Mexico. Beginning in the early eighties, Mexican politicians began to accept the neoliberal reforms urged on them by the World Bank and by economists trained at the University of Chicago, the birthplace of free market or *laissez-faire* economic theory. In what scholar Raj Patel calls "the triumph of a certain kind of thinking about 'development,'" which prioritized the attraction of transnational capital, Mexico took on massive loans through the World Bank.[39] When these loans went into default, Mexico agreed to "structural adjustment": the contraction of the social safety net— health care and assistance to the poor—and the mass privatization of formerly state-owned industries.[40] Privatization and the devaluing of the currency in Mexico led to the 1995 "Tequila Crisis" in which the United States and other capital-rich nations were able to scoop up Mexican assets at the crisis prices precipitated by the reforms they pressed on Mexico.[41] Unemployment soared and Mexican workers—especially small farmers who could not compete with the 1994 NAFTA (North American Free Trade Agreement) influx of subsidized American corn—suffered deeply in the wake of these events. More than 1.3 million people were driven by hunger and poverty from the lands they had farmed and into cities.[42]

Yet, many economists and politicians on both sides of the border continue to champion neoliberal policies in "developing" nations, arguing that extreme hardship for the poor is simply the price of growth. In the words of a retrospective piece on NAFTA: "Supporters say Nafta [sic] was not conceived to solve domestic problems for any member country. Instead, they say, the growth in the nations' G.D.P.'s speaks to the pact's positive effects."[43] The United States intervened in Mexico in the name of economic freedom facilitated by free trade, foreign direct investments, deregulation, and privatization, but the freedoms produced by neoliberal policy were not enjoyed by all. Of American complicity, geographer David Harvey noted, "While proclaiming its role as a noble leader organizing 'bail-outs' to keep global capital accumulation on track, the U.S. paved the way to pillage the Mexican economy."[44]

Foreign investment in Mexico ballooned after NAFTA, but Mexican industry contracted, and resulting unemployment, plus displaced farmers, produced the massive emigration of the 1990s and 2000s. Patel argues against a discourse that posits immigrants as willingly pursuing the material rewards that await them in the United States: "This trajectory, from country to city to border crossing, is one that has been imposed on them. Yet *campesinos* want a better life and they want it in rural areas, in the communities where they live."[45] When one hundred thousand rural protestors flooded Mexico City in 2003 to speak against NAFTA and Mexican leaders' neglect of the rural poor, "they were fighting not to have to move, to emigrate, if they could avoid it," but "Mexican migrants found themselves not only pushed off their land, but pulled forcefully to the United States."[46] Immigration from Mexico to the United States is spurred by geopolitical dynamics beyond NAFTA and US immigration reform, dynamics that shape immigration flows as well as produce what scholars call "disposable workers"—those migrants whose poorly paid work is so critical to the US service sector.[47]

In twenty-first-century Georgia, immigrants who have been "pulled" to the United States have found themselves at the center of local discourse about citizenship that vilifies immigrants for the jobs they take, the crime they invite, and, of course, the impact of their children on the schools. This discourse of citizenship and its attendant categories of "aliens" and "illegals" have produced and reinforced one of the nation's most draconian immigration policing apparatuses. Cobb County, where Marietta is located, has led the state in formulating a ruthless brand of immigration enforcement. Since 2006, Cobb County has collaborated with the national immigration authority, dreaded in many immigrant communities: Immigration and Customs Enforcement (ICE). Two tools have been important in developing the capacity of the county to identify and detain undocumented immigrants. House Bill (HB) 87, which Daniella mentioned, is one; the other is a task force program providing for local law enforcement to be trained by ICE to detain people, such as Daniella's mother, thought to be undocumented and begin deportation procedures.[48] Until 2011, Cobb County was one of a handful of other counties in Georgia to use the training and enforcement tools of the task force program, but the Arizona-inspired bill, HB 87, made those practices law statewide. In 2012, Cobb returned a sheriff to office who was voted one of the top ten "toughest immigration sheriffs" in the United States by Fox News.[49] Among his accomplishments was "turning over" more than ten thousand undocumented immigrants to ICE since 2007.[50]

"Tough" immigration policing like that in Cobb is a process and politics that have made fugitives of law-abiding community members and poisoned the relationship between immigrants and their adoptive cities, and, in some cases, between students and their schools across the South and across the country.[51] In response to increasingly oppressive state legislation and prolonged inaction at the federal level, at numerous protests in Georgia and across the United States, undocumented adults and students have mobilized for immigration reform.[52] In Cobb, the anti-immigrant crusader D. A. King works out of Marietta, planting "RubiObama Amnesty" signs along I-75 and planning protests countered by a small but committed group of pro-immigration-reform Mariettans.[53] They, unfortunately, aren't getting the same attention King is from *The New York Times*, by which he was deemed "one reason [Georgia] rivals Arizona for the toughest legal crackdown in the country."[54] In Marietta, anti-immigrant rhetoric pervades the public sphere and the media; students in Marietta are immersed in it regardless of whether they wish to be. A third grader from Mexico, Lidia, who attends one of the city's highest-poverty elementaries, told me she loved President Obama. I asked her why. "Because he doesn't want to send us all back."

The growth of Marietta High's Latino population has been the greatest factor in its progress toward resegregation, while support for Latino students is eroded by discourses of citizenship and transience in Marietta. In the school board's rhetoric, transience decimates the graduation rate and depresses test scores, and students who are not citizens drain public coffers and are unlikely to pursue higher education. The students and families of Franklin Road are the target of much of this language: stigmatized as a "menace," to quote a *Marietta Daily Journal* headline, the denizens and their homes were referred to in online comments and articles as "those people" and their "slums," responsible for "uncompensated health care" and "increased crime."[55]

At a crossroads in the new century, the city and school board leaders can choose redevelopment to move as many low-achieving, low-income students out of the system as possible, or instead, they can choose to do the much harder work of forming creative solutions for newly arising challenges, solutions that prioritize not just raising the academic achievement of students of color but educating them with an eye to their worth, humanity, and centrality to the school and the community. At a time when Latino students remain the fastest-growing constituency of the public schools and the county's immigration policies tack ever further to the right, whether and how MHS chooses to support its undocumented students will have profound consequences for the students, the school, and the city.

Citizenship is not just who has legal status and the rights and obligations entailed thereby: it is who counts. Being an American citizen entails not only the privileges and obligations of our democracy—it confers belonging.[56] To quote Frederick Douglass, it is a place "within the pale."[57] Citizenship confers, theoretically, not only protection from the state—from detention by ICE, for example—but a condition of protection *by* the state, and a sense of belonging to an America in which one's talents, intelligence, contributions, and spirit indeed pave the path of and toward the American dream.

Whether Latino graduates are native-born citizens, first-generation immigrants, or what researchers have called "1.5"ers (those who entered the United States as small children) deeply informs their perspectives on the purpose of education and the meaning of community.[58] A "1.5"er who crossed the border illegally with her parents, Sonia Hill (née Torres) arrived at Marietta High at a moment when Latinos were, like the handful of South Asian students, an unremarked-upon minority.[59] In the early nineties, the high school had almost even numbers of black and white students and very few Latinos: the class of 1995 had only about fifteen Latino graduates.[60] The Mexican-born Mariettans of Sonia's parents' generation were uniquely privileged and burdened—many were beneficiaries of the amnesty provision of the 1986 Immigration Reform and Control Act. Viewed from the perspective of immigration policy that has grown increasingly punitive since the Clinton administration, the "amnesty immigrants" in Marietta are the lucky few.[61] But they were also, like the Torreses, very often large families surviving on meager wages in a city where no infrastructure yet existed of community groups, businesses, and networks for immigrant families.

For early Mexican immigrants to Georgia like the Torres family, the American dream offered little more than life without fear of deportation:

owning a home or sending children to college was not part of the promise. "We were very, very poor," Sonia told me, "It was more of a 'get out there and work' [mentality]."[62] By the time she entered high school, Sonia was living in Marietta with her mother and two siblings, the fourteen-member family having been whittled down by divorce and the marriages of the older children. Her older brother was the household's earner, and she, too, was encouraged to get a job and provide for the family when she finished high school. "No one ever told me," she recalled, "that I was expected to go to college. No one. It's not part of our—at least with my generation—it wasn't part of our culture."

At Marietta High in the early 1990s, being Latino was a not-yet-defined difference; it was not black and not white, an anonymity both freeing and isolating. By the time Sonia entered middle school in Marietta, after moving from Houston, Texas, she was fluent in both English and the ways of the American teenager. She remembered that the relative cultural isolation in Marietta—she estimated her elementary school back in Texas was 80 percent Latino—was a "shock" to her. In the social hierarchy at MHS, Latinos had no prescribed place. "I was accepted by both [black and white students]," she mused, "and it was very black and white. But I didn't feel like I was part of either group. I was able to kind of be in between. And it was okay. I was okay with it." When I asked about stereotyping or discrimination, she suggested there simply weren't "enough" Latinos to provoke such reactions among the white and black students and parents of the community. Sonia hung out with classmates of both races; her boyfriend was a black football player. She enrolled in an internship program at school called "Black Youth Leadership"—"Well, I was a minority, I figured, even though I wasn't black"—a program that was instrumental in getting her the excellent job in insurance she had when we met.

The no woman's land of being Latino at the high school shaped Sonia's path after graduation. She married a man who had been "the only black student in [the Atlanta suburb of] Dunwoody," she confided with a chuckle. Code-switching, for example, came naturally to both of them. "If someone hears me on the phone, they have no idea that I'm Hispanic.[63] I don't have an accent. And my husband is the same way. Even though he's African American and people have a certain perception of what they sound like over the phone. He turns on that professionalism, and no one even knows that he's African American." The phone is one thing, but it's hard to imagine that the couple can go incognito in their neighborhood. They live in a tony development near the Marietta Square—one that the demolishing of public housing made way for—that sprouts terraces and gleaming rooftop patios. Its residents are mostly older whites. On buying what and where she did, Sonia reflected, "At the time, we didn't know we were going to be parents. Had we known that, we wouldn't have chosen that house. Part of that is the [Marietta] school system."

Sonia's own unlikely trajectory from Marietta High to her nicely appointed insurance office, unaided by a college degree, has influenced her attitudes toward education as a private tool versus a public good. When I asked her about the Marietta system, Sonia shook her head: "We considered the public schools . . . but Marietta's have a really bad reputation." I wondered if "bad reputation" held the same meaning for her that it did for white and black graduates—an allusion to racial and economic resegregation. "It's not really race that I'm worried about. It's all the kids on Franklin Road . . . that's the part I'm worried about, the kids that unfortunately don't have the parenting they need or whatever it is they're lacking. There's a lot of drug activity. You get those kids in with my kids and that's what concerns me." The specter of "those kids"—poor students of color from the wrong part of town, of whom she was one twenty years ago—stands for the peril of public schools for a "highly gifted" child like her son.

For Sonia and for many other affluent parents of color, there is, ironically, a perception of *no* choice for those who have the most choices: private school is deemed the only route for a bright child when the public schools are rife with guns in lockers and brawls in the lunchroom. Sonia was determined that her son's education would be guided by the stars of individual achievement and personal ambition without the complications of family obligation and cultural expectations that his mother knew—and those that struggling, low-income students at MHS still know. Through her insurance business, Sonia leads a program for Latino students in area high schools—including MHS—in which they learn how to open checking accounts, save for college, and overcome what she calls "the culture" of Latino parents who don't prioritize higher education.

Whatever may come of the Latino students at Marietta High who flip through bright binders labeled "Financial Literacy" and eat the pizza Sonia brings, their prospects have nothing to do with Sonia's son. He would not be fettered by knowing his mother didn't go to college after graduation or that his grandparents snuck across the border; in order for his native-born-ness to be a true gift, it needed to be undone from history; it needed to be citizenship without the shadow of alienness, of deprivation, of marginality. Although he's only three years old, he's already been accepted at a nearby private school—the one I went to—where the student body is approximately 80 percent white, 5 percent black, 2 percent Latino, and 0.8 percent "mixed."[64] The school's graduation and college acceptance rates for the class of 2012 were 100 percent. "How could I not send my child there?" as Sonia put it. Sonia's perspective illuminates a fundamental dilemma of public schools seeking to remain integrated and highly effective. In order to retain the support of a broad community, school culture and curriculum must enjoin battles on two fronts: they must challenge the discourses that undermine the effectiveness of public education for bright students and those that deny the worth of students who are not, traditionally, high achievers.

"Those Kids": Latino Students' Visions and Revisions of Citizenship

Resisting their construction as marginal or "alien" in citizenship and transience discourses in Marietta, Latino students are increasingly agents of change in their own right. They are national merit scholars, drug users, good Christians, thespians, soccer stars, college scholarship recipients, car wash employees, teen dads, and youth pastors. Scattered across as wide a spectrum of difference as when Sonia Hill was among them, they are yet teenagers of a new moment. They negotiate the distance between the ideals of citizenship in a democracy with the realities of being undocumented, or being documented but poor and of color. In Homecoming traditions, at school formals, through teams and clubs, Latino students have gradually staked claims of belonging at Marietta High.

"We're taking over!" cried Elena gleefully. On a spring afternoon in 2013, she was interrogating her friend, Bridget, about how much "Spanish" music was played at Marietta's junior-senior prom. Bridget reported that there was "still a lot of hip hop" but plenty of *bachata*. She and Elena dissolved into laughter over "white kids" attempting the dance at prom. "Hey, I can dance *bachata!*" countered one of their peers—a mixed race sophomore who loved to bust a move for his doting female friends. "Yeah, he can," they admitted, "because we taught him."[65] The music at school dances is only one way by which Latino students measured their impact on the school's culture. Much had changed in the two short decades since Latinos made their first real showing in MHS's demographics.

A daughter of the amnesty generation, 2013 graduate Bridget Reyes has never known the inconveniences, anxiety, and even terror of life without documents. Bridget is Georgia-born and Marietta-raised. Echoing Sonia Hill, Bridget describes the Marietta that her parents made a home back in the eighties as host to "only, like, four [Mexican] families [who] . . . were all very close."[66] She underestimates the size of the Mexican community in 1980s Marietta, but not by that much: there were 366 Latino residents counted in the 1980 census, in a population of more than 30,000. Bridget's father went to Marietta Junior High for a short time and dropped out. Her mother is US-born and a high school graduate and the child of migrant agricultural workers who immigrated from Mexico to Texas. Her bilingual parents' steady, remunerative jobs in construction and office administration and their citizenship status set them apart from more newly arrived, precariously situated families.

Second-generation privilege has material and cultural consequences. Though Bridget is far from spoiled—during her elementary school years, her family spent cramped months living with her grandmother in an apartment on Franklin Road—she has stability and prospects that elude many of her foreign-born Latino peers. As she became a student leader at the high school, founding clubs and heading up community service projects, she faced the ambivalent scrutiny of her peers.

BS: When people see me, they're like, "Oh you're not really Mexican." I'm like "Yeah I am."

RY: Does that annoy you?

BS: It kinda does cause it's like don't say, "Man you're so smart, you're such a unique Mexican, you're like white!"

RY: Who says that to you?

BS: Hispanics! Hispanics will be like "You're so white, you're so American you don't know about this!" And I'm like, "Are you kidding me, I know all about that!" And they're like, "You don't know how to dance!" And I'm like, "I'm a professional—what are you talking about?" [Both laugh.] Or "I can't believe you were at that party," and I'm like, "I party every weekend." Or they're like, "Your grades are so good, and you party all the time." And I'm like, "I study all the time, I actually care."

The cultural distance between white and Mexican students—measured in clubs, sports, academics, and friendships—is slowly shrinking at MHS. But as one of the standard-bearers of such changes, Bridget has had to move between those worlds, proving herself in each. Combating the stereotypes of low-income immigrant students as, at best, uninterested in school, and, at worst, gang members and thugs, MHS's leadership seeks venues to celebrate the achievements of individual Latino students. Bridget's high profile at the high school brought requests from the administration, most recently for a promotional piece about the diversity and accomplishments of the class of 2013. Before the filming, Bridget was handed a sheet of a few lines to say, followed by instructions for a fist-pumping "Yeah, we did it!" In her analysis of being chosen for the video simmers her sense that if only she, Bridget, and a couple of her fellow Latinos were deemed a suitable public face of "the Mexicans" at the high school, then something is very wrong.[67] As she put it: "What kind of bothers me a little is . . . they called three of each race to go down and make the video. And they chose me and I think it's funny because I don't know how they choose those people—you know? . . . Our principal was talking about how I represent the Hispanics. I like that I get a lot of credit for [my involvement] and I like thinking that I represent the Hispanic population, but then I don't like it because it makes it seem like the population is so bad, and 'we have this one girl who stands out' and stuff. It's good, but I think about it more and I wish it wasn't like that."

In Bridget's critique of the video, her discomfort with being "representative" when she knows she is unique is obvious. If what a student activist like Bridget seeks is to engage and galvanize the whole Latino population, being viewed by her principal and teachers as the "one girl who stands out" represents a kind of failure. Her criticism suggests both her disappointment that more of her Latino peers don't "stand out" and perhaps a nascent critique of the narrow definition of success that prevails at MHS and in contemporary public schools.

The American dream, premised on traditional definitions of individual accomplishment, exerts a powerful grip on immigrant students, at least those who find an academic and social foothold in their high schools. For those students, college both *is* the dream and the key to its chest of upper-middle-class comforts.[68] Although Bridget's service work at school and on Franklin Road seeks to expand the MHS "community," through expanding the definition of who "counts," her personal ethos is that college is what will make *her* count. That ethos that calls for exceeding the accomplishments of her parents and for broadening the horizons of education and achievement in her family shapes her expectations of her peers. Bridget insists that doing "better than your parents" should be the horizon toward which all her peers orient themselves. Just as much as "Hispanics who won't ask for [academic] help," an unwillingness among her Latino classmates to assimilate culturally exasperates her: "You'll see Mexican [students at MHS] with skirts and like traditional shirts and I'm like, dude, it's the twenty-first century, that's not right! You need to change!" Having balanced, as she sees it, the cultural demands of family, peers, and school, she deems certain ways of breaking with the past as essential to realizing a life that eluded her parents. What the equation of college with the American dream means in a highly undocumented community of Latinos presents a dilemma for high achievers like Bridget who are simultaneously guided by and uncomfortable with narrow definitions of who counts at school and in the community.

Bridget, like Sonia Hill, draws stark distinctions between her parents' generation, in which work and stability, not college, described their American dream, and her own, for whom going to college should, she feels, be at the very center of those ambitions. Her dynamism and charisma have helped draw students toward her service activities and club events, but she claims that the small number of students who come to the educational programs for Latinos is a testament to how few of them are, in Bridget's term, "motivated." Although she heartily critiques the shortcomings of the "too easy" college prep curriculum, and she wonders at why there are not more and better guidance counselors, she lays blame mostly at the feet of her Latino peers themselves. "They have no motivation to succeed. I see the same ESOL kids being in ESOL [throughout high school and] I'm like, 'Why are you in guys in ESOL? You speak perfect English!'" Asserting that effective intervention comes not in junior or senior year but before freshman year, Bridget doubts that many Latino students would enroll in the kind of intensive summer program that she thinks would help prepare them for a successful high school career. "They don't like to sign up for things; they don't like to pay for it; they don't have transportation." Alluding to undocumented students who cannot get driver's licenses, Bridget touches on the difficult truth that being a citizen has gotten and will get her much more than just a set of wheels. How do you change students' minds about what they accomplish if, as in the Jim Crow era, the barriers they perceive are enshrined in law?

Undocumented Latino students encounter many of the same hurdles as their documented peers—cultural difference, money, the expectation that everyone will work to support the family—but those difficulties are themselves encompassed in and even overshadowed by the greater threat: deportation. The day before I was supposed to meet and interview Bridget's friend, Paul, and his brother, Ernesto, Bridget texted me, "Ernesto is in jail. He didn't do anything bad. Driving without a license. Should be out tomorrow, but not sure." Ernesto had dropped out of Marietta High several years before—he was a leader in a local gang, but Bridget described the gang as more "the cool Hispanics who hung out together," not drug dealers who violently defended their turf. For years, Ernesto had been in and out of trouble, but his family was worried that this episode was the kind of trouble they'd always feared. When I met with Bridget, I asked why Ernesto had no license—"Is he undocumented?" She nodded. I gaped at her. "Will he be deported then?" She didn't know; she said that usually if immigration didn't come within twenty-four hours, the arrestee is released on bond. "It's been twenty-four hours," she said, "and they haven't come." She paused, "So I guess we'll see."

Immigration law and notions about who is deserving of citizenship and its privileges widen the gap between students like Bridget and Paul—both successful, involved graduates of Marietta High. Paul talks about college, too, but with a wistfulness you'd never hear in Bridget's voice. I met with him several days after Ernesto's arrest, and he assured me that Ernesto wasn't going to be deported—at least not this time.[69] A 2011 alum of MHS, Paul says almost everything with a smile—his sweetness has a pure, unaffected quality, and that smile emerges from under a mustache not much fuller than that of an adolescent. Bridget and Paul have been friends since middle school, but their friendship bears a burden of very different pasts. Paul is one of five children; the family immigrated to the United States without papers in the mid-nineties. The first of his family to graduate from high school in the United States, Paul outpaced his brothers academically: one year, Paul even found himself in the same homeroom as Ernesto, who is older by two years. Seen as a promising, talented student by his family and his teachers, Paul did not work during high school like so many of his peers did. When the men in his family moved to Alabama for a year for jobs harvesting and picking, Paul was allowed to remain behind, living with another family member and continuing his studies in Marietta.

In Marietta, school choice has increased racial and socioeconomic isolation in the elementary schools and has helped produce a single "white" elementary, West Side, in which few poor students of color can be found.[70]

By an accident of geography, Paul spent fifth grade there.[71] West Side has consistently produced more International Baccalaureate and Advanced Placement (AP) students than any nonselective elementary in the city.[72] Like many of his classmates there, he was funneled into the magnet program at the middle school. However, as Paul's classes emptied of black and brown faces, his enthusiasm for taking AP and IB classes in high school flagged. "I wanted to be in class with my friends," he explained.[73] So he took the college prep curriculum—"regular classes"—and joined JROTC, which is both an extracurricular at the high school and one of the vocational program's "career pathways." He thrived in JROTC and was honored at the annual summer academy. A good student with increasingly bright prospects, Paul never fell in with Ernesto and his friends. A class-cutter who resented authority, Ernesto pushed Paul away from his cohort, hoping Paul's fate wouldn't match his own—a dropout with few avenues out of low-wage work.

Unlike 60 percent of the Latino students Paul started ninth grade with at Marietta High, he graduated.[74] Two weeks after that, he got a job at an electronics store to which his family was connected (all the men had worked there at some point, except Ernesto). The owner didn't mind that the Gomez boys had "no socials," said Paul, using the undocumented community's shorthand for "Social Security numbers." Having no social had ramifications far beyond employment. Paul's grades were good enough to get state aid for college and government loans. Encouraged by his JROTC teachers to go into the Navy or the Air Force, he had to answer their exhortations *"It'll pay for college!"* with a shrug. The faculty and administration at MHS are not equipped with the information they need to support students like Paul; when we were talking about opportunities for undocumented students, the principal pointed out that "You can become a citizen if you serve in the military." That's true, you can, but you must be a permanent resident—that is, have a green card—or be on a current visa in order to enlist. For Paul, that would mean returning to Mexico to apply for a visa, without any guarantees he could get one and without any surety of eventual return to his family, community, and life in the United States.[75] Distinctions like those that define eligibility for the military are critical to offering good, useful counsel to an undocumented student like Paul, who suffered in the knowledge that he was just the kind of kid who would flourish in the service. But without enormous risk, he couldn't attempt to enlist—just like he couldn't get a driver's license or health insurance or a college scholarship for a state school. All roads led right back to the electronics store.

In the 2010s, in the desolate terrain of congressional inaction on their behalf, undocumented students continue to toil toward the mirage of higher education and reliable work. The crucial rights afforded immigrant children by the 1982 decision in *Plyler v. Doe*, including the right to a K-12 education, also entailed a "false promise" of continued opportunity after they graduated—to join their peers heading off to college or even the military, participating in AmeriCorps programs, or obtaining internships.[76] Some researchers assert that a college degree is the high school diploma of the twenty-first century: the bare minimum required for a shot at economic security for students who don't come from affluence.[77] In the provisions of the DREAM Act (Development, Relief, and Education for Alien Minors) is compassion for students like Paul, but Georgia's immigration laws entrench a brutal caste system in which undocumented students find their ambitions and hopes to be so much red clay crumbling between their fingers.[78]

"Motivation"—what Bridget deemed as the great lack among her peers—has its own cultural politics: immigration policy that intentionally erects obstacles for undocumented students gives the lie to the link between excellence in school and success after graduation. Even for Paul, who has quickly ascended from maintenance to a sales position at the electronics store, the horizon becomes fuzzy beyond the daily grind of the shop. The opportunities that Bridget has before her, the college degree she can practically reach out and touch, are the stuff of fantasy for Paul. Winning honors through JROTC and garnering the admiration of his teachers and peers—creating opportunities for himself—made the denial of higher education harder. "I guess it brings you more down," he said. He went on: "It was like why study, or why do good if it's not even going to matter? . . . I really . . . like school . . . [and] I really wanted to go to college . . . but I don't want to use the money I have 'cause it's mostly paycheck by paycheck 'cause I live with a roommate. Because of being [categorized as] 'international,' [the tuition] is a lot more money. So it's like I'm going to take one credit and it's going to take me a long time."

Georgia is one of the three worst places in America to be an undocumented student. In twenty states in the United States, Paul could qualify for in-state tuition due to university system policy or legislation geared toward opening up higher education to undocumented students. But

Georgia isn't one of these. In fact, Georgia is one of only six states to ban undocumented students from receiving in-state tuition.[79] Beyond even that, in 2010, Georgia joined South Carolina and Alabama in banning undocumented students from attending any state university that turns away qualified, in-state applicants.[80] Supporters of the bill argued that "it's wrong for illegal immigrants to take slots at these schools since they can't legally work in the country after graduation."[81]

State law, however hostile to undocumented youth, doesn't dictate what forms of intervention and support secondary schools can offer students. Paul's graduating class—the class of 2011—was Marietta High's first GEAR UP (Gaining Early Awareness and Readiness for Undergraduate Programs) cohort; the program ostensibly provides summer activities, college counseling and scholarship assistance, educational field trips, and tutoring support. Paul remembers going on college campus trips with GEAR UP. On the trip to nearby Kennesaw State, he imagined himself there easily—strolling to class with peers and hanging out on the campus green. However, Paul could only enroll as an international student, paying out-of-state tuition rates three times higher than in-state tuition, with no hope of federal or state aid to defray the almost $20,000 cost of an academic year.[82] In 2010, undocumented Kennesaw State student Jessica Colotl—a high-achieving junior who was nearly deported after campus police stopped her for a minor violation—caught the attention of the nation. Colotl's was a cautionary tale for students like Paul.[83] Not tailored to the concerns and needs of undocumented students, GEAR UP was not helpful in addressing the obstacles Paul faced. As of 2013, MHS offered no institutional support specifically for undocumented students.

It is through the "stolen" benefit of public education that undocumented children discover the meaning of citizenship, like a photographic negative—taking shape in the dark room of classes, clubs, sports, and college applications—that proves for certain their place outside the frame. Refusing that place outside the frame, some noncitizen students strove to make their status irrelevant to their social and academic lives and to their future plans. As a Marietta student, 2011 graduate and undocumented Brazilian immigrant Lauren Garcia went about the recruitment of her Latino peers to student government, clubs, football fandom, and even the International Baccalaureate program's challenging courses with a missionary's zeal.[84] Perhaps unconsciously, Bridget and Lauren Garcia cultivated "social capital" through the activities, programs, and classes to which they strove to lure their Latino classmates.[85] Social capital is critical for Latino students who are so often likely to be isolated in English Language Learner (ELL) classes and less likely to join clubs and go out for teams for reasons of money, the demands of an afterschool job, the lack of a car, and a sense of outsiderness.[86]

For Latino students, citizen and not, the race and class integration that many extracurricular activities offer is an important antidote to academic tracking and the uneven and unequal flow of information to immigrant students and families about scholarships, special programs, and postgraduation opportunities. MHS offers no specific support for first-generation college aspirants, a gap that is already being filled by private for-profit "educational service" companies, one of which Bridget and her parents paid two thousand dollars to join.[87] Sometimes peers fill the knowledge gap that school programs should and private companies aim to; it was Lauren who pushed Cesar Verde, whom we met in Chapter 3, to apply for the elite IB program. Lauren integrated him into the majority-white IB cohort's social world, which was anchored on the city's affluent west side.[88] She recalled that as a student leader her "biggest thing was [greater] Hispanic student involvement, because you really don't see that. We're [a] very, very diverse [student body], but it's also very split. Hispanics wanna be involved and they get involved in some things, but in some things they don't even try."[89]

Like Bridget, Lauren was deemed "very Americanized," as she put it, by her Latino peers: that kind of citizenship had costs. Bridget had to defend her cultural authenticity among her Mexican friends; for Lauren, being "Americanized" was part of a trajectory that entailed sacrifice. After balancing the spheres of school and family for most of high school, Lauren had to choose, her senior year, between staying at MHS—where she had so carefully cultivated the social capital that would, she hoped, mean college acceptance—or moving to Florida with her parents, who were taking new jobs there. Ultimately, she decided to live with a friend in Marietta until graduation, and that summer, her private college scholarship took her several states away from her close-knit family. Amy Rocha, who graduated with an International Baccalaureate diploma and enrolled as an international student at a college in Canada, would never have a visit from her undocumented parents, and for a while, it was not clear that she could come home to them, either.

The high cost of social capital for Latino students raises the equally fraught issue of "human capital." Human capital is an idea familiar to us from the rhetoric of every modern American presidential candidate: it posits that students are the capital that US schools produce for "growth and competition" in "the global knowledge economy."[90] The concept of "human capital" predates, but fits squarely into, contemporary neoliberal education reform agendas, in which students are not only free market consumers of education, but also the products themselves. In terms of readiness for the global market, Latino students in the United States are deemed by some to be faulty products. In the words of a report by a reputed education research organization, explaining its use of white students' scores to calculate global competitiveness: "We compare U.S. white students' [scores] to *all* students in other countries. We do this . . . to consider the oft-expressed claim that education problems in the United States are confined to certain segments within the minority community."[91] In this calculation, Bridget and other students of color like her quite literally do not count, regardless of their striving and of their individual academic performances vis-à-vis their white peers. If American public schools are unable to mold Latino students into competitive global products, what then should be the relationship between the student and her education, the school and its constituent population? Education historian Joel Spring admits human capital is "the driving force in public school policies," but wonders if, in the context of an already dispiriting ratio of college graduates to jobs they can live on, the point of schooling shouldn't perhaps be "to prepare students to improve the quality of society and their own happiness."[92]

Many community-rooted activists, such as the late Grace Lee Boggs, believe that schools and communities can cultivate a diversity of opportunities for students to contribute to community vitality and solve shared problems, especially those students who cannot find meaning or inspiration in the curriculum and culture of their classrooms.[93] In such a model for reorienting the focus of schooling, public education does not seek the social reproduction of one class of student: an affluent, high-scoring, potentially high-earning child.[94] Rather it seeks to link students, teachers, and families to their environments—treating the city as a classroom in which problems of infrastructure, or pollution, or food scarcity can be approached in a spirit of collaboration and with a "love of place" that fuels each student in his or her own role and produces greater sustainability—in terms of equity, environment, and economics—in communities of color.[95] However, even these broader parameters for a "good education" also encompass making the desired future self within reach for each student. In this sense, the lack of institutionalized support for immigrant students, and especially for those who are undocumented, renders "love of place" and stewardship of the community a difficult endeavor.

Undocumented students who excel often make such difficult trade-offs, bravely accepting exile—measured in cultural distance or actual miles— from the places in which their sense of citizenship and community steward-ship was forged. Regardless of their tenacity, those students are enmeshed in a cumbersome immigration apparatus at the national and state levels. Because immigration reform and legalization are such a partisan matter, there is no consensus in the research about the impact of immigration on the economy or the "price tag" on citizenship for the estimated 11 million undocumented—calculated through taxes paid by new citizens versus the cost of public benefits they can access.[96] While some research suggests immigrant labor is reducing work opportunities for the native-born, other researchers claim low-wage immigrant workers do not negatively impact the job market for US citizens but rather complement the native work force and bring down the cost of production.[97] Similarly, some studies show that documented immigrants constitute a "fiscal drain" in their use of social ser-vices, while others demonstrate that they pay taxes, spend a great per-centage of what they earn, and, once eligible, are less likely to use public benefits like food stamps.[98] Despite a seeming ideological gridlock, the immigration reform effort gained momentum in 2013. The possibility of a pathway to citizenship and the long-awaited adoption of the DREAM Act filled undocumented immigrants in Georgia and across the country with hope for their own futures and for that of their communities.

Redefining Community at and beyond the High School

What community means at Marietta High is in constant revision; one thing is for certain, however: the high school's future is bound up with that of its most vulnerable students. Although the political climate in the county has long been a toxic one for undocumented students and their families, the role that Marietta High plays can and should be a critical one in mediating the relationship between the city and its undocumented and low-income denizens, who increasingly fill the classrooms at MHS. When I asked a documented Latino graduate recently what the administration was doing to support struggling Latino students, especially those without papers, he said he didn't really know—nothing, really, he guessed. After a pause, he went on, "but maybe it's students who will do it, they are the ones who start things."[99] My questions had revolved around what teachers, administrators, and school leaders were or weren't doing; his insight showed me that I was looking too hard for institutional change. I had forgotten that change rarely starts with the institution.

Change at the high school is inextricably connected to social and economic change outside its walls; across metro Atlanta, Latino students have grappled with the same kinds of marginality in very different high schools and cities. The student-founders of AH! (Asociación Hispánica!) had this much figured out: how students cultivate belonging and community—and render their identity legible and meaningful within it—has everything to do with feeling that their education matters and their challenges are not unique. The place I go to think about belonging at MHS is certainly the most obvious, but also one of the best: the most integrated place in Marietta—Northcutt football stadium on a fall Friday night. On one such evening, a gaggle of exuberant Latino students were winding through the crowd in bright T-shirts. "AH!" read the front of their T-shirts and on the back "Asociación Hispánica!"[100] I stopped them to ask about the group, but practically bouncing with the night's energy, they couldn't be slowed for long. A girl with a beribboned ponytail lingered a moment and told me that the group's leader "didn't go to school here," and that her name was "Rosa . . ." she hesitated: "I think—I don't really know. This is our first year!" she crowed before darting off to rejoin her friends.

As at most area high schools, there was no organization at MHS that purported to unify Latino students for greater integration in the student body and better preparation for life after graduation. The 2012–2013 school year was, indeed, AH!'s first year at MHS. The founders of AH! are not from Marietta, but they came through the public schools in a county nearby, which has seen Latino growth similar to that of Marietta. At their high school, they felt the same frustration that Lauren Garcia did. As cofounder Rosa recalled, "I was the only Latina in AP classes, honors, cheerleading, everything. . . . A lot of students want to be in their comfort zone," safe from the stress of being stereotyped.[101] "If you don't take a risk," said Rosa of her peers' reticence, "then you won't fail and confirm [people's] stereotypes." Not only were social pressures uniquely acute for Latino students, but family and school administrations also presented challenges. Parental involvement, said Miguel, Rosa's friend and cofounder, is difficult in families where demanding work schedules and limited understanding of English render supporting their children's academics a Herculean task. At school, even well-meaning teachers and administrators who can be trusted with the confidence that a student is undocumented "don't know how to help," attested Miguel. Faculty and administrators "aren't trained" to offer guidance to undocumented students; they don't know "which scholarships don't require a Social Security number" or how best to navigate college admissions without a green card. Miguel and Rosa saw that just as much as their peers needed administrative help, they needed each other: a network of students who shared their hopes and difficulties and could aid one another with the logistics, the preparation, and the encouragement many first-generation college hopefuls require.

Ever since, and likely before, Sonia Hill's resourceful appropriation of "black leadership" opportunities, Latino students at MHS and other high schools have improvised creatively, either assuming roles in preexisting organizations or leveraging personal relationships with school leadership for assistance with scholarships and jobs. Organizations like AH! are intended to "change the culture," as Miguel put it, at high schools where Latino students are marginalized, by establishing the formal infrastructure of mentoring, service, and leadership events that the Latino community needs. Rosa and Miguel see their project as training student leaders— young people who will be resources for their fellow Latino students and engines for administrative change at their high schools. Marietta High's AH! chapter has more than one hundred members (Bridget and Paul among them). As Miguel informed me proudly, "That chapter has bloomed, and the administration has been very open to it. The level of engagement of the students is phenomenal; it's like all of them were waiting for it."

While AH! is focused primarily on Latino students' social and academic experiences of community at the high school, YELLS (Youth Empowerment through Learning, Leading, and Serving) seeks to expand the very notion of what "community" is. YELLS began as a school-based club, like AH!, but in 2008, it became an independent nonprofit working exclusively with Marietta students and families. Who composes YELLS, where it is based, and what it seeks to accomplish challenge traditional definitions of the MHS community. YELLS's mentoring program convenes every Tuesday of the school year in a donated unit in Liberty Pointe Apartments where mostly black or Latino MHS students work with their assigned students from one of the city's high-poverty elementary schools. The high school students act as mentors, or "Bigs," to their students—their "Littles"—and the pairs plan service projects for the residents of Franklin Road.

In the rhetoric of school leaders, the school "community" refers to staff, faculty, students, and their families; in that sense, integration at the level of school community indexes socioeconomic and racial heterogeneity in the classroom, in extracurriculars, and in social groups. However, in the work of the student groups described in this section, community is inclusive of the city's poor, jobless, ill, and, of course, undocumented. Integration in this broader *comunidad* is a form of resistance to the transience discourse that posits the poor and undocumented of Franklin Road as outside the embrace of citizenship. In places like Liberty Pointe, a low-income development among several just like it on Franklin Road, the next generation of black and Latino MHS graduates are growing up in a community from which the city schools have strived to distance themselves. Linking the low-income elementary school students on Franklin and their families with high school students and city resources, YELLS insists upon Franklin Road's denizens as members of a broad and inclusive Marietta City Schools community.

Among the raft of community service and leadership organizations at MHS, YELLS is different in its mission and its means; it prioritizes students and their struggles within the larger context of the community's challenges. On one Tuesday, Gael, a third-grade YELLS mentee, was absorbed in illustrating the week's theme—forming good habits. Carefully, he drew two flowers, a blue curl for wind, and a little boy with a bike. "I should exercise and play outside more," he explained. "I play video games and Legos a lot instead of playing outside, but our playground isn't good; it's dirty and people have written inappropriate things on it." I couldn't help but smile at Gael's precocity; earlier, he listed "being proactive" as a good habit. I hadn't heard his mentor, a senior at Marietta named Anthony, say that word so I wondered where it, and much of what Gael said, had come from. When Gael sprung from his chair to intercept a bag of popcorn heading into the other room with a group of fourth-grade girls, Anthony turned to me, "Isn't he great?" Although Anthony's parents are Guatemalan and Gael's are Mexican, the two have the same light brown coloring, heart-shaped faces, and disobedient dark hair. Although he isn't the role model one might imagine for Gael—Anthony's academics suffered from moving around—his calm manner and sweetness worked wonders on Gael's tantrums. While Anthony struggled through MHS and didn't manage to graduate with his 2013 class, Gael has thrived in the classroom, across his subjects. They are not a conventional pair, but in the context of YELLS, they make sense.

Service on and to Franklin Road is the centerpiece of YELLS. One service day I attended in 2013 attracted more than two hundred residents, who danced, ate, played games, and worked in the YELLS-founded community garden. The Bigs who had planned it were justly proud. Like Anthony, very few of the Bigs have straight A's or are club presidents, and that isn't an accident. Laura Keefe, a young white woman who used to teach English at Marietta High, founded the program in 2007 because she perceived a gap in extracurricular offerings. She told me: "I felt like there were a lot of programs for those 4.0, IB, top-of-the-line students—National Honor Society, Beta Club, a million organizations that have a GPA requirement and are sort of elite, in a sense. When I was forming [YELLS] I wanted to have those students who are not typically at the top of their class—the guidelines [of my organization] being passion, commitment, and desire to be a leader. . . . [I sought the students] who might not have been getting the attention they deserve."[102]

As a result of Keefe's selection ethos, the Bigs of YELLS are a diverse bunch. But for one white student, they are all black and Latino, and there is substantial diversity of background—from students who live on Franklin Road itself to those who grew up in Marietta's wealthiest neighborhoods, from evangelical Christians to Buddhists, from those born and raised in Marietta to those who hail from Ethiopia or El Salvador.

As at the high school, the relationships across race and class in YELLS can't be painted in broad strokes—real integration occurs friendship by friendship, in collaborating on projects, planning workshops, and shaping new YELLS initiatives. Along with tutoring and supporting their Littles, Bigs spend the school year planning spring service projects for the residents of Franklin Road (all of the Littles live on Franklin Road). The process is entirely student led, from fundraising, to advertising, to staffing and executing the events. Through their service work, the students are pushed to hold each other accountable and to design projects that address a need in the Franklin Road community: the Field Day and "Taste of Franklin" projects aimed not only to engage residents and celebrate the community's ethnic diversity, but also to continue to chip away at assumptions and stereotypes that render Franklin and its "transient" population marginal and disposable in local discourse. The gardening group sought to explore—through their community garden and plans for a farmers' market—the idea of fostering a "local economy," where, in Wendell Berry's formulation, interdependence, local knowledge and skills, and local production and consumption redefine the economic and social landscape.[103]

In these ways, community service at YELLS challenges discourses of citizenship and transience that narrowly circumscribe "community." The projects the students execute explore racial and class inclusion in practice, not just theory. Pushing beyond their at-school peer groups and collaborating in a commitment to the people of Franklin Road as part of the Marietta City Schools community, the Bigs explore integration as a social value. Lower-income YELLS mentors like Anthony, who will be the first in his family to attend college, forge relationships with Bigs like Delia, a black junior who comes from one of Marietta's nicest neighborhoods and has been aiming for admission at an Ivy League institution since she was a freshman. But like any mechanism for belonging, clubs produce insiders and outsiders; the definition of "community" at YELLS may not align with that of AH! or any number of religious groups, teams, or associations in which students participate.

YELLS brings together MHS students who may not have otherwise become friends, and those friendships often lead to difficult grappling with stereotypes and ingrained prejudice. One black student in YELLS told me her only Latino friends are the "AH! Hispanics" (many of whom are in YELLS) because they are the ones whose "lives are going somewhere."[104] On the surface, this student's notion that only Latino students in AH!— about a fifth of the total population at MHS—are "going somewhere" seems to simply reflect a stereotype of Latino students as without ambition. Yet, at another level, her perceptions illustrate how YELLS and AH! challenge the discursive construction of Latino students as uniformly disengaged from the school community and its norms of achievement and success. Before YELLS and AH!, resistance to that discourse solely took the shape of individual Latino students' achievements—a Latino class president or star athlete—but the groups have produced collective modes of refusing the transience and citizenship discourses that relegate Latino students and the communities they come from to the margins.

Tensions around difference course through every high school, and community is made, and even expanded, as students explore how relationships in school—like opportunities, achievement, values, and customs— are structured by discourses outside it. Bulbs of social connection blink in and out, not necessarily via some circuit breaker with levers for race, class, and nation, but rather through particular currents: from sexuality or sports or religion, to a way of dressing, or dancing, or simply working together on an assignment. These flash through students' school lives, bringing them together, urging them apart. Certainly the lunchroom is peppered with "white," "black," and "Hispanic" tables, but also with tables where no color or class logic is discernible. Bridget's Mexican friends may rib her for her "whiteness," but in watching her among them, she seems to have the unusual combination of their affection and respect; when she invites them to YELLS service days, they come in a cheerful cadre. Exploring what community means on Franklin Road defies the separation of the schools from the broader citizenry and challenges students to defy the logics of transience and discourse of citizenship that would exclude Franklin Roaders from the Blue Devil family.

Community is what has to happen, or those discourses of citizenship produce "aliens" and "illegals" instead of neighbors and friends. Bridget's little black car is often pulled up outside Liberty Pointe Apartments on Franklin Road. She applied to be a mentor with YELLS early in her high school career, and along with a couple of other YELLS teens, Bridget founded the community garden in 2010. When I first met her she was in the garden, informing the elementary student she mentors that getting dirty is part of growing food as she secured a pair of huge work gloves on a pair of very small hands. An ongoing collaborative project of the YELLS students and Liberty Pointe's residents, the community garden represents an alternative vision of sustainability, of education, and of the people of Franklin Road themselves.

In the garden at Liberty Pointe, everyone is a student. "Now would you look at those collards," exclaimed Ms. Kerry, an older black resident of the complex. She had been moving slowly along the garden's perimeter, expressing concern about the state of the pepper plants and admiring the lush leaves of the broccoli. She drew my attention to the collards, sprouting out of the compost pile, right as I was about to dump an armload of weeds on them. "We'll eat those!" she reprimanded gently, and plucked an iridescent broad frond right out of the heap. She rescued all the renegade greens, whose health benefits my Mississippi-raised grandmother would have lectured me on and then eradicated by cooking them with bacon. A mentor to the children who come to Liberty Pointe, Ms. Kerry chastises stompers of rows and gives quizzes on plant identification, rubbing sprigs of rosemary and mint under their noses. With me and the high school students, she retraces the ways of her mother and grandmother—how they grew, cooked, and healed their bodies, what of their knowledge has been lost, and what's being rediscovered, right there in Liberty Pointe's fertile soil.

The community garden is beguiling in many ways: as a welcoming and pretty respite from the gray uniformity of the complex's buildings, as a lesson in the hardy patience of chard and spinach overwintering, as a means for residents to learn (or remember) how to grow their own food, but most of all as a metaphor for Franklin Road. Circular and composed of an inner and an outer ring, with four raised beds on the north side, the garden is reminiscent of an opening eye—or perhaps a rising sun. Although it sees its challenges in the form of chipmunks, trouble-seeking kids, and neighborhood cats, its very existence, like that of Liberty Pointe and the Franklin Road Association, was unthinkable in the early aughts, when few of the residents themselves considered Franklin Road a community.

Among Marietta's politicians, school leaders, and residents across race and class, Franklin Road plays a particular role discursively: not unlike the football field, it is a site where narratives about the city and the school's past and future are constructed and contested. At the nexus of those discourses, the people of Franklin Road are construed as rootless and outside "the pale," without a say in their future or that of the community, framed in local media and by city leaders as blighted and beyond redemption.[105] In 2013, city leadership embarked on a campaign to cultivate support for the redevelopment of Franklin Road—"for the sake of our schools," intoned the mayor.[106] The students of YELLS and their community partners, the Franklin Road Association, sought to demonstrate that the complexes were sites of community building and that they were orchestrating the transformation of Franklin Road into a safe, affordable neighborhood where, in the words of Franklin Road Association member Robin Montgomery, "people are organizing to improve their lives."[107]

The unpredictability of work and good wages means that the poor families on Franklin Road find themselves constantly on the move—this paradox of being moved about and held in place is a signature of human struggle in the neoliberal economy. The discourse of transience frames the low-income residents of Franklin Road as a liability for the city: tallied in emergency room visits, calls to fire and police departments, and the defection of affluent families from an increasingly high-poverty school system. Extricating the schools from the poverty and strife on Franklin, rather than ameliorating that poverty and strife, is how the city council and school board articulate the dilemma of the corridor.

Transience discourse shapes how city leaders and school leaders formulate "solutions" to the problems of Franklin Road, but transience also indexes the difficulties of unanchored lives and the efforts of "highly mobile" poor students to form community and stay afloat academically.[108] As Marietta High's principal pointed out to me, students who move a great deal during high school must "start all over" at each school, often "never find[ing] that thing that engages them."[109] In a survey of 236 graduating seniors in the class of 2013, almost 10 percent cited "moving a lot" or "changing schools" as the greatest challenge to graduating.[110] Supporting the principal's insistence that becoming rooted at school and finding a sense of identity in the community is critical to students' success, almost 25 percent of students cited events like pep rallies, proms, and football games as their "favorite parts" of high school, and nearly 30 percent listed activities like chorus and band and sports such as basketball, track, and football as integral to their high school experience. Perhaps, among 236 respondents (the graduating class was 324), 10 percent of students reporting transience as a challenge is not many. But as the principal intoned with a shake of her head, "These are just the ones who made it." In the class of 2013, the Latinos "who made it" numbered only forty-five, half of whom reported that they would be going to college.[111] The destinies of those graduates bound for college, those not, and those who did not make it to graduation are bound up with discourses of citizenship and transience in Marietta.

The students of Franklin Road know the topography of poverty in Marietta—crime, drug use, prostitution—better than students anywhere else in the city. Along with those hazards and the absence of crosswalks and safe play spaces—what many residents deem evidence for the necessity of community building instead of redevelopment—Franklin Road is also what's called a "food desert."[112] Although there are a handful of restaurants, there is nowhere residents can reliably get fresh produce. The YELLS students founded the garden with those very conditions in mind. In contrast, the city's solution is not community-based initiatives but rather redevelopment: if not a world-class stadium, then at least a "mixed-use development," which will ostensibly draw back upper-middle-class professionals and the Whole Foods groceries that follow those markets.

Student-led community "greening" and community-based learning are core values of YELLS, and all YELLS youth are both teachers and students in the nascent paradigm. Darrell, a junior at MHS, was a patient teacher at YELLS; his truculent third-grade Little adored him. He was also a student of the garden, slowly but surely finding his footing in brand new territory. "Uh, ma'am, is this a poisonous lizard?" Three of the YELLS Bigs and I were volunteering at a local nature center, intending to bring back new know-how to the community garden at Liberty Pointe. Darrell was pointing, horrified, at a tiny green anole, the pink coin of its throat puffing in and out. The garden manager assured him of the lizard's harmlessness, but he watched dubiously as it lithely scaled a pot of chives. The kids harvested greens and carted compost, learned how tomatoes can be grafted to produce stronger root systems, weighed the take of the day's work, and, of course, talked. About school. About breakups. About parents who'll "whup" you if you talk back. About siblings *you* have to whup. They talked about what I hoped wasn't happening to them because I like them so much and admire their resourcefulness, wit, and sweetness in the face of split-up families and abusive stepparents, not enough money or work, moves in and out of state and from apartment to cheaper apartment. But as they talked, they also wondered aloud about how you'd cook the chard, and at the intricately knuckling roots of the kale plants they pulled up, and the delicacy of the pea seedlings. They liked their work, and Darrell's usual fatigue, his shyness, and his seeming sadness fell away as he rinsed another batch of herbs and watched for the anoles.

What would happen if the Franklin Roaders of Marietta City Schools were situated at the very center of local education reform? If instead of treating students of Franklin Road like the symptoms of an illness affecting school performance, they were viewed as central to reenvisioning what schools do and how they do it? If they were deemed students deserving of the resources, legislative attention, and community support that are, comparatively, lavished on the better-heeled residents of communities east and west of Franklin Road? Instead of kids about whom something must be done, can they be seen as students who *do* something—as agents of change, rather than victims of it? Scholar Ruth Gilmore further observes, "If agency is the human ability to craft opportunity from the wherewithal of everyday life, then agency and structure are products of each other. . . . Actors in all kinds of situations (farms, neighborhoods, government agencies, collapsing economies, tough elections) are fighting to create stability out of instability. In a crisis, the old order does not simply blow away, and every struggle is carried out within, and against, already existing institutions: electoral politics, the international capitalist system, families, uneven development, racism."[113] Gael, who wants to be an engineer (due to prodigious talents with Legos), and Anthony, who aims to study nursing at a community college, are crafting opportunity for themselves inside and through the old order. What will be the new?

There is no panacea when it comes to Marietta High and the struggles of public schools in general, but if there were, it might resemble community gardening. Community gardening as a movement has spread across the country, not only in parts of Philadelphia, Boston, Detroit, Baltimore, and New York City that were economically and physically denuded by deindustrialization, but also across the Pacific Northwest and the Southeast. Gardening as pedagogy and politics in poor communities gained ground in the 1970s when "guerilla gardening" and urban homesteading emerged in neighborhoods where jobs, food, and hope were scarce but abandoned lots were plentiful.[114] According to the American Community Garden Association, in 2012 there were more than 18,000 community gardens in the United States.[115] In the garden at Liberty Pointe, the cultivation of a safe space amid the danger and clamor of the broader city, the fostering of responsibility to the community and the garden, the attracting of local support, and the planning for the long term by organizing peers and residents are all the results of the students' ownership of and pride in the garden and its broader purpose.[116] Community gardening offers education with no tracking, no high-stakes testing, and no race to retain the rich or mask the scores of the poor.

The "community schools" model, an idea that has seen several iterations over the twentieth century, similarly emphasizes the interdependence of community and school.[117] Whether it be in the form of wellness check-ups provided at school or in community building and service programs—what YELLS embodies and what scholar Novella Keith calls "new citizenship discourse"—community schools represent a tradition of deep engagement with the struggles of local people.[118] In her work *The Next American Revolution,* Grace Lee Boggs critiques school reform that privileges the shaping of docile subjects for the global economy over the cultivation of citizens who develop the skills needed in their own communities. She describes projects as diverse as tracking soil erosion, rehabbing local homes, building greenhouses, documenting water quality, assembling solar panels and wind turbines, and, of course, running urban farms and farmers' markets as enterprises that engage students in meaningful work and provide "alternative value-oriented means of securing [a] livelihood."[119] As research on "service learning" has consistently demonstrated, children and teens who live in troubled households and communities in crisis are engaged far more effectively by projects that address the problems they encounter every day.[120] Contemporary supporters of service learning and other community-focused curricula are reprising what educational philosopher John Dewey observed nearly a century before—that "educational aims" should be "natural to [the students'] own experience" rather than merely "those [to] which they are taught to acquiesce."[121]

The question of what a community-relevant curriculum looks like is a focus of mainstream education reform debates. The STEM curriculum (science, technology, engineering, and math) has long been hailed as the mechanism for making American students ready for a global workforce. However, a recent report from the National Education Policy Center suggests that a curriculum that focuses on addressing challenges in one's own community can be critical to making school feel useful and important to students. Education researcher William Mathis writes that "soft skills," such as the ability to work with those different from oneself and to "embrace cultural diversity," are seen as increasingly valuable in the workplace.[122] Outlining the "Four Cs" (critical thinking, communication, creativity, and collaboration), Mathis's policy brief suggests that these "Cs" should be linked with a more traditional "top down" curriculum in math and science.[123] This "linked learning" rejects tracking in favor of "universal acceleration" and conventional testing in favor of "a broad array of assessments"; it encompasses "a range of sites of learning beyond the walls of the high school" and "flexibility in the school day and year."[124] Rationale and goals for "linked learning"—the ability to work with those from different backgrounds, for example—should sound familiar: they align with mainstream views about why maintaining desegregation is important in public schools and racial isolation is harmful.

Although racial isolation has demonstrably negative effects on the health, happiness, civic participation, and academic success of the low-income students of color who are most likely to be cordoned off in segregated districts, desegregation is more often talked about in terms of how students from diverse educational settings will have greater success in the work world.[125] These are terms that limit our capacity to reimagine the contours of public education, but desegregation's once cluttered negotiating table— city-suburb district consolidation, broad-scale busing, and nonvoluntary redistricting—was nearly bare by the early 2000s. In the context of those closed avenues, the language of linked learning makes desegregated learning environments a priority. What must go further, however, are the arena and means through which schools integrate and students experience integration.[126]

The projects that YELLS undertakes are fundamentally integrative, in a way that is broader than the distribution of students of color in the advanced placement classes of the high school. There is work for everyone in the garden, and the proof of know-how and commitment is not in test scores, but in the strawberry leaves finally revealing their bright red prizes, in the arugula reaching skyward in spicy shoots, in two hundred community members turning out for fairs and field days in what used to be an empty courtyard. At the garden at Liberty Pointe, Marietta High students and Liberty Pointe residents discover their roles through their strengths—whether those are writing proposal letters and grants or building raised beds and fine-tuning the timed irrigation system. As Latino students redefine what it means to be integrated and practice citizenship in ways that draw school and community closer, the powerful grip of neoliberal reform slackens. The legacy of *Brown* as a shared ideal can't be reduced, in the words of Little Rock Nine integrator Ernest Green, to "sitting next to white students."[127] Rather, the principles of *Brown* embodied by the "new integrators" at MHS make it clear that community is an expanding family, citizenship is commitment to that community, and education is the power to take part in realizing deeper dignity and greater justice for the whole community, at and beyond the school.

CONCLUSION

Reclaiming *Brown:* Integration Is Not a Policy Goal—It's a Movement

RESEGREGATION IS a numerical, demographic reality in Marietta and many other cities and suburbs across the county. Resegregation is also a cultural moment, a kind of test in a test-obsessed era, for communities and for school and city leaders. I initially posed the following question: can Marietta High resist resegregation and remake its public school system, and if so, how? The "how" of resisting resegregation is somewhat like the "how" of desegregation: an acceptance that in the great tide of change, the old ways won't serve. The feat of desegregation was the undoing, albeit uneven and certainly incomplete, of centuries of "racial learning": a sea change in the quotidian practices, beliefs, and customs that constitute a culture. The battle against resegregation will require institutionalizing a broader vision and definition of integration, one that reframes what public education can and should do in communities, like Marietta, unmoored by demographic, economic, and cultural change.

Resisting resegregation is about memory as much as about school reform policy—about whether the rupture and reconciliation of the early *Brown* era can be brought to bear on tensions over retaining white students and guaranteeing equity for students of color in contemporary Marietta. Ways of remembering—and forgetting—the desegregation era have influenced how city leaders and residents confront the transformation of both the city and the high school from majority white and middle class to places of

153

greater poverty and ethnic diversity. A story about desegregation that acknowledges injustice, loss, and hard negotiations is a more useful tool for social change than a narrative that enshrines colorblindness through a too-simple tale of individual heroism and courage. Just as the ethos of color-blind camaraderie limits possibilities for radical change, instituting reforms such as school choice and the application-only International Baccalaureate program relies on a model of integration institutionalized in the sixties and seventies, a model that hobbles educational equity at Marietta High School and social justice in the city at large. I have attempted to show that, thus far, IB and school choice—intended to slow the attrition of affluent white families—have not positioned MHS to confront the major challenge of the contemporary era: providing the best possible education to the low-income students of color who increasingly compose the school-age population.

Retaining middle- and high-income families and ensuring educational equity for low-income students of color are inextricable projects, but this fact should not absolve school leaders of the responsibility for increased racial isolation in the elementary schools and intensified tracking in the high school. Although nostalgia and deeply embedded structures of race and class prejudice shape the reforms that city and school leaders enact, efforts to stave off socioeconomic resegregation are important to ensuring just and excellent education for *all* Marietta's students. In 2013, MHS was a high-poverty high school by the standards of federal education policy and Title I funding, but MHS's low-income students numbered 55 percent of the school population, just barely a majority. MHS has yet to reach a point of no return; it can remain an income-diverse place, given the will, creativity, and determination of the community.

Recent studies have demonstrated how powerfully class affects what happens at a school: teacher turnover, academic excellence, community support, and, often, racial isolation of the student population are all heavily influenced by income diversity.[1] A socioeconomically mixed school system is and should remain a priority in Marietta, but contemporary constructions of what constitutes class diversity place priority on affluent (usually white) students. What will bring them back to public schools? What will keep them once they return? Or put another way, what will reduce the numbers of poor students of color in the city's schools?

The 2013 redevelopment bond was, in the interpretation of some denizens, the city's answer to the last of those questions. The community's response to the bond proposal was swift and racially charged. At the public hearing about the bond, the Cobb County NAACP president was the first to speak among the anti-bond contingent, calling redevelopment a poorly disguised effort to rid Marietta of "the citizens who are not welcome."[2] Before sitting, she turned toward the council again: "Someone is going to make money [off] Franklin Road, and it will be on the backs of the people on Franklin." Another critic of the bond, an older black Franklin resident, stood next. "I am not a transient!" she declared, responding to the monolithic label applied by school and city leaders to the residents of the corridor.[3] Describing positive change on Franklin, she talked about the involved and committed members of the Franklin Road Association and the activities of YELLS. As she sat down, I recalled seeing her calmly manning a registration table overwhelmed by families and children at YELLS's Franklin Road Field Day. Insisting that city leaders needed to "give Franklin Road a chance to prove itself," a local coach and mentor testified to his faith in his fellow residents.[4]

In the spate of speakers criticizing the bond, only two white attendees came to the podium. One was former MHS faculty member, Ken Sprague, whom we met in Chapter 3. Condemning the bond, he drew the audience's attention to a revealing document produced by the city's redevelopment office that listed the apartment complexes on Franklin with their corresponding "price tags"—that is, the amount of money the city school system spends educating the children who live there.[5] The other critic was a conservative Cobb County resident; he suggested both that the bond was a "big government" intrusion and that it represented an effort to drive poor people out of Marietta.[6] Even the council room felt subtly segregated, with most of the black Mariettans in attendance on the right side of the podium, and the white residents on the left.

Black critics of the bond refuted the portrait of a crime-ridden ghetto—critical to the case for demolition and redevelopment—furnished by several white speakers. A young white man, a former assistant district attorney for the county, flourished a sheaf of statistics as proof of the "criminal culture of the area" and claimed he would drive on Franklin Road only in the company of "an armed officer."[7] "I don't see the Franklin that he sees," countered a black Franklin denizen seated behind him, and another longtime resident echoed her. "My son grew up on Franklin and he's doing very well," she told the council.[8] Although bond proponents talked about economic revitalization and new industry on a remade Franklin Road, the public debate intensified around the issue of the schools.

Redevelopment for the "sake of the schools," in the mayor's words, was also redevelopment to halt resegregation. More than one thousand Marietta City School students were living on Franklin Road in 2012–2013; that's one in every eight students in the system. The middle and high school students of Franklin Road attend, of course, the sole middle and high schools; elementary school students are divided among three high-poverty schools, with the lion's share assigned to Lockheed.[9] It is possible, said Principal Leigh Colburn, that without the Franklin Roaders, the high school would no longer have Title I (high-poverty) status.[10] Although it seems clear that the bond initiative had its roots in the long and troubling history of urban renewal and redevelopment in the United States, it would also have the effect of displacing at least part of the population that was seen as depressing test scores and graduation rates and fueling resegregation in the city schools.[11]

The redevelopment bond passed in November 2013 by a slim margin; a photograph in the *Marietta Daily Journal* showed the superintendent of schools and the mayor congratulating each other on the victory.[12] In December, I went to the grand opening of YELLS's "community action café" in the Woodlands Park Apartments. The café would serve as a study, arts, and service-learning space to be staffed and patronized by the high school students of Franklin Road, and it would complement YELLS's successful tutoring program in Woodlands Park. A month later, in mid-January of 2014, the city bought Woodlands and a neighboring complex with bond money and notified residents of the impending demolition.[13] Having spent months rehabbing and transforming their Woodlands Park rental space into the action café, Laura Keefe and the students of YELLS never anticipated that Woodlands would be the first to face the bulldozers—many of Franklin Road's properties were in and out of foreclosure and thus priced very low. At an inaugural "teen night" at the café, Keefe caught me gazing at the bright, freshly painted walls, the book shelves and comfy couches, and the charming highboy tables arrayed with snacks and games. "We put so much work into this," she said quietly, "I'm just trying not to think about it."

Redevelopment as a response to resegregation changes nothing about the structural position of the denizens in question; it represents a solution only for school and city leaders and the affluent families those leaders hope to draw back.[14] It is no solution for the students of Franklin whose levers for educational and social justice—the programs of YELLS and the community organizing of Franklin residents themselves—are imperiled by it. Redevelopment in the name of the public schools is a betrayal of *Brown* and of the spirit of *Brown's* righteous successor, *Green v. New Kent County*, the 1968 Supreme Court ruling that demanded not only that segregation be banished but that integration eliminate "racial discrimination . . . root and branch."[15]

The great strength of the Marietta school system is its deep-rootedness, a wellspring of tradition that so many graduates spoke of and that touches more than just those students whose families are "Old Marietta." But that same rootedness can turn to inflexibility and an inability, on the part of city and school leaders, to imagine an MHS sustained by a constituency other than the white families who have sent generations of children there. Keeping MHS in step with the strategies of No Child Left Behind—implementing school choice and founding charter schools and application-only academies—has forestalled an organic, fruitful collaboration between the community and the school, in which the school is responsible to and engaged with, rather than in constant flight from, Marietta's poor residents.

Reimagining an institution's role in its community and in the lives of its students is far easier said than done, especially when skepticism and doubt about the efficacy and quality of public education reign. In Marietta, the tensions and contradictions inherent in this process are evident in "Graduate Marietta," a 2013 initiative to raise the high school's graduation rate. Criticism of Marietta High reached a fever pitch in 2011–2012. That year, MHS was reeling from the mandatory transition to the "adjusted cohort" calculation method, which, as discussed in Chapter 3, brought the Latino graduation rate down below 40 percent, the black graduation rate below 60 percent, and the white graduation rate to just above 80 percent— dramatic decreases from just one year prior.[16] According to Principal Colburn, a white 1983 graduate herself, the new rates are so low because they include "every child who enrolls for even a day" in the ultimate calculation.[17] Reflecting the new method, MHS's overall graduation rate plummeted from 80.5 percent in 2010 to 59 percent in 2011. "B-A-D, bad," was the verdict offered by then-School Board Chair Jill Mutimer of the new rates.[18] Even as the system continued to be pummeled by the effects of the global recession, Mariettans were demanding more of the high school, and as Mutimer's grim assessment suggested, the low graduation rates damaged the cause of public education in the city.

Mariettans—like so many Americans—are "indicator" obsessed. Not just graduation rates, but standardized test scores, end-of-course tests, Advanced Placement and IB enrollments, and the achievement gap had local parents raising their eyebrows. "I don't think they have [the community's support]," said one parent when asked how the city schools were broadly perceived by local families. This judgment, from an upper-middle-class Latino mother and MHS alum, reflected a particular set of anxieties and assumptions about MHS's transformations, its student body, and its future, but also a willingness, like that of some other affluent Mariettans, to release their alma mater to its anticipated demise.

Principal Colburn insisted that it doesn't have to be that way. "I want to say to everyone 'Stop criticizing us and *help* us,'" she exclaimed. Exasperation, indignation, and hope all washed across her face in her sunlit office. We met on a July afternoon, Colburn having shed her school-year suits and heels for jeans. She unwrapped a granola bar, flashing me a high-wattage smile that betrayed, just barely, her fatigue. She'd spent the previous days poring over the "graduation surveys" of the 2013 seniors; it was the first time she'd surveyed a graduating class, and she'd do it annually now, she said. The surveys documented the students' "graduation stories"—their biggest challenges and best moments of high school. I read through them, feeling that I had opened the diary of the institution, noting the careful "i"s dotted with hearts in some places and straining to make out the hurried scrawl in others.[19]

What was your favorite part of high school? "The pep rallies, the faculty . . . the family setting." —Daneesha B. "Being able to be a part of the family of Blue Devils." —Sarah W. "Being a Blue Devil, making memories with new people, and Friday nights at Northcutt." —Binh H. "Bonding as a whole class and family." —Ana Luisa V. "Participating in activities with my friends, the rich traditions around the school." —Bobby M. "Meeting new friends, the Blue Devil spirit." —Jamilah H. "The people and the Marietta traditions." —Adil T. "Making memories with my friends and being a part of the amazing Blue Devil family." —Jennifer M. "Celebrating the Blue Devil spirit . . . attending pep rallies . . . bringing the spirit into other people's lives." —Dervon P. "Being a part of a group of students who value their school and classmates more than anything." —Wunmi I. "Cheering my Marietta Blue Devils. I truly enjoyed being a part of a long-lived tradition." —Shaquelle R.

What was your greatest challenge? "Being homeless more than once was difficult. Living in a shelter. My biggest challenge was losing sight of graduation and losing faith in myself and giving up a few times." —Alejandra M. "My biggest challenge to reach this goal was starting my senior year pregnant and becoming a teen mother. My transition from the high school to [the alternative graduation program], having the baby, recovering from a c-section, working, taking care of my daughter, and keeping up with work had its moments but I did it!" —Destiny H. "I've struggled with depression and sophomore year it got really bad. I felt like I was suffocating constantly and waking every morning felt like a battle. It got to the point where I cared about absolutely nothing. . . . I'm surprised that I'm even still alive, let alone graduating." —Aliyah H. "Overcoming drug abuse and depression" —Marquis S. "Relocating from state to state at least five times before high school. Moving from school to school due to chronic homelessness." —Malik T. "Moving to seven high schools and maintaining my GPA. Freshman year my mom's [boyfriend] was shot and killed in our house during a home invasion." —Jayla M.

The "greatest challenges" described by the students were bigger problems than "math and English class," as Colburn put it; they were problems "the school can't solve." Inextricable from race and class, traumas like homelessness, drug addiction, mental illness, and family crises were dramatically more common among black and Latino graduates. After two more years of equally distressing graduation outcomes in 2012 and 2013, the principal, superintendent, and a team of educators came up with "Graduate Marietta," an initiative to engage the whole community in guiding the most vulnerable students to graduation.

Following more than three decades of tremendous demographic shifts, the community still didn't have, as Colburn and her colleagues determined, the appropriate infrastructure for the high school's students. "We have lawyers in this community, psychiatrists and therapists, community groups . . . we need [their] help," she explained. What Colburn envisioned—a teen homeless shelter, mental health counseling at school, a lawyer and special adviser to immigrant families who are trying to get citizenship—were forms of expertise and services that went far beyond the high school's responsibilities. Such services were the responsibilities of the state. Being unmet, they had fallen to Colburn and her teachers (who were known to take students in to live with them), the in-school social worker, and the guidance counselors with their already staggering caseloads—to, in short, the Blue Devil "family."

A rather straightforward campaign to build support for students on the academic and economic margins, Graduate Marietta's "collaborative school system-community initiative" is, potentially, a nascent challenge to the paradigm of free market education reform. The campaign is animated by the idea that the students of the community's high school are everyone's children—to keep healthy, to encourage, to watch over. Gesturing toward Northcutt Stadium where graduation is held, Colburn put it this way: "My plea to them is this: realize that all those students who cross [that] field and receive their diplomas *and* those who do not become the adult members of our community." In cultivating broad support, the high school may develop the capacity for reimagining its relationship to that community and innovating the curriculum in ways that invite greater success for struggling students. Much depends on how Graduate Marietta is framed and how community members engage with its mission.

Graduate Marietta is also a public relations campaign. Hamstrung by a catch twenty-two familiar to school leaders in the age of "standards and accountability," Colburn needs the combined resources of the community to guide struggling students to graduation, but that support is, in great part, contingent on metrics like graduation rates. A deeply compassionate woman, the principal finds herself defending the rights and needs of marginalized students in one sentence, while praising the possibilities of redevelopment in the next. Dropouts who cause trouble and "get arrested" create a "negative image of the school district," according to Colburn. Yet they are also "her kids," and she is grieved by the dangers, stresses, and pains they face that she and Marietta High's staff can't keep at bay. Such students often hail from Franklin Road. Colburn reflected on redeveloping Franklin: "It may be that we can work with the city council [on redevelopment plans for Franklin Road]. [The current state of the complexes] is honestly not good for our students to live in. I've been asked by people in the community, 'Well, where are the people on Franklin gonna go?' And I say, 'I don't know, but I hope not [back to] Franklin Road.'"

Like Blue Devil football or the IB program, or even school choice, Graduate Marietta is another ritual reconstruction of MHS's identity, with complicated racial and class politics and consequences for poor students of color. One of the campaign's new videos (Graduate Marietta "went live" in August of 2013 with online videos, flyers, and a pitch from the superintendent) featured a former Franklin Roader. Decked out in cap and gown, Bridget Reyes spoke into the camera: "Because I'm a high school graduate, we *all* benefit."[20] Months before, she had wryly recounted being called to the guidance office and given a sheet of paper with a few sentences about the opportunities her diploma would bring her. Pausing the video and emblazoning Bridget's charming, vaguely sardonic smile on her computer screen, Colburn talked about the importance of "mobilizing our community to support student achievement," echoing her own lines from the promotional video. The superintendent called Graduate Marietta a "collaboration," and "partnership" between city and school to confront graduation as a "community concern." This insistence by school leaders on a collective response to climbing dropout rates in the form of increased resources for marginalized students is encouraging, but the conversation around Franklin Road, and areas like it, must move beyond crime, transience, and blight for the vision of Graduate Marietta to be broad enough to embrace the students of Franklin.

My meeting with Colburn sprang from questions about the bond between community and school I'd been mulling all year, but that had crystalized on the May morning of Marietta High's graduation. After the ceremony, I went looking for Bridget and found her ringed about by her family, who wept and hugged her as if she was departing for college that very afternoon. As the oldest, and the first in her family to pursue her education beyond high school, she'd spent years urging her siblings—who were twisting themselves in her gown and cavorting around her—to follow her path to college. "Thanks for coming, Miss Ruthie," Bridget said, throwing her arm over my shoulder. I searched for the words to thank *her*. Anything I'd given her—a hand with college applications, a ride after school, a slice of pizza on the square—seemed so scant next to all she'd given me. Wielding her already-bedraggled faux diploma ("They're just rolled-up pieces of blank paper, *Jefa;* they'll send us the real thing in the mail," she'd assured her mom), she rapped me on the head affectionately. "See you later!" she hollered with a grin as the family headed to the parking lot.

I scurried away, dabbing my eyes surreptitiously and scanning the remaining clusters of graduates for Sumsi, a YELLS mentor from The Gambia, whose sweetness and even keel had been so valuable in the hubbub of big service days. I discovered her still celebrating on the field with the women in her family. They had spread a brightly patterned cloth on the grass, which Sumsi danced across in delicate, shy steps as her aunts and mother stood around her, holding a brass pot they tapped a rhythm on while they sang. I clapped along and so did Delia, a black junior and one of YELLS's (few) straight-A students, who had come to congratulate her graduating friends. Bidding goodbye to Sumsi, we made our way to our cars, and Delia reminded me to come see her in the fall production of

A Raisin in the Sun at the school's new arts facility. The product of yet another multi-million-dollar education bond, the auditorium would make Marietta High a "home for the arts," as Principal Colburn put it—the Georgia Ballet and the state's symphony orchestra were already partners, and other collaborations were in the works.

Thinking about Delia, YELLS, and the elegant complex rising out of the construction site at the high school, I cynically turned over in my mind the ballerinas and young violinists school leaders hoped to draw to the new theater. How many of *them* would be Franklin Roaders? But in the deepening day, in almost-empty Northcutt Stadium gussied up for graduation and bedecked in balloons and Blue Devil banners, I realized it didn't matter, really, for whom the auditorium was intended. It mattered that once again local voters had committed their money to their public school, and it mattered that all the students who enrolled could take classes that would bring them into the gleaming new space. It mattered that those students would have the tools they needed for whatever creative projects called them, and it mattered that Marietta High was making itself better for the next decade of Blue Devils, different as they may be from those of fifty, or twenty, or just ten years before.

Embedded in the relationship between the school and the community, signaled by events as seemingly disparate as the passage of education bonds and the instituting of Franklin Road Gardening Days, is the enduring possibility of greater educational justice. What Mariettans taught me is that to inaugurate a broad educational justice movement we need not look to court decisions, national legislation, state-level reforms, or even district-implemented school policies, but instead to local people who seek to expand the "school community" and foster a newly broad integration era. In cities like Marietta—which have been remade by decades of cultural, political, and economic change since *Brown v. Board*—this new integration era will be student-driven and community-based. It will be fueled by the work and vision of "new integrators" like undocumented Latino students and low-income students of color and by veterans of social change as well—progressive educators, local activists, and committed community members like those of Franklin Road. Instead of school "reforms," local revolutions are taking shape through groups like YELLS. Such student groups transform "colorblindness" and "diversity" from rhetoric that denies the salience of structural racism into practices that challenge it by cultivating activism within the current majority at MHS—a majority that is not white and privileged and likely never will be again.

For school integration in the twenty-first century to be as radical as that of the *Brown* era, as shattering to the customs and beliefs entrenched by the status quo, then it must encompass and engage with parallel justice struggles: movements to end deportation, to pass the DREAM Act, to increase the living wage, to develop sustainable food systems, to combat discrimination in the justice system and abuse at the hands of police, to safeguard the franchise of marginalized voters, and to protect the air, soil, and water of the places where low-income families and their children live. In the sense that educational justice is inextricable from these several spheres of social justice, so too is integration about work, food, housing, representation, and education—about community, in the broadest sense of the word.

I lingered a bit longer in the warm morning, reflecting on the Mexican American students in Arizona who successfully protested the banning of their ethnic studies curriculum and the cadre of white and black students in South Georgia who, after decades of segregated proms, organized their first integrated dance in 2013.[21] And I thought, of course, of Darrell and Bridget and Kendra and Anthony and all the YELLS youth and the students of AH! who didn't need the school board or the city council to shape a new MHS for them because they were already doing it themselves. I looked toward the stadium. How many thousands of fans had endured Georgia's cold, rainy autumns; had stood hopefully, faithfully through games that went from bad to worse; had stuck by a team that, like the *Brown* era, saw its major triumphs decades ago? Yet every fall brings a new opportunity to break that losing streak; every August ushers in renewed hopes for the future. Surely it's time for a new era for the Blue Devils— time for a reinvention of integration for today's Mariettans, and for the students who will fill the stands with their cheering and the May sky with their tasseled caps in the generations to come.

EPILOGUE

IN EARLY AUGUST of 2015, on an afternoon made cool by rain, Bridget and I gazed across the fencing that encircled what once was Woodlands Park Apartments. Woodlands Park is the former home of two of three YELLS programs. For a time, the apartment buildings had remained in various states of destruction, as if demolition was a disease that worked faster on some than others, leaving one cluster gutted but still standing, another half-razed, hunkering in the dust among the encroaching kudzu and the spindly, spared pines. But by the time Bridget and I found ourselves at the site—the familiar blinking red of my recorder between us, and Bridget rifling through my bag for chewing gum (gone were the formalities of that first slightly stilted interview four years before)—there was no vestige, amid the detritus and dumpsters, of YELLS's facilities, playground, and cheery signage. An orange "danger" tape still fluttered along the fence, a plaintive echo of the ribbon-cutting at the grand opening of the Community Action Café, just months before the city bought Woodlands Park and slated it for demolition in redevelopment's first salvo.

We went, in part, because I wanted to take some photographs of Bridget there—for my own tracking of redevelopment on Franklin, but also as a kind of leave-taking. Bridget hung on the fence and looked back at me, cartoonishly furrowing her eyebrows and turning down her mouth, saying things like, "Do I look sad enough?" I played along: "Wistful—we're going for wistful." Later, as we sat in the car in the Woodlands Park entrance and talked about redevelopment, she was unguarded and no longer joking. Her gaze fell on the muddy base of the building—the leasing office—that had housed the Community Action Café. I pried: "The café? Is that what you miss? Since the leasing office was demolished?" Bridget had helped make the café what it was—a bright, bustling space, with a steady stream of teens and parent "customers" just a couple of months after opening. "That wasn't ever the leasing office," she told me. "When I lived here in middle school, it was a community center with a computer lab, and my Girl Scout troop—we were called *Unidas Latinas*—we met there. And Miss Ruthie, no one ever calls this Woodlands Park. Its Las Colinas. That's how we all know it."

Bridget had me there. For me, the names of complexes didn't signify anything except the endlessly revolving door of management companies. During my fieldwork, the name of the complex where YELLS's mentoring program was housed changed three times. But Woodlands Park would always be Las Colinas for Bridget's generation and for their parents, not because it was Las Colinas longest, but because the people who lived there, and the community members who worked there, produced a culturally meaningful space out of the complex. In a period when crime was highest on Franklin and its apartments had become a shorthand for all that was wrong with Marietta, there was, at Las Colinas, a Latino Girl Scout troop, a community computer lab, and a clothing exchange and food pantry.

The *Marietta Daily Journal* offered a different interpretation of Woodlands Park and its neighboring complexes: "This stretch of the city has been faced with higher than normal crime stats and other issues. . . . [T] he city has been able to purchase extremely dilapidated apartment complexes, help those residents find other housing, and demolish that property to market to other businesses."[1] In the *Marietta Daily Journal*'s rendering, Franklin Road's complexes constitute what Henri Lefebvre called "abstract space": a site of social interaction and political life rather than a space productive of it. Through the lens of abstract space, the actions of Franklin residents register as quotidian acts in the context of existing discourses, not actions that can change and appropriate them. Franklin Road as abstract space informs the rhetoric of champions of redevelopment: in that context, the demolition of apartment buildings—and with them the YELLS programs housed there—is a politically neutral act with positive net economic gain, even, in the more morally righteous moments at City Hall, an act of extreme benevolence on the part of city leaders.

Only in seeing YELLS's programs for what they were and are— "counter-spaces," to borrow again from Lefebvre, on Franklin Road—is it clear that despite the seeming innocuousness of a mentoring, service, and leadership program, YELLS's mission and praxis are a rebuke. They are a rebuke to the notion that the people of Franklin are at best rootless and at worst criminal, as well as to the falsehood that demolition produces opportunity on Franklin rather than destroying the very spaces where Franklin Road students cultivated opportunity for themselves. Woodlands Park, for YELLS youth, was not abstract space as property awaiting its moment on the market, but a place they experienced as a palimpsest, in which the layers of community history, communal action, and identity construction were perceptible, powerful, and socially real.

In the summer of 2015, redevelopment came to Franklin in earnest. The city's purchase of Woodlands Park was followed by two more complexes in fairly quick succession. The mayor—the graying Blue Devil who had handily won a second term and the battle of the redevelopment bond two falls before—donned a construction helmet for the festive demolition derby that marked the razing of the first complex. "An iconic step," said Mayor Tumlin, "[for the city] as we actually start the redevelopment process. . . . Once you get this building down, it's easier to get folks closer to the signing table. We have a lot of interest [in the area], which has increased the more we get to tearing these two [complexes] down. The attractiveness of 50 acres in the center, near Interstate 75, is creating a lot of excitement."[2] The kickoff of the Franklin Gateway Revitalization Project was "symbolized by the road's name change to 'Gateway Boulevard,'" reported the *Marietta Daily Journal.*[3]

What city leaders hoped would bring investors to Franklin is what brought so many undocumented families there. Bridget's parents and those of her friends sought the centrality of Franklin; those employed in construction and maid work had easy interstate access to jobs across the metro area. And Franklin was cheap—some of the only truly affordable housing in the city for many years. For the documented but low-income students of Bridget's generation, being in Marietta High's district was a potential ticket to college, boasting as it did one of only two International Baccalaureate (IB) programs in the county and one of only twenty-seven IB public school diploma programs in Georgia.[4] Bridget reflected on how Franklin Road was home to many of Marietta High's recent IB graduates. She reeled off a list of names—"Remember Carlos and Marie? Remember David?"—Latino students I had met at YELLS service days—"All graduated *full IB.*" The connection that Bridget drew between Woodlands Park and Latino IB graduates was more than a claim that Franklin Roaders could "make it"—Bridget was more tired of this narrative than anyone. Rather, it demonstrated how little Franklin resembled the corridor of violence, neglect, and squandered promise that city leaders called upon to justify the violence of demolition and displacement.

The YELLS afterschool program at Woodlands Park was the centerpiece of the organization's efforts to build community in the Franklin complexes, community that would provide low-income parents free afterschool care, tutoring, and enrichment for their children, and provide children with what matters when you are seven or eight—playgrounds with slides you can slide on and plenty of popsicles when the afternoons grow hot. The infrastructure that makes possible such simple pleasures for Franklin's kids did not exist widely before YELLS brought funding, volunteers, teachers, supplies, and programs to Woodlands Park. If you were a grownup new to YELLS, as I was in 2012, you got a "welcome tour" from participants. My guides, third graders Mariana and Elena, showed me the leadership room, the art lab, the library, and the classroom spaces with proud smiles and highly polished explanations (particularly about their own contributions to the YELLS ART! exhibition in the main room). Because Woodlands Park was home to the afterschool program, it was also host of many of the community meetings that helped set a new tone for the relationship between the school superintendent, her staff, and the Spanish-speaking families of Franklin.

Bringing the Community Action Café to Woodlands Park helped create critical continuity—it would focus on high school residents, but would also attract middle school students. As YELLS founder Laura Keefe saw it, in Woodlands Park after the opening of the café, whether you were five years old or fifteen, there was something for you. At the café ribbon-cutting in December of 2013, Keefe and the rest of the YELLS youth still held out some hope that Woodlands Park would be rescued or at least its demolition delayed. The alternate scenario, accepting the loss of buildings, was that some small part of the 68-million-dollar bond might be set aside for a new home for YELLS. If there were 11 million dollars in the budget to buy and demolish Woodlands Park—and YELLS programs with it—would there perhaps be a few hundred thousand for a new YELLS site?

Even beyond the loss of YELLS facilities for the afterschool program and Community Action Café, the demolition of Woodlands Park spelled financial trouble for YELLS. In an arrangement with the City of Marietta and the complex owners, YELLS had enjoyed free use of the complex's community center for its activities, channeling the thousands of dollars that would have gone to utilities, rent, and renovation into programming for the students of Franklin. In the summer of 2014, YELLS signed a lease for a new building on Franklin, a commercial office building with limited outside play space and no street frontage to attract people to the community café. Although the county offered funding for a down payment on the building, the owner wanted $200,000 more than the building's assessed value, a price tag that made the city balk and dashed YELLS's dreams of owning. The fantasies of a new Franklin bedecked in high-end development and new industry mean that Franklin property owners are no longer willing to sell at present market rate. YELLS was, effectively, already being priced out of the neighborhood in which it had, for eight years, functioned as a purveyor of critical services and an anchor, helping to root families on Franklin and fashioning for those children a foothold in their local schools.

Although local coverage of the redevelopment of Franklin Road was uncritical—and often laudatory—farther flung journalists pointed to the Franklin Road Corridor as a project with historical baggage: an urban renewal effort reminiscent of the 1960s, aimed explicitly at purging the area of many of its brown and black residents and pricing out those who remain. In a piece called "Why Aren't We Talking about Marietta, Georgia?" economist Joe Cortright of the Portland-based think tank City Observatory called redevelopment on Franklin "a pretty cut-and-dried case of gentrification and displacement."[5] He notes the absence of the kind of public outrage and "media attention" in Marietta that attend less "egregious" gentrification in places like New York and San Francisco.[6] Echoing Cortright, New York–based writer Eric Jaffe of *City Lab* (an online affiliate of *The Atlantic*) pointed to the absence, in Marietta's public discourse, of any condemnation of the city for forcing out residents without any services or compensation.[7] Cortright calls gentrification in Marietta too short on "hipsters" to be "sexy enough" to suit the narratives attached to, for example, the transformation of Brooklyn's neighborhoods.[8]

Why this is true—that Marietta doesn't rank with Brooklyn or San Francisco despite what Cortright accurately describes as the "explicitly stated strategy" of the city government—is simple.[9] Discourse around the value of neighborhoods is rooted in notions of the "historical" and "cultural" that are deeply class and race inflected. It attaches in particularly pernicious ways to developments like those on Franklin, where commercial properties with decreasing market value are seen to have correspondingly little cultural or historical value, even if inhabitants accord significant meaning to them. For that reason, the construction of counter-spaces on Franklin is inextricable from other forms of resistance to the redevelopment of Franklin Road.

In the broader context of community building and integration, planting gardens on Franklin, rehabbing swing sets, gathering at community meetings, and staging stop-the-violence rallies are all manifestations of resistance, even if they don't stall or halt the passage of legislation.[10] Many residents of Franklin Road questioned redevelopment, and some openly condemned it, but their voices were given few venues, and they had little political clout to shift the agenda. Many had no democratic recourse, as the undocumented residents of Franklin couldn't vote against the bond.

Just as suburban school resegregation and its repercussions for students of color are hidden in plain sight, resistance to redevelopment on Franklin is similarly invisible.[11] In both cases, the value, vitality, and power of poor communities of color—of students particularly—is the necessary lens for perceiving both alternative responses to resegregation and resistance to redevelopment. As writer and activist Alice Walker lamented, "I wonder if America will ever have a place for poor people. It appears they are doomed to be eternal transients."[12] It is precisely against this destiny that the work of place-making happens on Franklin, and this work is integral to broader efforts to make the city schools into sites of transformation and meaningful opportunity.

What the students of Franklin and their allies face is bigger than bulldozers. The connection between redevelopment and resegregation is thrown into relief through the byword of contemporary education reform—the market. In the calculations of the city's economic development team, investment would spur investment—one win on that front would produce another. When the Atlanta Braves announced, in the spring of 2013, their plans to move from a stadium downtown (built as part of the 1996 Olympic boom that devastated historic black neighborhoods there) to a new site a few miles from the Franklin Corridor, spirits soared at City Hall. They soared higher still when, in the fall of 2015, Home Depot opened up a technology center on Franklin Road.[13] Finally, in the waning days of 2015,

Atlanta United—the soccer franchise bought by Arthur Blank (Home Depot cofounder and Falcons owner)—decided to pull out of a proposed contract with DeKalb County for a multi-million-dollar practice complex and instead build on Franklin Road.[14] This unexpected victory for the mayor and his economic development team was followed closely by an even more surprising one for the teens of YELLS's Community Action Café, both of which heralded a new chapter for the students of Franklin Road.

On a much anticipated January night in 2016, the four teen hosts of the YELLS Mayoral Forum stood before a packed house. All day, the YELLS site on Franklin had been abuzz with preparations for the mayor's first ever visit—a town hall hosted by the teens of the Action Café, during which the mayor would take questions from community members about redevelopment and the proposed name change from Franklin Road to Gateway Boulevard. The mayor came accompanied by two city council members, his staff, and a *Marietta Daily Journal* reporter. In preparing to host the event, the YELLS teens had crafted questions in concert with their peers, neighbors, and family members, and planned a program that specifically prioritized the concerns of the Franklin Road community. Issues such as the demolition of four complexes, the likelihood of rent hikes, and the city's stated goal to increase home ownership with no plan for engaging current residents in such a "rental to ownership" conversion were powerfully voiced by the teens themselves on their own, hard-won turf at the YELLS facility on Franklin.[15] Although there were very few softballs—one of the opening questions from teen host Lawrence was "Are the changes [on Franklin Road] considered redevelopment or gentrification?"—the teens deftly pursued their delicate mission. Seeking to articulate the pressing concerns of the community members and the students themselves, they were also cultivating a working relationship and open dialogue with the mayor, his staff, and the city council. For the teen hosts, relegating to the shadows issues important to Franklin Roaders (for example, the absence of any material or logistical support to residents displaced by demolitions) was out of the question, but the mayor's presence on Franklin and willingness to engage with YELLS youth was a clear and important gesture toward building that collaborative relationship.

Much of the city's bond-related public relations had centered "quality of life" improvements for Franklin Roaders, and the mayor's staff came prepared with visualizations of crosswalks, new traffic signals, long-awaited parks, and sports facilities—one of which will be located across from and host events in partnership with YELLS's new neighbor, Atlanta United. Although the brandishing of attractive maps featuring splash pads and walking trails didn't bespeak of a public official being taken to task by his constituents, the teen hosts weren't, in fact, the ones who needed to do that work. As they laid out the concerns of the assembled with rehearsed courtesy and charming nervousness, they also opened door after door for defiant community members to make clear the stakes of redevelopment. A black resident—in oblique reference to the mayor's portrait of displaced residents as "the heroes" who "stepped aside" to make way for improved quality of life on Franklin—recalled seeing children playing in a trash-littered lot near a demolished complex and leaned into the microphone, "Are you going to do anything for your people? I believe in development, but are you going to do anything for your people, Mr. Mayor?" Another resident offered the story of her own daughter—a single mother of two returning to school and trying to find affordable housing; she reminded the audience that the city had demolished all its public housing and asked the mayor, "Can there be a place that accommodates these single mothers?" Acknowledging that affordable housing is "a challenge," he suggested she turn to Section 8 housing—the very kind of voucher-accepting apartment complexes that have been bought and demolished through the bond. Finally, a parent, mother to one of the evening's hosts, rose to inveigh against the name change and, more broadly, celebrate the work of YELLS. "I've seen these children get up early in the morning to clean Franklin Road" and seen the Action Café grow as a community hub, she professed. "They're not doing this [work] for Gateway Boulevard. They're doing this for Franklin Road."

At the root of the assembled Mariettans questions, demands, and entreaties was that rub: community. Who composes it? And what are the mechanisms of its survival? Those questions animate the work of YELLS; they are dramatized in every season of Blue Devil football; they dog the IB program, and they shadow the votes of the school board on choice programs and charter schools. They are the vexing questions that must be engaged as central to battling resegregation.

The relationship between community on Franklin and community as understood through the lens of Marietta's public schools was implicit in moments of the evening's discussion, but toward the end of the night, the mayor reflected quite directly on the subject: "We need to be more inclusive; I'm not talking about dialect or the color of your skin . . . we are all the

same . . . we [need to know each other]. You go to Marietta High?" he asked
Lawrence, who nodded. "I went to Marietta High, a little bit before you."
The audience tittered appreciatively. The mayor concluded: "We have so
much in common." The mayor's invocation of Marietta High as both literally
and figuratively common ground draws attention to how the high school
endures as a potentially powerful touchstone for the "shared vision" that the
teen hosts articulated at the forum. But an assertion of sameness also marks
out the space where continued movement building and community self-
determination remain so essential: the energetic and rooted place-making
of YELLS insists that Lawrence and the mayor are, indeed, not at all the
same, and in terms of the experiences that make them who they are, they
have very little in common. Their shared identity as Blue Devils produces
the possibility of dialogue and creative collaboration through, not despite,
difference. Turning to the eloquent words of the YELLS mother contesting
the name change: it is for Franklin Road, not Gateway Boulevard, that
Lawrence speaks, works, and imagines a next chapter.

After the City Council voted a month later on the renaming of the corridor, the *Atlanta Journal-Constitution* reported "a compromise was
reached to keep 'Franklin' in the name—thanks to the insistence of young
people from the Franklin Road area."[16] Until the teen-led forum, the
mayor had never been to YELLS's home on Franklin (Tumlin quipped that
he doubted a mayor had been on Franklin Road "in twenty years"), nor had
he been held accountable for the impact of redevelopment on its residents
by those residents themselves. The name-change vote made a democratic
ideal at least fleetingly concrete: an officeholder listened and acted on the
voices of his constituents—not those with the most money or the greatest
conventional influence, but those with a demonstrated and deep commitment to their neighbors, their city, and their schools.

Out of the Rubble: The Community Action Café

"Will you be comfortable there?" asked Dmitri, a Community Action Café
team leader, as he escorted me to my stool at the back of the cafe. The
YELLS teens had trolled the complexes to drum up attendance at the community meeting, which YELLS was hosting. Dmitri looked around periodically to see who, of his recruits, had already arrived. A sixteen-year-old
with a cherubic face, Dmitri's interests are primarily fashion-related, but

he has a place in the café; his energy and poise earn him respect. Like the other teens, he loves calling the café his own—an enterprise that relies on their work, their creativity, and their vision. The café, like Franklin Road broadly, is a space of negotiation, embodying the query: how can YELLS and its youth be integral to, rather than cast aside by, the transformation of Franklin, and how can they make the process of revitalization their own? The kind of social reproduction that takes place in the café is different from, but connected to, that of the schools. The work of the café presents a fruitful contradiction—teens who come straight to the café from a shift at McDonald's or Wendy's take off their name tags just in time for Dmitri to remind them to put on their gloves to ice the tea for the community meeting attendees. What makes service in the café so different from work in a service sector that has come to embody labor exploitation in the developed world? The teens seek balance, power, and joy in work at the café, work that enables them to grapple on the ground with the YELLS conception of servant leadership: service by and for community members that binds together local institutions, grass roots leadership, and families in the process of self-determination.[17]

The café consumes the second story of YELLS's new home; when you are having a coke or a cup of tea in the café lounge, the ambience is something between a Starbucks and a Gymboree, as the cheery chaos of the afterschool program floats upstairs to join the sounds of the teens, usually arguing playfully over a question of aesthetics in the lounge or about the theme for the next youth-hosted workshop. The impossibility of purchasing the building at its $600,000 sticker price has meant that YELLS has not been able to do the extensive kitchen renovations the teens had hoped for, since both programs will have to find a new home at the end of the current three-year lease. But the teens are adept in making do; microwaveable treats and fresh fruit covered the tables, next to couches strewn with bright pillows.

The Action Café survived a rocky start—the loss of the Woodlands Park site was followed by a transition year during which Laura Keefe struggled to find YELLS a new home, recruit staff, and attract new teens in the midst of uncertainty about redevelopment's next targets and Franklin Road's future. But as the community meeting began, a familiar rhythm developed: focused discussion of the upcoming event—a back-to-school bash providing school supplies to the children of Franklin—followed by more informal brainstorming about security in the complexes, the calendar for the café, and the ways that the assembled parents and residents could support the teens' hard work. There was talk of redevelopment and of the future—a future in which YELLS remains integral to Franklin and its children and teens; in which amid the tumult and uncertainty, Dmitri takes his team to the street to spread the word about café events; in which the YELLS mentors and their mentees host community dinners at rotating complexes; and in which the garden continues to produce its squash and cucumbers and students from the nearby complex track their growth and pick their prizes.

I was reminded of the portrait of Las Colinas that Bridget drew while I gazed out the window of the Action Café at the apartments' former site, now beckoning green stretches composing the sixty-million-dollar Atlanta United practice fields and headquarters.[18] Place making and community building on Franklin Road arise out of necessity, ingenuity, and courage. Those, too, are the ingredients of the new integration movement. The redevelopment bond may have meant the destruction of YELLS's original home, but if capital is patient and wily, so too are Franklin Roaders. YELLS exists in the tradition of community resilience and resistance in a place where those qualities have always been the conditions for survival. The integration movement contemplated in these pages is, in fact, no different from those very forms of survival; the flourishing of Franklin Roaders and the shape of their resistance are and will be the shape of integration in communities across the country. The families of YELLS and the teens of the café insist through work that roots them, that gives them joy, and that binds them to each other and to their community that the future of Franklin Road and of Marietta's schools is theirs too. It is at this register—the integration of school and community—that we might see Franklin for what it is: not a place worth saving, but already saved, by the work of its people and by the courage of its students.

Notes

Acknowledgments

Index

NOTES

Introduction

1. Kenneth Norwood and Jan Robles, interview by the author, digital recording, Marietta, GA, July 30, 2013. All other quotes from Robles and Norwood date to this interview.

2. The previous incarnation of Lockheed Martin was Bell Aircraft, which produced fighter planes during World War II. Bell was the first workplace to desegregate in Marietta, as it was encompassed by Executive Order 8802, which established the Fair Employment Practices Commission and banned discrimination in hiring in the defense industries. Thomas Scott, *Cobb County, Georgia, and the Origins of the Suburban South* (Marietta, GA: Cobb Landmarks and Historical Society, 2003), 168–69.

3. "Characteristics of the Population, 1960," US Census Bureau, accessed April 10, 2017, http://www.census.gov/prod/www/decennial.html.

4. Cobb County's White Citizens for Segregation (WCS) staged a 1960 boycott of businesses refusing to place an "S" for segregation on their doors, a boycott that received heated reactions in the *Marietta Daily Journal* from both supporters and critics. Scott, *Cobb County*, 283.

5. Characteristics of the Population, 1960," US Census Bureau, accessed April 10, 2017, http://www.census.gov/prod/www/decennial.html. In 1960, most of the black men of working age were service workers and laborers, who drove, cook, built, and repaired for white Marietta. A modest share worked in better-paying manufacturing jobs, and a handful, like in most every Southern

town, engaged a loyal black clientele as barbers, tailors, and the like. Consistent with many Deep South cities, more than 50 percent of employed black women worked as "domestics" in white households. Median years of education for black adults was 7.6 versus 11.5 for whites; median black family income was $2,898, and median white family income was $5,677.

6. By 1980, more than a third of black adults over age twenty-five had graduated high school versus only 14 percent in 1960. "Characteristics of the Population, 1960, 1980," US Census Bureau, accessed April 10, 2017, http://www.census.gov/prod/www/decennial.html.

7. American FactFinder, "US Census, Community Facts, ACS Demographic and Housing Estimates, 2011–2015," accessed May 9, 2017, https://Factfinder.Census.Gov/Faces/Nav/Jsf/Pages/Community_Facts.Xhtmlm.

8. The trial of Leo Frank, accused of killing thirteen-year-old Mary Phagan who worked in his pencil factory, aroused the nativism and anti-Semitism that convulsed many mostly protestant communities in that era. As scholars have observed, it was deeply ironic that Frank's fate was sealed by the inconsistent testimony of a black worker, in a time and place when the words and deeds of black citizens were suspect at best. After a series of appeals that led eventually to the commuting of his death sentence to life imprisonment, Frank was seized from jail and lynched by a group of white Mariettans calling themselves the Knights of Mary Phagan. The defense of white Southern womanhood, the vilification of prosperous Jewish capitalists, and the (ineffective) racist paeans offered by Frank's defense typify the political, social, and economic climate so hospitable to the rebirth of the Ku Klux Klan. Just months after Frank was murdered, the new Knights of the Ku Klux Klan met around a flaming cross on nearby Stone Mountain. Scholar Nancy MacLean asserts that a direct link between the Knights of Mary Phagan and those "knights" called to order under the cross on Stone Mountain—a connection Marietta's white political leadership ambivalently claims—is mostly "popular myth." Yet the lynching of Frank by prominent white Mariettans and the leveraging of the event by influential Southern politicians like Tom Watson suggest that Marietta was a powerful wellspring of the "vigilante spirit" that gave birth to the second Klan. Nancy MacLean, *Behind the Mask of Chivalry: The Making of the Second Ku Klux Klan* (New York: Oxford University Press, 1994), 12.

9. Daphne Delk, interview by the author, digital recording, Atlanta, GA, February 12, 2012. Unless otherwise noted, all other quotations from Delk date to this interview.

10. In doing so, I follow Susan Eaton, who makes this distinction clear in her powerful work on segregated education in Hartford, Connecticut, *The Children in Room E4: American Education on Trial* (Chapel Hill, NC: Algonquin, 2007).

11. A too-often overlooked example of successful desegregation litigation outside the South that predated *Brown* is the 1947 decision in *Mendez v. Westminster*, which condemned the segregation of children of Mexican descent in the schools of Orange County, California. Philippa Strum, *Mendez v. Westminster: School Desegregation and Mexican-American Rights* (Lawrence: University Press of Kansas, 2010); Martha Menchaca, *The Mexican Outsiders: A Community History of Marginalization and Discrimination in California* (Austin: University of Texas Press, 1995). For local desegregation efforts in the South that predate the *Brown* era, Liva Baker's excellent study of desegregation in New Orleans details efforts dating back to the nineteenth century and to the infamous decision *Brown* overturned, *Plessy v. Ferguson* (1896), which ruled "separate but equal" Jim Crow laws constitutional. Liva Baker, *The Second Battle of New Orleans: The Hundred-Year Struggle to Integrate the Schools* (New York: HarperCollins, 1996). And for the history of cases that paved the way for the decision in *Brown*, Richard Kluger's volume is definitive: *Simple Justice: The History of Brown v. Board and Black America's Struggle for Equality* (New York: Random House, 1975).

12. Horace Mann and his ilk helped to make their states the leaders of the common schooling movement, and by the end of the century, their peers in states across the Northeast and Midwest saw substantial success in their crusade for systematized and state-supervised education. The South is notably absent from this narrative; for reasons debated by education historians, the movement was slower to gain political traction and support below the Mason-Dixon. Historian Carl F. Kaestle argues that the slave economy and the system of values, customs, and politics that undergirded it were hostile to the forms of state control—and "Yankee" influence—that developing free and universal public education required. Kaestle also observes that slave owners were uncomfortable with the notion of widely available books and growing literacy. The belief that learning made slaves ungovernable was universal across the South, and thus was punishable by law in many places. Unless they were free or (in rare cases) permitted by their owners, black children had no education at all. White children of privilege and some poorer whites were taught at home or went to community-supported schools. On the eve of the Civil War in the slave-holding South, only North Carolina had anything resembling a tax-funded, centralized, public school system. Carl F. Kaestle, *Pillars of the Republic: Common Schools and American Society, 1780–1860* (New York: Hill and Wang, 1983), 203, 213.

13. Kaestle, *Pillars of the Republic*, 23.

14. Katherine S. Newman, Cybelle Fox, David J. Harding, Jal Mehta, and Wendy Roth, *Rampage: The Social Roots of School Shootings* (New York:

Basic, 2004); Douglas Foley, "The Great American Football Ritual:
Reproducing Race, Class and Gender Inequality," in *Contemporary Issues
in Sociology of Sports*, ed. Andrew Yiannakis and Merrill J. Melnick
(Champaign, IL: Human Kinetics, 2001).

15. As Newman et al. write, in a one-high-school town, the school is "the com-
    munity's most public stage," and it is athletes who most often enjoy adula-
    tion on that stage, from both peers and adults, often to the exclusion of
    students with other abilities and interests. *Rampage*, 127.

16. Education historian Joel Spring asserted that the history of American
    public schooling is that of a century-long project to secure "the domina-
    tion of a Protestant Anglo American culture in the United States." Carl
    Kaestle adds that nationally entrenching capitalism, as both a philosoph-
    ical and economic commitment, was part and parcel of early school
    reform. Quoted in William Hayes, *Horace Mann's Vision of the Public
    Schools: Is It Still Relevant?* (Lanham, MD: Rowman & Littlefield,
    2006), 75.

17. As institutions, schools have played a distinct historical role in shaping
    Americans' ideas about broad democratic notions—such as civic participa-
    tion, social cooperation, and responsible citizenship—and also about the
    issues that trouble these democratic ideals: race, class, and belonging.
    Why schools have such a critical function in their communities and how
    once-radical ideas—like racially integrated education in the South—
    became commonplace characteristics of public schooling are explained, in
    part, by what educational historians Larry Cuban and David Tyack call the
    "distinctive institutional character" of schools. David Tyack and Larry
    Cuban, *Tinkering Toward Utopia: A Century of Public School Reform*
    (Cambridge, MA: Harvard University Press, 1995), 7. Anthropologist
    Mary Douglas helps illuminate the nature of this "institutional character":
    as she points out, institutions order the social world and shape the human
    actions that constitute it. Mary Douglas, *How Institutions Think*
    (Syracuse, NY: Syracuse University Press, 1986).

18. In the mid-twentieth century, "multiculturalism" and "cultural pluralism"
    were radical ideas about de-institutionalizing the Eurocentric and usually
    racist values of the early reformers; they have since become domesticated,
    innocuous metaphors gracing the pages of education textbooks—the
    American citizenry as "tossed salad" versus "melting pot," Hayes, *Horace
    Mann's Vision of the Public Schools*, 76, 78. Work in the last decade that is
    critical of multiculturalism as "deracialized" and apolitical offers a salient
    and necessary critique of "pro-diversity" curriculum, politics, and reform
    that do not take structural inequality and systems of power as their points
    of departure. Barry Troyna, "Beyond Multiculturalism: Towards the

Enactment of Anti-Racist Education in Policy, Provision and Pedagogy," *Oxford Review of Education* 13, no. 3 (1987): 307–20.

19. President Truman's 1948 executive order 9981 desegregated the armed forces. Howell S. Baum, *Brown in Baltimore: School Desegregation and the Limits of Liberalism* (Ithaca, NY: Cornell University Press, 2010); Robert L. Hayman Jr. and Leland Ware, eds., *Choosing Equality: Essays and Narratives on the Desegregation Experience* (University Park, PA: Penn State University Press, 2009); Tracy K'Meyer, *Civil Rights in the Gateway to the South: Louisville, Kentucky, 1945–1980* (Lexington: University Press of Kentucky, 2009).

20. Amy Stuart Wells's excellent study *Both Sides Now: The Story of School Desegregation's Graduates* draws on more than five hundred interviews with graduates of the class of 1980 at desegregated high schools in six cities. Almost all of "desegregation's graduates" reflect positively on attending desegregated schools, citing lessons in tolerance of those who are different and appreciation of diverse experiences and perspectives as benefits of desegregated schooling. Amy Stuart Wells, Jennifer Jellison Holme, Anita Tijerina Revilla, and Awo Korantemaa Atanda, *Both Sides Now: The Story of School Desegregation's Graduates* (Berkeley: University of California Press, 2009).

21. Drawing on the work of legal scholar Patricia Williams, I allude here to the way in which progressive racial discourse is always dogged by what Williams calls in her work, *Seeing a Colorblind Future,* "the false luxury of a prematurely imagined community," or, in the case of many of my interviewees, nostalgia for an imagined community Patricia J. Williams, *Seeing a Colorblind Future: The Paradox of Race* (New York: Farrar, Straus and Giroux, 1997), 5. It is in the name of this "prematurely imagined community" that so many quote Martin Luther King Jr., and it is the perverse veneration and ubiquity of that "character not color" dogma assigned to King that primes the cultural soil for the powerful critiques voiced by scholars like Williams and by community members and activists across the country.

22. School segregation was never unique to the South or to black students, nor were efforts to dismantle segregated schools. In a recent, excellent work, Thomas Sugrue documents school integration struggles in the North in *Sweet Land of Liberty: The Forgotten Struggle for Civil Rights in the North* (New York: Random House, 2008). In California, Texas, and Arizona, many Mexican students attended segregated schools, and few of these segregated districts were successfully desegregated under *Brown.* Scholarship on desegregation efforts in Latino communities in the Southwest has been growing since the 1990s. Martha Menchaca, *The*

Mexican Outsiders: A Community History of Marginalization and Discrimination in California (Austin: University of Texas Press, 1995); Guadalupe San Miguel Jr., *Brown, Not White: School Integration and the Chicano Movement in Houston* (College Station: Texas A&M University Press, 2005); Guadalupe San Miguel Jr., "The Impact of Brown on Mexican American Desegregation Litigation, 1950s to 1980s," *Journal of Latinos and Education* 4, no. 4 (2005): 221–36.

23. A popular slogan of the immigrant student movement and the title of a 2012 publication from UCLA's Dream Resource Center about two young DREAM activists, Tam Tran and Cinthya Felix, accessed on May 9, 2017, https://books.labor.ucla.edu/p/79/undocumentedunafraid.

24. Education historians Tyack and Cuban point out that public schools today are the product of almost two centuries of reform and that some reforms were so deep and so successful that they are no longer thought of as reforms, but simply what all schools are and do. They also observe that schools shaped reforms, just as reforms shaped schools (Tyack and Cuban, *Tinkering Toward Utopia*, 9–10).

25. Consistent with the literature on resegregation, I use the term to refer to the process by which a once-integrated institution becomes majority single race again.

26. Cuban and Tyack, *Tinkering Toward Utopia*, 140.

27. An article in the *Atlanta Journal-Constitution* in the spring of 1960 featuring a state map showing majority "open schools" versus "closing schools" counties declared what most Georgians knew to be true: "In general, the higher the ratio of the Negro population to white, the more likely [the county was to favor closing schools in order to maintain segregation]." Bruce Galphin, "Straws in Sibley Study?" *Atlanta Journal-Constitution,* April 3, 1960. Historian Kevin Kruse's account of the Sibley Commission reminds us that public hearings turned up more staunch segregationists than open schools advocates, but not by much. Kevin Kruse, *White Flight: Atlanta and the Making of Modern Conservatism* (Princeton, NJ: Princeton University Press, 2005), 144.

28. Kruse gives the example of West Fulton High School, which had two black students in 1962 and was majority black by 1964. He writes, "as [whites] fled from the schools in record numbers and at record speed, [schools] passed from segregation to resegregation with barely any time spent on true 'integration.'" Ibid., 168.

29. In 1960, only 5 percent of Marietta's white school-aged children were in private school; in 1970, after the city schools had all desegregated, the percentage had dropped. "Characteristics of the Population, 1960, 1970,"

US Census Bureau, accessed April 10, 2017, http://www.census.gov/prod
/www/decennial.html.

30. Gary Orfield and Chungmei Lee, "Historic Reversals, Accelerating
Resegregation and the Need for New Integration Strategies" (A Report of
the Civil Rights Project, University of California, Los Angeles, 2007).

31. By 2005, the percentage of black children in majority white schools had
declined to 27 percent. Orfield and Lee, "Historic Reversals," 23.

32. As Orfield and Lee write, "During the desegregation period, the long
exodus of blacks from the South ended and a reverse migration of blacks
from the North beginning in the 1970s was a sign of the changes in the
region. Blacks moving from New York or Chicago or Detroit to Charlotte
or Nashville or Orlando were moving from a far more segregated to a far
more integrated school system and to societies far more open than in the
past." Ibid., 14.

33. Matthew Lassiter, *The Silent Majority: Suburban Politics in the Sunbelt
South* (Princeton, NJ: Princeton University Press, 2006), 278.

34. Amy Stuart Wells and Robert L. Crain, "Perpetuation Theory and the
Long-Term Effects of School Desegregation," *Review of Educational
Research* 64, no. 4 (1994): 531–55. Roslyn Mickelson's meta-analysis of
more than 500 desegregation studies demonstrates the academic differ-
ence made by *Brown* for black students and the "social outcomes" of
Brown for black and white students in their adult lives. Rosyln Mickelson,
"Twenty-First Century Social Science Research on School Diversity and
Educational Outcomes," *Ohio State Law Journal* 69 (2008): 1173–228.

35. "Should Anything Be Done to Integrate Schools?" *Face the Nation, NPR*,
August 28, 2012, http://www.npr.org/2012/08/28/160185201/
should-anything-be-done-to-integrate-schools.

36. The Seattle suit was brought by a white parent who believed her daughter
had been discriminated against in a school assignment process in which
race was used as a factor to assign students in a manner that sustained
integration in the city's schools. Jonathan L. Entin, "*Parents Involved* and
the Meaning of *Brown:* An Old Debate Renewed," *Seattle University Law
Review* 31 (2008): 923–36.

37. Plurality opinion in *Meredith v. Jefferson County Board of Education*
(2007); this case was decided with *Parents Involved in Community Schools
v. Seattle School District No. 1,* 551 U.S. 701 (2007).

38. A section entitled "Promoting Socioeconomic Diversity and School
Choice" in the Obama administration's 2017 budget draft proposes $120
million in competitive grants available to districts "interested in exploring
ways to foster socioeconomic diversity," accessed on December 28, 2016,

www.whitehouse.gov/sites/default/files/omb/budget/fy2017/assets
/opportunity.pdf. Richard D. Kahlenberg and Halley Potter, "A Better
Affirmative Action: State Universities That Created Alternatives to Racial
Preference" (A Report of the Century Foundation, Washington, DC, 2012).

39. Orfield and Lee, "Historic Reversals."

40. Beth Hawkins, "Lawyer Hired by Eden Prairie Group Has Deep Pockets,
History of Anti-Desegregation Cases," *MinnPost*, January 31, 2011,
accessed April 10, 2017, https://www.minnpost.com/learning-curve/2011/01
/lawyer-hired-eden-prairie-group-has-deep-pockets-history-anti
-desegregation-c.

41. Most Southern districts never addressed the racial isolation of Latino students, and desegregation suits in Phoenix and Houston, which held
promise, were dropped by the Reagan administration. Orfield and Lee,
"Historic Reversals," 35.

42. Ibid., 32. According to the Pew Research Center, at the turn of the twenty-first century, the fastest growing Latino populations in the country were
those of Georgia, North Carolina, Tennessee, Arkansas, Mississippi, South
Carolina, Alabama, and Virginia. "The New Latino South: The Context
and Consequences of Rapid Population Growth," Pew Research Hispanic
Center report released July 26, 2005, http://www.pewhispanic.org
/2005/07/26/the-new-latino-south/. "Southern States Manifesto: Update
2012," Rural Women's Health Project, accessed April 10, 2017, http://
rwhp.org/extra/Southern-States-Manifesto-Immig2012.pdf, 18.

43. Raymond A. Mohl, "Globalization, Latinization and the Nuevo New
South," *Journal of American Ethnic History* 22, no. 4 (2003): 31–66.

44. Renee Stepler and Mark Hugo Lopez, "Ranking the Latino Population in
the States," Pew Research Center: Hispanic Trends, September 8, 2016,
http://www.pewhispanic.org/2016/09/08/4-ranking-the-latino-population-
in-the-states/. Latinos in Georgia's schools—especially in metro Atlanta—
are increasingly vulnerable to resegregation and racial isolation. Because
Latinos never experienced desegregation in the South at the scale that
black students did, the increase in Latino students attending majority-
minority schools does not seem large, growing from 70 to 78 percent
between 1968 and 2005. However, it indicates a distressing trend. In the
West, where Latino students saw some desegregation gains in the *Brown*
era, those gains have been reversed, and resegregation has exploded,
increasing 40 percent in as many years. In 2010, the South and the West
represented the two most segregated regions for Latino students. Orfield
and Lee, "Historic Reversals," 34–35, 42.

45. As scholar David Kirp opined after *Brown*'s 2012 anniversary, "it was hard
not to notice that desegregation is effectively dead," despite the difference

it made in the lives of students, especially poor students of color. "Making Schools Work," *New York Times,* May 19, 2012, accessed April 10, 2017, http://www.nytimes.com/2012/05/20/opinion/sunday/integration-worked -why-have-we-rejected-it.html?_r=0. Roslyn Arlin Mickelson, Martha Cecilia Bottia, and Richard Lambert, "Effects of School Racial Composition on K–12 Mathematics Outcomes: A Metaregression Analysis," *Review of Education Research* 83, no. 1 (March 2013): 121–58; Stephanie Southworth, "Examining the Effects of School Composition on North Carolina Student Achievement Over Time," *Education Policy Analysis Archives* 18 (2010), accessed April 10, 2017, doi:http://dx.doi .org/10.14507/epaa.v18n29.2010.

46. Tyack and Cuban, *Tinkering Toward Utopia,* 6.

47. Susan Eaton and Steven Rivkin, "Is Desegregation Dead? Parsing the Relationship Between Achievement and Demographics," *Education Next* 10, no. 4 (Fall 2010), accessed April 10, 2017, http://educationnext.org /is-desegregation-dead/.

48. This phrase is a popular one in education research and often accompanies privatization projects. For example, the National Math and Science Initiative, a "public-private partnership" funded by entities like Exxon Mobil and the Bill and Melinda Gates Foundation, refers to the low scores of American students in math and science as the "STEM (Science, Technology, Engineering, and Math) crisis." Without addressing the crisis, American schools and students will not be "globally competitive." National Math and Science Initiative, "Transform Education," accessed on May 9, 2017, https://www.nms.org/Education.aspx.

49. Jennifer Hochschild identifies the tension between believing that all chil- dren should have equal opportunities to succeed and wanting one's own child to have advantages beyond those of other children as the "paradox" of the American dream. "That circle cannot be squared," she writes. Jennifer L. Hochschild and Nathan Scovronick, *The American Dream and the Public Schools* (Oxford, United Kingdom: Oxford University Press, 2003), 2.

50. Jennifer Hochschild, "Is Desegregation Still a Viable Policy Option?" *PS: Political Science and Politics* 3, no. 30 (1997): 458–66, 464.

51. As desegregation scholar Susan Eaton commented, "Educators have long testified and research has long demonstrated that schools with large shares of economically disadvantaged children become overwhelmed with chal- lenges that interfere with education. Racially segregated high-poverty schools tend to be overrun with social problems, have a hard time finding and retaining good teachers, are associated with high dropout rates, and are less effective than diverse schools at intervening in problems

outside of school that undermine learning." Eaton and Rivkin, "Is Desegregation Dead?"

52. Claudia Sanchez, "School Closures Pit Race and Poverty against Budgets," *NPR*, March 23, 2013, accessed April 10, 2017, http://www.npr.org /2013/03/23/175104850/race-poverty-central-to-national-school-closure -debate. More than twenty school closures in Washington, DC, under the leadership of Michelle Rhee, twenty in Philadelphia under the state-run school reform commission, and more than fifty in Chicago sparked pro- tests and drew widespread news coverage, but as Sanchez notes, school closures are increasingly common in districts across the country and are consistent with the Obama administration's support for replacing "failing schools" with charter schools. Susan Saulny, "Detroit Plan Would Close 45 Schools," *New York Times*, March 17, 2010, accessed April 10, 2017, http://www.nytimes.com/2010/03/18/education/18detroit.html; Rhonda Cook and Alan Judd, "Beverly Hall, 34 Others Indicted in Atlanta Schools Cheating Scandal," *Atlanta Journal-Constitution*, March 29, 2012, accessed April 10, 2017, http://www.myajc.com/news/news/local/beverly -hall-34-others-indicted-in-atlanta-schools/nW7mX/.

53. Erika Frankenberg and Gary Orfield, eds., *The Resegregation of Suburban Schools: A Hidden Crisis in American Education* (Cambridge, MA: Harvard Education Press, 2012), 2.

54. Ibid., 219.

55. Orfield and Lee, "Historic Reversals," 42.

56. "Characteristics of the Population, 1980, 1990, 2000," US Census Bureau, accessed April 10, 2017, http://www.census.gov/prod/www/decennial.html.

57. Title I funds—federal funding for high-poverty schools—are accorded when 40 percent or more of the student body is classified as low-income. "Improving Basic Programs Operated by Local Educational Agencies (Title I, Part A)," US Department of Education, accessed April 10, 2017, http://www2.ed.gov/programs/titleiparta/index.html. "Downloadable Data," accessed April 17, 2017, https://gosa.georgia.gov/downloadable -data. During this research, all data since 2004 were available through school "report cards" accessible via the Georgia Department of Education website. In 2014, however, all data for school years after 2010-2011 were moved to a new platform, the Governor's Office of Student Achievement, https://gosa.georgia.gov/downloadable-data. For data concerning school years prior to 2010, a data request form must be submitted electronically to http://gosa.georgia.gov/webform/report-card-data-request.

58. See Note 57.

59. Of the 180 school districts in Georgia, 109 have been or are under court order to desegregate. Thirty-five districts that were under court order

have been declared unitary. Thirty of those achieved "unitary status" in the years since the 1991 decision in *Oklahoma v. Dowell,* which essentially stripped the phrase of its meaning by ruling that a desegregation injunction could be removed by a district court if "the school system was being operated in compliance with the Equal Protection Clause, and was . . . unlikely . . . to return to its former ways." *Board of Education of Oklahoma City v. Dowell* 498 S. Ct. 237 (1991). "Desegregation of Public School Districts in Georgia: 35 Public School Districts Have Unitary Status, 74 Districts Remain Under Court Jurisdiction," Georgia Commission Report, Georgia Advisory Committee to the US Commission on Civil Rights, December 2007, accessed April 10, 2017, http://www.usccr.gov/pubs/GADESG-FULL.pdf.

60. From the perspective of critical race theory, confronting resegregation with strategies to bring back affluent whites is consistent with historical desegregation plans that prioritized white families and, in many cases, brought advantages of advanced academic or extracurricular programs to white children. Gloria Ladson-Billings suggests, in a seminal article, that critical race theory as applied to desegregation studies demonstrates that "the dominant logic is that a model desegregation program is one that ensures whites are happy (and do not leave the school system altogether)." "Just What Is Critical Race Theory and What's It Doing in a Nice Field Like Education?" *International Journal of Qualitative Studies in Education* 11.1 (1998): 7–24.

61. "Characteristics of the Population, 2000," US Census Bureau, accessed April 10, 2017, http://www.census.gov/prod/www/decennial.html. I do not mean to suggest that private schools are any kind of idyll either. Drug use and drug dealing, for example, are not confined to public school campuses. The comparatively affluent students of private schools have traditionally been portrayed as eager customers of higher-end narcotics such as cocaine. Although the most readily available drug is marijuana, not cocaine, statistics have begun to bear out such a stereotype. The annual survey results released by the National Center on Addiction and Substance Abuse showed that in 2012, a majority of American private school students reported that there were drugs on their school campuses. "National Survey on American Attitudes on Substance Abuse XVII: Teens," National Center on Addiction and Substance Abuse, August 2012, accessed April 10, 2017, http://www.casacolumbia.org/addiction-research/reports/national-survey-american-attitudes-substance-abuse-teens-2012.

62. Coined by French philosophers Gilles Deleuze and Felix Guattari, the concept of "deterritorialization" has become important to the anthropology of globalization. Arjun Appadurai uses the concept to frame an

argument about the role of imagination in the way deterriorialized groups consume, produce, and reshape the culture of the "homeland." *Modernity at Large: Cultural Dimensions of Globalization* (Minneapolis: University of Minnesota Press, 1996), 37–39. Here, I mean to suggest that the private school very often cultivates institutional culture that is separate from its host community or city.

63. I borrow this phrase from Greg Dening, *The Death of William Gooch: A History's Anthropology* (Honolulu: University of Hawaii Press, 1995).

64. Only the students of Chapter 4, some of whom had not yet graduated when I interviewed them and some of whom are undocumented, are all identified by pseudonyms. Some graduates or community members I had assumed would want anonymity instead insisted they be named. As historian Michael Frisch suggests, "shared authority" is integral to oral history that honors the interviewee's narrative and perspective. Michael Frisch, *A Shared Authority: Essays on the Craft and Meaning of Oral and Public History* (Albany, NY: SUNY Press, 1990). In my oral history research, I was guided, as well, by Alessandro Portelli's description of interviews as "dialogic exchanges" that produce an oral source "co-created by the historian." Alessandro Portelli, "A Dialogical Relationship: An Approach to Oral History," accessed April 10, 2017, http://www.swaraj.org/shikshantar /expressions_portelli.pdf, 1.

65. All people, writes Mary Douglas, "use their institutional commitments for thinking with." *How Institutions Think* (Syracuse, NY: Syracuse University Press, 1986), 7.

66. John L. Jackson Jr, *Real Black: Adventures in Racial Sincerity* (Chicago: University of Chicago Press, 2005), 24. During my fieldwork, I often returned to John Jackson's *Real Black: Adventures in Racial Sincerity,* as well as Carol Stack's *Call to Home: African Americans Reclaim the Rural South,* which acknowledge that the production of knowledge about a community is a project fraught by the fact that the people have already crafted a story about who they are and what their memories, beliefs, and actions mean. Stack writes, "Our influence on each other was mutually felt; they learned from me what I wanted to find out, and I learned from them what they wanted me to know." Carol Stack, *Call to Home: African Americans Reclaim the Rural South* (New York: Basic, 1996), xviii. For Jackson, this dynamic is about "anthropological sincerity," which he describes as "the ways in which we might displace subject-object equations within the ethnographic project to make room for . . . the agency and interiority of one's interlocutors" (23–24). Anthropological sincerity frees fieldwork from the goal of authenticity and reminds us that interviews and conversations in the field are performances on both sides. In documenting desegregation

and exploring the meaning of integration in Marietta, community members held and shared divergent and competing "truths" about their high school and the meaning of community and equity in and outside its walls.

67. David Cecelski, *Along Freedom Road: Hyde County, North Carolina, and the Fate of Black Schools in the South* (Chapel Hill: University of North Carolina Press, 1994); Barbara Shircliffe, "'We Got the Best of That World': A Case for the Study of Nostalgia in the Oral History of School Segregation," *The Oral History Review* 28, no. 2 (Summer–Autumn 2001): 59–84; Vanessa Siddle Walker, *Their Highest Potential: An African American Community in the Segregated South* (Chapel Hill: University of North Carolina Press, 1995). Jack Dougherty's *More Than One Struggle: The Evolution of Black School Reform in Milwaukee* (Chapel Hill: University of North Carolina Press, 2004) also contributes to scholarship asserting that *Brown* was not the alpha and omega of black struggles for educational equality.

68. The work of journalist-scholar Jonathan Kozol and desegregation researcher Susan Eaton has unflinchingly portrayed the human toll of "apartheid schooling." The sobering power of Kozol's and Eaton's work is that the conditions Kozol documents in his fourth-grade class in Boston in the mid-1960s—where crumbling buildings matched the morale and hopes of students and teachers—are shockingly echoed in Eaton's account of another fourth-grade classroom circa 2000, where her precocious protagonists come to understand their slim odds of escaping Hartford's resegregated, struggling public schools. Jonathan Kozol, *Death at an Early Age: The Destruction of the Hearts and Minds of Negro Children in the Boston Public Schools* (New York: Houghton, 1967); Jonathan Kozol, *The Shame of the Nation: The Restoration of Apartheid Schooling in America* (New York: Crown, 2005); Susan Eaton, *The Children in Room E4: American Education on Trial* (Chapel Hill, NC: Algonquin, 2007). Much more recently, journalist Nikole Hannah-Jones documented the resegregation in the schools of Tuscaloosa, Alabama, in her compelling ProPublica article, "Segregation Now: The Resegregation of America's Schools," ProPublica, April 16, 2014, accessed April 10, 2017, https://www.propublica.org/article/segregation-now-the-resegregation-of-americas-schools/#intro. Other scholarly work includes: Robert L. Hayman Jr. and Leland Ware, eds., *Choosing Equality: Essays and Narratives on the Desegregation Experience* (University Park, PA: Penn State University Press, 2009); Gary Orfield and Chungmei Lee, *Why Segregation Matters: Poverty and Educational Inequality* (Cambridge, MA: Civil Rights Project, Harvard University, 2005); Amy S. Wells, Jennifer J. Holme, Anita J. Revilla, and Awo K. Atanda, "How Society Failed School Desegregation Policy:

Looking Past the Schools to Understand Them," *Review of Research in Education* 28 (2005): 47–99.

69. The exception is Tracy K'Meyer's oral history documenting desegregation's local trajectory in Louisville, Kentucky, over the long term. "Remembering the Past and Contesting the Future of School Desegregation in Louisville, Kentucky, 1975–2012," *Oral History Review* 39, no. 2 (2012): 230–57; *From Brown to Meredith: The Long Struggle for School Desegregation in Louisville, Kentucky, 1954–2007* (Chapel Hill: University of North Carolina Press, 2013).

70. Jacquelyn Dowd Hall's conception of the "long Civil Rights Movement," which examines the radical roots of the movement in the 1940s and its trajectory through the 1970s, has influenced a decade of civil rights research. It informs my theorization of a "long integration era" at Marietta High, stretching from initial desegregation in 1964–65 into the resegregation decade of the 2000s. "The Long Civil Rights Movement and the Political Uses of the Past," *Journal of American History* 91, no. 4 (2005): 1233–63.

1. Blue Devil Pride: Marietta Football in the Long Integration Era

1. James Aaron Gullatte, interview by the author, digital recording, Marietta, GA, February 9, 2012. Unless otherwise noted, all quotes from Gullatte date to this interview.

2. The 1966 "twin bids" by Lemon Street and Marietta High for their respective state championships (Lemon Street played in an all-black league), the closing of Lemon Street High the following year, and the black-student-orchestrated Homecoming protest of 1969 at MHS are the subject of Ruth Yow, "Shadowed Places and Stadium Lights: An Oral History of Integration and Black Student Protest in Marietta, Georgia" *Oral History Review* 42, no. 1 (Winter/Spring 2015): 70–95.

3. Horace Crowe, "Imps, Hornets Go for State Crowns," *Marietta Daily Journal,* December 2, 1966. The closure of black institutions during desegregation and the cost to those black communities are detailed in a rich body of scholarship. In *Along Freedom Road: Hyde County, North Carolina and the Fate of Black Schools in the South* (Chapel Hill: University of North Carolina Press, 1994), historian David Cecelski chronicles the struggles of black residents of Hyde County, North Carolina, to resist the closing of their schools in the late-sixties desegregation process. Barbara Shircliffe documents the efforts of a coalition of black activists to

reestablish a formerly all-black school closed during Tampa's desegregation process ("Desegregation and the Historically Black High School: The
Establishment of Howard W. Blake in Tampa, Florida" *The Urban Review*
34, no. 2 [June 2002]: 135–58). In a grim irony typical of Jim Crow politics, black communities that had for years insisted that the inferiority of
their institutions be addressed were then told, when trying to save them
from demolition, that those all-black institutions were too dilapidated,
small, or outdated to serve as integrated schools. It is interesting to note
that the Marietta branch of the Cobb NAACP was crusading for school
improvements in 1956, two years after the decision in *Brown v. Board of
Education*. Perhaps they knew that once desegregation made it to
Marietta, Lemon Street High—lacking adequate bathrooms, laboratory
facilities, a library, and gym space—would be deemed outmoded and
closed. An eight-room addition to Lemon Street High was completed in
1960—only to be abandoned to desegregation seven years later. Marietta
School Board Meeting Notes, September 11, 1958, Marietta City School
System Archives.

4. In Little Rock, football culture and its traditions were battlements against
progressive change: an all-white team and its white fans emblemized resistance to desegregation and black students' inclusion. In the fall of 1957,
when the black students of the Little Rock Nine integrated Central High,
the Central High Tigers, a longtime powerhouse in Arkansas, had an
undefeated season—some say their best ever. Ralph Brodie, star player on
the Tigers and the student body president that year, grieved the loss of
that season to history: where the team's triumphs should have been, the
trials of the black desegregators—the Little Rock Nine—dominated the
headlines. In his book *Central in Our Lives*, a revisionist history asserting
the innocence of most of Central High's white students, Brodie writes that
the Tigers' underrecognized stellar 1957 season "gave the student body a
positive boost and helped keep morale high inside the school" (quoted in
Jay Jennings, *Carry the Rock: Race, Football and the Soul of An American
City* [New York: Rodale, 2010], 137). The image of Elizabeth Eckford,
one of the Little Rock Nine, making her way gamely through heckling
white hordes is etched into American collective memory, but photographs
like those in *Life Magazine* of the 101st Airborne on their feet at Quigley
Stadium cheering wildly for the Tigers are obscure by comparison.
("Backing the School They Guard, Paratroops Cheer Central High
Touchdown Against Baton Rouge," photo caption from "What Faubus
Wrought: The Mob Action and the Pacification of Little Rock," *Life
Magazine*, October 7, 1957.) In 1959, Central High was closed, but at the
suggestion of Governor Orval Faubus, the Tigers still practiced and

competed, placing second in the state that year. Unlike at Marietta, at Central, the winning team's destiny was entirely unbound from that of the high school, where the discord and violence of desegregation endure as Central High's—and Little Rock's—civil rights legacy.

5. For a detailed discussion of Ben Wilkins's role in the desegregation era and his lasting influence in Marietta, see Yow, "Shadowed Places."

6. Black Mariettans use "Baptistown" and "the projects" to refer to the government housing complex, Lyman Homes, which was demolished in 2007, as well as the surrounding neighborhood of single-family homes. The razing of Lyman Homes dramatically altered the geography of Baptistown. Black interviewees of the desegregation generation often mentioned the fact that the Lyman Homes site was still an empty field in 2012, five years after the demolition. Bill Kinney and Joe Kirby, "MHA Officials Hoping Lyman Homes Successor Is 'A Real Knockout,'" *Marietta Daily Journal,* December 4, 2012.

7. "Sunday Gamblers Have a Fight: Knives and Rocks Used and Blood Flows Profusely," *Marietta Daily Journal,* February 26, 1903.

8. Warren Duffee, "Disease, Suffering Thrive in Slum Areas: Broken-down Houses, Poor Sanitation, Regarded as Menace to City's Health, Morals," *Cobb County Times,* March 28, 1940. (Marietta Housing Authority Archive, Department of Museums, Archives and Rare Books, Sturgis Library, Kennesaw State University, not yet processed or catalogued.)

9. Jim Dante, a black 1977 graduate and football player, recalled of his childhood move from government housing to a single-family home: "You could still walk in five or ten minutes to where we used to live, so it was just—like I said, we always lived close to other types of people anyway. . . . In our neighborhood it was all black. You go a block or two over and you get other people." Jim Dante (pseudonym), interview by the author, digital recording, Peachtree City, GA, July 9, 2012.

10. Horace Crowe, "Friday," *Marietta Daily Journal,* November 7, 1974.

11. Lemon Street Elementary and Lemon Street High are referred to in Marietta using the shorthand, "Lemon Street"; only Lemon Street High's main building was demolished in 1967. Up until 2013, the elementary building housed the Hattie G. Wilson Library, named after a local black educator and activist.

12. Jennifer Ritterhouse, *Growing Up Jim Crow: How Black and White Southern Children Learned Race* (Chapel Hill: University of North Carolina Press, 2006), 110. Jonathan S. Holloway's memoir-cum-cultural history *Jim Crow Wisdom: Memory and Identity in Black America since 1940* explores the cultural and historical power—at both the individual

and structural registers— of "racial memories" (Chapel Hill: University of North Carolina Press, 2013), 7.

13. Oscar Brinson, class of 1972, and Steve Head, class of 1971, similarly testified that they retained their pre-desegregation peer groups. As Head put it, "when [I] got to Marietta . . . my black friends were still my . . . friends . . . you kind of brought your friends with you [to Marietta High]."

14. Katherine Newman refers to key personalities in the community and its institutions as "front stage actors." Katherine S. Newman, Cybelle Fox, David J. Harding, Jal Mehta, and Wendy Roth, *Rampage: The Social Roots of School Shootings* (New York: Basic, 2004), 137.

15. Jim Overstreet, "Richards Heads College Lists, to Sign with Gators Saturday," *Marietta Daily Journal*, December 9, 1971. Division I schools must field a certain number of men's and women's sports teams in order to qualify for Division I; they also dole out the most scholarships and field the most competitive football teams.

16. Crowe, "Friday."

17. "Downloadable Data," accessed April 17, 2017, https://gosa.georgia.gov /downloadable-data. During this research, all data since 2004 were available through school "report cards" accessible via the Georgia Department of Education website. In 2014, however, all data for school years after 2010-2011 were moved to a new platform, the Governor's Office of Student Achievement, https://gosa.georgia.gov/downloadable-data. For data concerning school years prior to 2010, a data request form must be submitted electronically to http://gosa.georgia.gov/webform/report-card -data-request.. Schools are eligible for Title I federal funds when 40 percent or more of their students come from low-income families. "Improving Basic Programs Operated by Local Educational Agencies (Title I, Part A)," US Department of Education, accessed April 10, 2017, http://www2.ed.gov/programs/titleiparta/index.html.

18. Hansell "Hap" Smith, interview by the author, digital recording, Marietta, GA, May 25, 2012. Unless otherwise noted, all quotes from Smith date to this interview.

19. Sonny Birch (pseudonym), interview by the author, digital recording, Marietta, GA, May 2, 2012. Unless otherwise noted, all subsequent quotes from Birch date to this interview.

20. Amy Stuart Wells, Jennifer Jellison Holme, Anita Tijerina Revilla, and Awo Korantemaa Atanda, *Both Sides Now: The Story of School Desegregation's Graduates* (Berkeley: University of California Press, 2009).

21. Merrell Sperling, interview by the author, digital recording, Marietta, GA, May 23, 2012. All subsequent quotes from Sperling date to this interview.

22. According to City-Data.com, 50.8 percent of people in Cobb County (Marietta is the largest city in Cobb) identify as evangelical Christians. "Cobb County, Georgia, Religion Statistics Profile," accessed April 10, 2017, http://www.city-data.com/county/religion/Cobb-County-GA.html.

23. Sperling described to me his "calling" to coach through an anecdote about watching a high school friend who worked as a local coach guide some players through a drill. "Somebody spoke to me," he said, "if you want to bring religion into it," and he realized that he was meant to leave his retail job and go back to school for a master's degree in education.

24. White 1990s graduate Chris Poston said that to join the ranks of "OMs," you must have three generations of Mariettans on one side of the family, but most Mariettans use "OM" as a shorthand for wealth and local political power. Black 1989 graduate and current faculty member Teisha Fooster also said, "People consider me to be Old Marietta," in the course of our conversation about the social capital of being from Marietta. Fooster is a longtime Mariettan; her mother is a Lemon Street High graduate, and her family is among the known and respected black families, but she is ambivalent about being "OM." Teisha Fooster, interview by the author, digital recording, Marietta, GA, April 19, 2012.

25. Such an act of self-definition is similar to what Elijah Anderson documented among the denizens of Jelly's in *A Place on the Corner*, all of whom, from the itinerant to the businessmen, claimed they were "respectable." Elijah Anderson, *A Place on the Corner* (Chicago: University of Chicago Press, 1976).

26. Jim Dante (pseudonym), interview by the author, digital recording, Peachtree City, GA, July 9, 2012. Unless otherwise noted, all subsequent quotes from Dante date to this interview.

27. Rod Garman (pseudonym), interview by the author, digital recording, Marietta, GA, May 9, 2012. All subsequent quotes from Garman date to this interview.

28. White students are far less likely to have a race-focused analysis of social life at MHS; among graduates of color between 1975 and 2012, the majority assert that they consciously associated with those "different from them," suggesting that having a diverse social circle "prepares you" for work and school in diverse environments and "develops character" and "values." Of those graduates of color, only two described specific racist incidents in high school and said those incidents affected the way they interacted with white people in general. While insisting race is not a pertinent social category, the majority of graduates also acknowledged that outside of class, at lunch, and before and after school, many students "naturally" affiliate with "those like them," that is, with those of their racial and

ethnic group. In my sample, it is safe to generalize that white and black graduates placed value on diverse peer groups and credited themselves with having such, often using the idea of "colorblindness" or basing friendship on "character."

29. Patricia Williams, *The Alchemy of Race and Rights: Diary of a Law Professor* (Cambridge, MA: Harvard University Press, 1991), 119.

30. Audre Lorde, "Age, Race, Class, and Sex: Women Redefining Difference" in *Sister Outsider: Essays and Speeches* (Berkeley, CA: Crossing Press, 1984), 115.

31. Sammie Dean Williams, interview by the author, digital recording, Marietta, GA, December 19, 2011. All further quotes from Williams date to this interview.

32. Robert Crain, Rita Mahard, and Ruth Narot, *Making Desegregation Work: How Schools Create Social Climates* (Cambridge, MA: Ballinger, 1982), 72. The authors compare black male and female academic improvement in integrated settings to come to the conclusion that black male students experience more social and academic stress, and therefore earn lower test scores, than do black female students. Although test scores seem too reductive a basis for conclusion, the difference between male and female test scores in the research is substantial. The data are specific to male students in recently desegregated schools, not students who have been in desegregated settings since elementary school.

33. Lena Bennett Evans-Smith, interview by the author, digital recording, Atlanta, GA, August 18, 2012. Unless otherwise noted, all quotes from Evans-Smith date to this interview.

34. Terri Arnold, interview by the author, digital recording, Kennesaw, GA, March 11, 2009. In the 1969 yearbook, her graduation year, Terri Arnold (nee Ferguson)'s picture is shown with the traditional caption of activities, which include "Basketball, 1,2, Track, 1,2, Cheerleading, 2." These were not, in fact, her activities at Marietta High; these were her activities at Lemon Street High. Some of her fellow black seniors, like Oscar's brother Harold Brinson, did the same: a small but important assertion of Lemon Street's place in their identities and lives.

35. Cynthia Lewis and Susan Harbage Page, "Secret Sharing: Debutantes Coming Out in the American South," *Southern Cultures* 18, no. 4 (2012): 6–25.

36. Lindsay Field, "For Blue Devils—Tradition Rules," *Marietta Daily Journal,* October 15, 2012.

37. Jeannelly Castro, interview by the author, digital recorder, Marietta, GA, May 10, 2012. Unless otherwise noted, all quotes from Castro date to this interview.

38. Shikera Cook, interview by the author, digital recording, Marietta, GA, May 16, 2012. Unless otherwise noted, all quotes from Cook date to this interview.

39. Historian and University of North Carolina (UNC) alumna Glenda Gilmore pointed out that Marietta's fight song was cribbed from that of the UNC at Chapel Hill (perhaps penned as early as 1897) with the words "Blue Devil" substituted for "Tar Heel," a galling appropriation given that UNC's archrivals are the Duke Blue Devils.

40. In this comment, Tumlin was assenting that the demolition of the projects had hurt Marietta's football fortunes. "But is that real or apocryphal?" I asked. "Maybe both," he replied. Steve "Thunder" Tumlin, interview by the author, digital recording, Marietta, GA, August 29, 2012.

41. Black informants never referred to government housing projects by their names; instead, they referred to the part of town where they were raised. In Baptistown, the public housing development was called Lyman Homes (demolished in 2007); in Louisville, the given name of the project was Johnny Walker Homes (demolished in 2004); and on Lemon Street, it was Fort Hill Homes. Baptistown and Lemon Street were separated by just a third of a mile; Louisville was a little more than a mile from Lemon Street—all easily navigable on foot or by bike.

42. Janel Davis, "Activists Object to Public Housing Closing in Marietta," *Atlanta Journal-Constitution,* August 8, 2012, http://www.ajc.com/news /cobb/activists-object-to-public-1494247.html. This article erroneously names James Gober as James "Grober." Gober did an extensive interview with historian Thomas Scott during which he spoke about his childhood in Baptistown and his years at Lemon Street. James Gober, interview by Jessica Drysdale, Jay Lutz, and Thomas Scott, Marietta, GA, July 30, 2010, accessible via Kennesaw State University Digital Archives, http://archon .kennesaw.edu/?p=digitallibrary/digitalcontent&id=31.

43. James Richards grew up in the projects, but black Mariettans' discomfort with the policies of the Housing Authority seem to cross class lines; Condace Pressley, a black 1982 graduate who grew up in a middle-class neighborhood near Lemon Street, referred to Fort Hill as "the [projects] they're trying to save." The projects figure prominently in her childhood geography, although she didn't live in them. Condace Pressley, interview by the author, digital recording, Atlanta, GA, April 9, 2012.

44. "HCV Use Distribution Map," obtained from MHA Director Ray Buday, by e-mail, March 6, 2012. The map illustrates where former public housing residents moved with the "HCVs," or housing choice vouchers, which are provided through a program of Section 8 of the Federal

Housing Act of 1937. Forty-six percent of residents were relocated within the city limits.

45. Fort Hill Homes was built for "negroes" just after the construction of its counterpart Clay Homes, the first "white" project and one of the first two government housing projects in the United States. Jon Gillooly, "Last to Go: Bulldozers Bringing Down Fort Hill Homes," *Marietta Daily Journal*, March 21, 2013, http://mdjonline.com/view/full_story/22030949/article -Last-to-go--Bulldozers-bringing-down-Fort-Hill-Homes. When faced with the claim that longtime residents would feel the pain of displacement, the president of MHA's board, a white 1970s graduate and die-hard Blue Devil, was uninterested in sentimental appeals. Public housing, she asserted, represents a failure by both its residents and the city. She explained: "Public housing . . . was never meant to be a generationally supported housing. The idea of somebody being born in public housing and then their grandchildren being born in public housing is not the way it should be set up." Fran Sutton, interview by the author, digital recording, Marietta, GA, April 12, 2012. Actually, at its New Deal inception, low-income, federally funded public housing was conceived as just the opposite—a stable community where working families could afford safe housing with modern amenities and guaranteed maintenance, no longer subject to the caprices of negligent, exploitive landlords. According to the 1953 Annual Report of the Marietta Housing Authority, in Fort Hill, in the fifties, the community of black residents instituted cooking and sewing classes and founded a nursery for working mothers. Far from a temporary last resort, public housing was framed by its proponents of the early forties as an ethical imperative that would positively shape the destinies of poor families, white and black: "It will make for healthier people and will enable them to give their children better advantages," opined Otis Brumby, in the November 3, 1939 *Cobb County Times.* Marietta Housing Authority Archive, Department of Museums, Archives and Rare Books, Sturgis Library, Kennesaw State University, not yet processed or catalogued.

46. In Atlanta, for example, thousands of low-income, mostly black residents were displaced to make way for interstates, stadiums, and the development of Olympic Park facilities. Charles H. Heying, "World Class: Using the Olympics to Shape and Brand the American Metropolis," in Melanie K. Smith, ed., *Tourism, Culture, and Regeneration* (Cambridge, MA: CAB International, 2007); Larry Keating, *Atlanta: Race, Class and Urban Expansion* (Philadelphia: Temple University Press, 2001); Jon Teaford, *The Rough Road to Renaissance: Urban Revitalization in America,*

1940–1985 (Baltimore: Johns Hopkins University Press, 1990). Race has been inextricable from urban renewal and from the discursive construction of "the projects." From the postwar period up through the aughts, "black" and "projects" went hand in hand—despite the fact in 1950s Marietta, of the five segregated housing projects the MHA was administering, three were white. "The Fourteenth Annual Report of the Marietta Housing Authority, 1953," Marietta Housing Authority Archive. In Marietta, as elsewhere, public housing was conceived to stimulate the economy, create jobs, and serve as "housing for the working and 'deserving' poor," as scholar Myron Orfield puts it. *Metropolitics: A Regional Agenda for Community and Stability* (Baltimore: Brookings Institution Press, 1997), 75. Yet in cities like Marietta where postwar projects endured into the twenty-first century, government housing is viewed almost universally as a blight, as evidence that not everyone is upwardly mobile and not everyone will graduate, get a job, and buy a home.

47. A record of eighty-one senior athletes' grade point averages (GPAs) in 2001–2002 indicates that the dozen students with the lowest GPAs were, with the exception of one, black males; there were only six black male athletes with GPAs above 3.0. Records obtained through former MHS faculty member Ken Sprague, files loaned to the author, February 18–23, 2013. By the 2010s, the team had had a difficult couple of decades, and black students at Marietta High had too. School leaders strived to address what the raft of assessments required by No Child Left Behind consistently revealed: the achievement and graduation gaps separating white students and students of color. Marietta High's black students have scored below white students in nearly every assessment during the decade between 2001 and 2011, the period for which there is accessible demographically disaggregated data for End of Course Tests, Georgia High School Graduation Tests, the SAT, and the ACT. See Note 17.

48. Here, I draw again on Katherine Newman's formulation of high school as the community's "public stage" where status, identity, and power are negotiated. Newman et al., *Rampage.*

49. In a striking anomaly, two senior Blue Devil players in the class of 2013 were recruited by Division I schools (the elite teams of the National Collegiate Athletic Association that are allowed to dole out full scholarships to eighty-five recruited players). It was deemed a banner year, and MHS quarterback Anthony Jennings, who was recruited by Louisiana State University, was likened to 1990s MHS quarterback Eric Zeier, who went on to Bulldog fame at the University of Georgia and a career in the NFL. Carlton D. White, "Marietta QB Jennings Commits to LSU," *Marietta Daily Journal,* June 7, 2012, http://mdjonline.com/view

/full_story_sports/18906873/article-Marietta-QB-Jennings-commits-to
-LSU?instance=lead_story_left_column.

50. Anthony White, "Q&A with Newest Marietta Council Member Ruben
Sands," *Marietta Daily Journal*, July 23, 2016, http://www.mdjonline.com
/news/q-a-with-newest-marietta-council-member-ruben-sands/article
_7f31b734-5148-11e6-8103-2f46d6681d7d.html.

51. Since the election of Hugh Grogan Jr. in 1978, the first black member of
City Council, and until the election of Michelle Kelly Cooper in 2013,
joining historically black Ward 5 councilmember Anthony Coleman, there
had never been more than one black council member at any given time.
Interview with Hugh Lewis Grogan Jr., October 23, 1984, Cobb County
Oral History Series, https://soar.kennesaw.edu/handle/11360/1981; phone
conversation with longest-serving councilmember, Philip Goldstein,
February 20, 2017. Mr. Goldstein was first elected in 1980 and has served
continuously since. The names of all city council members, dating back to
the establishing of the city council in 1877, are available online at https://
www.mariettaga.gov/DocumentCenter/View/29, accessed May 9, 2017.

52. Ruben Sands, interview by the author, digital recording, Marietta, GA,
April 23, 2012. Unless otherwise noted, all quotes from Sands date to this
interview.

53. Theorist Mikhail Bahktin describes the work of Carnival this way: "[It]
celebrated temporary liberation from the prevailing truths and from the
established order. . . . A special form of free and familiar contact reigned
among people who were usually divided. . . . People were [able to access]
new, purely human relations . . . [and] a type of communication impossible
in everyday life." Bahktin suggests that liberation from the hierarchy
meant not that it was inverted, but that all were temporarily "equal" and
released into a newly free way of relating. *Rabelais and His World*, trans.
Helene Iswolsky (Bloomington: Indiana University Press, 1984), 10.

2. Fifty Years of "Freedom": School Choice and Structural Inequality in Marietta City Schools

1. Daphne Delk, interview by the author, digital recording, Atlanta, GA,
February 12, 2012. All further quotations from Delk are drawn from this
interview, unless otherwise noted.

2. This detail is from historian Thomas Scott's account of Delk's desegrega-
tion experiences, *Cobb County Georgia and the Origins of the Suburban
South: A Twentieth Century History* (Marietta, GA: Cobb Landmarks and
Historical Society, 2003), 357.

3. Loyd C. Cox, Superintendent, "Text for Annual Letter to Parents, for Use During 30-Day Spring Choice Period," April 1, 1966. Part of a collection of copied documents housed at Marietta High, obtained through faculty member Kristina Nesbitt, documents borrowed and copied on September 4, 2012. (Ms. Nesbitt uses the documents in her social studies classes.) Original archived school board documents are housed at the Marietta City Schools Central Office.

4. Several excellent accounts of desegregation detail the politics and local repercussions of freedom of choice plans: R. Scott Baker, *Paradoxes of Desegregation: African American Struggles for Educational Equity in Charleston, South Carolina, 1926–1972* (Columbia: University of South Carolina Press, 2006); Joseph Crespino, *In Search of Another Country: Mississippi and the Conservative Counterrevolution* (Princeton, NJ: Princeton University Press, 2007); Howell S. Baum, *Brown in Baltimore: School Desegregation and the Limits of Liberalism* (Ithaca, NY: Cornell University Press, 2010); Kevin M. Kruse, *White Flight: Atlanta and the Making of Modern Conservatism* (Princeton, NJ: Princeton University Press, 2005); Davison M. Douglas, *Reading, Writing, and Race: The Desegregation of the Charlotte Schools* (Chapel Hill: University of North Carolina Press, 1995); Matthew D. Lassiter, *The Silent Majority: Suburban Politics in the Sunbelt South* (Princeton, NJ: Princeton University Press, 2006).

5. In his introduction to the now classic work by Numan V. Bartley, *The Rise of Massive Resistance,* historian Paul Gaston credits the phrase "massive resistance" to its architect, Virginia senator Harry F. Byrd Sr., *The Rise of Massive Resistance: Race and Politics in the South during the 1950s* (Baton Rouge: Louisiana State University Press, 1969), x.

6. Kruse, *White Flight,* 132.

7. Ibid.

8. Elizabeth Jacoway, *Turn Away Thy Son: Little Rock, the Crisis That Shocked the Nation* (New York: Simon and Schuster, 2007).

9. Massive resistance was inaugurated in 1956 with the signing of the "Southern Manifesto" by a majority of Southern congressmen and the adoption by five Southern states of the doctrine of interposition, whereby the state "interposes" between its citizens and the federal government to protect those citizens from federal tyranny. That same year, Virginia passed a package of massive resistance laws that mandated that the public schools in any desegregating district be closed. Schools in two communities—Charlottesville and Norfolk—were closed in 1958 but reopened with the disavowing of massive resistance by Governor Lindsay Almond in 1959. Prince Edward County schools, closed in 1959, did not reopen until

1964. Matthew D. Lassiter and Andrew B. Lewis, eds., *The Moderates' Dilemma: Massive Resistance to School Desegregation in Virginia* (Charlottesville: University of Virginia Press, 1998).

10. An example is the correspondence between Leon Dure, a major player in Virginia's desegregation politics, and John Sibley, of the Sibley Commission, which conducted public hearings on desegregation across Georgia in 1960. In a letter to Sibley, Dure condemned school closures in Virginia, calling them a "misadventure," but insisted that tuition vouchers represented a viable option for concentrating control in local districts. Leon Dure, letter to John Sibley, December 9, 1961; "Leon Dure Finds the Whole South Turning to Freedom of Choice as Schools Solution," *Daily Progress,* March 29, 1961, John Sibley Papers, Manuscript, Archives, and Rare Book Library, Emory University.

11. Timothy J. Minchin and John A. Salmond, *After the Dream: Black and White Southerners Since 1965* (Lexington: University Press of Kentucky, 2011).

12. *Green v. County School Board of New Kent County* 391 US 430 (1968).

13. Ibid.

14. In 1965–66, a handful of black students joined Delk at MHS, but no formal system-wide desegregation was under way. After five attempts, the desegregation plans of the Marietta School Board were approved by HEW (the Department of Health, Education, and Welfare, which was established during the Eisenhower Administration and eventually replaced by the Department of Health and Human Service and the Department of Education). In the 1966–67 school year, a "free choice plan" was instituted. Under the plan, every black and white student in the city had to submit a form indicating what school he or she wished to attend. In 1966, the city still had dual systems, and the Board, unsurprisingly, argued that Lemon Street was underenrolled and too costly to maintain. Consequently, in 1967, Lemon Street Elementary and High were closed and those students funneled into MHS. Scott, *Cobb County,* 361–64.

15. Cobb's black population of 7,997 in 1960 constituted 7 percent of the county's total citizenry. Almost half of Cobb's black residents resided in Marietta in 1960; the city was about 15 percent black. "Characteristics of the Population, 1960," US Census Bureau, accessed April 10, 2017, http://www.census.gov/prod/www/decennial.html.

16. Diane Ravitch, *The Death and Life of the Great American School System: How Testing and Choice Are Undermining Education* (New York: Basic Books, 2010); Andrew J. Coulson, *Market Education: The Unknown History Vol. 21* (Piscataway, NJ: Transaction Books, 1999); Peter W. Cookson, *School Choice: The Struggle for the Soul of American Education* (New Haven, CT: Yale University Press, 1995).

17. Before its 2011 restructuring by the Obama administration, the No Child Left Behind (NCLB) Act stipulated that children at schools deemed "failing" could transfer to another school in their district. After restructuring, Georgia held onto choice, but didn't fund it: Georgia's new policy—as defined by an NCLB "waiver" granted to the state—eliminates the choice provision required by NCLB, which was that any student in a Title I school that failed to make Adequate Yearly Progress for two consecutive years could request transfer to another district school, with transportation provided by the district. (As of February 2013, Georgia and thirty-four other states had been granted NCLB waivers. Kathryn Baron, "Districts to Seek NCLB Waiver Whether or Not They're Invited," EdSource, February 10, 2013, https://edsource.org/2013/districts-to-seek -nclb-waiver-whether-or-not-theyre-invited/26943.) However, Georgia continues to offer intradistrict transfer (a program established in 2009) to students who wish to enroll in another school in their district that can accommodate them. Transportation, essential for low-income families hoping to use school choice, is *not* provided. "Title I, Part A Public School Choice," Georgia Department of Education, accessed April 10, 2017, http://www.doe.k12.ga.us/School-Improvement/Federal-Programs/Pages /Public-School-Choice.aspx.

18. The Supreme Court has, claim Alexander and Alexander, eroded the separation between church and state and created greater legal latitude for private and parochial school vouchers in decisions such as *Zobrest v. Catalina Foothills School District* 509 US 1 (1993) and the Cleveland Voucher Case of 2002 (see next note). Klint Alexander and Kern Alexander, "Vouchers and the Privatization of American Education: Justifying Racial Resegregation from *Brown* to *Zelman,*" *University of Illinois Law Review* 5 (2004): 1147.

19. Alexander and Alexander called the Supreme Court's validation of Cleveland's voucher program "re-segregation's Trojan horse." Ibid., 1135. Cleveland's program provides vouchers on a sliding income scale and explicitly includes religious schools—thus the contentious 2002 case. Thomas Ott, "Cleveland Students Hold Their Own with Voucher Students on State Tests," Cleveland.com, February 22, 2011, http://blog.cleveland .com/metro/2011/02/cleveland_students_hold_own_wi.html.

20. All of this language is drawn from a document entitled "Managing the MCS Brand," which addresses the importance of protecting the city schools' "brand" in the form of its "school seal, logos, and slogans." Accessed on May 8, 2017, https://www.marietta-city.org/cms/lib /GA01903590/Centricity/Shared/files/newsroom/Managing%20the %20MCS%20Brand_Identity%20Guidelines.pdf. The document was

likely produced by the school system's former director of communications, Thomas Algarin, a marketing and branding expert, who worked with IBM, General Electric, Bellsouth, and Marshalls.

21. Danny K. Weil, ed., *School Vouchers and Privatization: A Reference Handbook* (Santa Barbara, CA: ABC-CLIO, 2002).

22. Marietta's only successfully established charter school was short-lived. In 2006, Imagine Schools, a Virginia-based company that runs "publically funded, privately operated" charter schools, opened Marietta Charter School for kindergarten through fifth grade. After four years, citing financial mismanagement and low enrollment, the Marietta School Board voted not to renew the charter, and the state commission on charter schools concurred. Jon Gillooly, "Marietta Charter School Renewal Request Rejected," *Marietta Daily Journal,* December 17, 2010, http://www .mdjonline.com/view/full_story/10700574/article-Marietta-Charter -School-renewal-request-rejected. In 2016, a group of Cobb County citizens and business leaders sought to found a dual-language charter school on Marietta's Franklin Road, but were not able to raise sufficient funds. Mary Kate McGowan, "Dual Language Academy's Charter Terminated By Marietta School Board," *Marietta Daily Journal,* July 12, 2016, http:// www.mdjonline.com/news/dual-language-academy-s-charter-terminated -by-marietta-school-board/article_d8b9ecbe-48a5-11e6-b702- 1b3ed51f0bc3.html.

23. The first voucher program in the country was launched in 1990 in Milwaukee and directed at low-income students (Milwaukee's is now the largest in the country with 20,000 participants). As of late 2016, thirteen states and Washington, DC, have some kind of voucher program. Of those, Louisiana, Ohio, Indiana, Arizona, and the District of Columbia have successfully implemented voucher programs for students in failing schools and, in the case of North Carolina, Louisiana, Indiana, the District of Columbia, and Ohio, with provisions for low-income students explicitly. Colorado also piloted a voucher program that was court invalidated. Of the thirteen, the remaining states—such as Georgia, Mississippi, and Utah—have voucher programs that allocate funds for students with disabilities to attend private schools. "School Voucher Laws: State-by-State Comparison," National Conference of State Legislatures, accessed April 10, 2017, http://www.ncsl.org/research/education/voucher-law-comparison. aspx. Additionally, Georgians can choose to direct their state tax dollars to private schools through "student scholarship organizations" (SSOs), just a step short of a tax-payer-funded voucher program. Vouchers are a complicated articulation of choice. Although vouchers for low-income students ostensibly expand their choices, they usually offer a set amount of money

to be put toward private education—in many cases, parochial schools. Vouchers tend to lure low-income students with involved parents out of public schools, prompting opponents of the programs to insist that already struggling schools will be further damaged by the departure of these students and the public funds that follow them out. Although vouchers as a tool of school choice are increasingly popular politically, the verdict is still out. Dramatic impacts on either student achievement or levels of racial desegregation that were predicted by critics and proponents have yet to materialize. Research on voucher programs has not offered strong evidence of a positive academic impact for students or a dramatic negative impact for school systems; the writers at *Journalist's Resource* out of Harvard's Kennedy School offered a synthesis of university, policy institute, and advocacy group studies of vouchers and concluded that voucher programs' "benefits are deeply contested." David Trilling, "School Vouchers and Student Achievement: Reviewing the Research," *Journalist's Resource*, September 14, 2016, https://journalistsresource.org /studies/society/education/school-vouchers-choice-student-achievement. However, the battle over vouchers is pitched, and the stakes, as far as adoption of programs across the country, are high indeed. As Alexander and Alexander assert, "the result of this privatization has been the erosion of the public school ideal, the proliferation of private segregated academies, and the balkanization and racial re-segregation of American education with the government's help." Alexander and Alexander, "Vouchers and the Privatization of American Education," 1135.

24. Marietta City Schools instituted open enrollment provisionally in 2007 at three schools including West Side, and then expanded it system-wide the following year. With these changes came the "branding" of the elementaries as "choice academies," each with its own focus, such as performing arts or math and science. Jon Gillooly, "Marietta Schools Initiate Limited In-district Choice," *Marietta Daily Journal*, February 17, 2007. Marietta was not first in "rebranding" and targeting upper-middle-class parents as "customers." A well-known example is Philadelphia's Central City Schools Initiative (CCSI), created in the early 2000s to bring high-earning professionals back into the downtown schools. Scholar Maia Cucchiara describes the CCSI as exemplifying "a new 'academic imaginary,' a subset of the city's schools that was distinct from the district as a whole and possessed its own identity, deliberately constructed and managed to appeal to professional parents. Creating this new imaginary involved changing the image of Center City schools as a group and crafting compelling, attractive identities for individual schools." "Re-branding Urban Schools: Urban

Revitalization, Social Status, and Marketing Public Schools to the Upper Middle Class," *Journal of Education Policy* 23, no. 2 (2008): 169.

25. Except in years when it had fewer spots than A.L. Burruss, West Side received the most students by a margin of about twenty students, with Burruss sometimes a close and sometimes a distant second. Over the years between 2007 and 2013, West Side has received 153 students, Burruss has received 132, and the other five schools are more than 100 students behind Burruss. Choice statistics for 2007 to 2013 obtained through Marietta Schools Central Office, compiled by Executive Assistant to the Superintendent, Cheryl Hood, and received by e-mail on March 19, 2013.

26. All testing, enrollment, and FORPL (free or reduced-price lunch) data from 2010–2011. I chose the fifth-grade CRCT (Criterion-Referenced Competency Test) in reading as a representative benchmark assessment. The students also take the CRCT in third grade, and in both third and fifth grades, they are tested in reading and several other subjects on material specific to Georgia's state standards. The three categories of achievement on these tests are "Exceeds Expectations," (a score above 850) "Meets Expectations" (a score between 800 and 849), and "Does Not Meet Expectations" (a score below 800). "Downloadable Data," accessed April 17, 2017, https://gosa.georgia.gov/downloadable-data. During this research, all data since 2004 were available through school "report cards" accessible via the Georgia Department of Education website. In 2014, however, all data for school years after 2010-2011 were moved to a new platform, the Governor's Office of Student Achievement, https://gosa.georgia.gov/downloadable-data. For data concerning school years prior to 2010, a data request form must be submitted electronically to http://gosa.georgia.gov/webform/report-card-data-request.

27. Superintendent Emily Lembeck told me that the school board seriously considered providing busing as part of the choice program, but ultimately didn't. She cited the cost ("Transportation is one of our most escalating costs, and the state only pays maybe 4 percent of it") and the logistics ("We're too spread out") as the rationale against free busing for choice students. Emily Lembeck, interview by the author, digital recording, Marietta, GA, March 21, 2013. Unless otherwise noted, all quotes from Lembeck date to this interview.

28. Amy Stuart Wells and Robert L. Crain, "Do Parents Choose School Quality or School Status? A Sociological Theory of Free Market Education," in Peter Cookson, ed., *The Choice Controversy* (Newbury Park, CA: Corwin Press, 1992), 65–82.

29. Choice statistics for 2007 to 2013 obtained through Marietta Schools Central Office, compiled by Executive Assistant to the Superintendent, Cheryl Hood, and received by e-mail on March 19, 2013.

30. Ibid.

31. Scholar Thomas Schelling introduced the term "tipping" in reference to residential segregation dynamics in "Models of Segregation," *The American Economic Review* 59, no. 2 (May 1969): 488–93. Charles Clotfelter applied it to desegregating public schools experiencing white flight in "School Desegregation, 'Tipping,' and Private School Enrollment," *Journal of Human Resources* 11, no. 1 (Winter 1976): 28–50.

32. Jill Mutimer, interview by the author, digital recording, Marietta, GA, March 15, 2012. Unless otherwise noted, all quotes from Mutimer date to this interview.

33. Mary Ansley Southerland, interview by the author, digital recording, Marietta, GA, March 3, 2012. Unless otherwise noted, all quotes from Southerland date to this interview.

34. See Note 26.

35. Johnny Sinclair, interview by the author, digital recording, Marietta, GA, March 21, 2012. Unless otherwise noted, all quotes from Sinclair date to this interview.

36. Steve "Thunder" Tumlin, interview by the author, digital recording, Marietta, GA, August 29, 2012. Unless otherwise noted, all quotes from Tumlin date to this interview.

37. During the 1980s, enrollment at MHS was between 20 and 25 percent black and about 70 percent white, approximately mirroring the city's demographics at that time. In the early eighties, there were small numbers of Asian and Latino students, but substantial numbers of international students didn't come to Marietta until the late nineties.

38. Lisa McGirr documents the remaking of conservatism by suburban activists in 1960s California who used local elected bodies—like school boards—as platforms to articulate a new national vision for the Republican Party. Although Mutimer is what McGirr would call a "kitchen-table activist," in the sense that she is a linchpin of local political networks, she does not connect her local politics to her national politics, at least not through an overarching political agenda. *Suburban Warriors: The Origins of the New American Right* (Princeton, NJ: Princeton University Press, 2001), 6.

39. Lassiter, *The Silent Majority.*

40. Lassiter and Lewis, *The Moderates' Dilemma,* 19.

41. These are the words of another white 1980s graduate in referring to what he sees as the disingenuous assertions by parents of color that they don't

have the resources to donate to the Touchdown Club and other school causes.

42. Mickey King (pseudonym), interview by the author, digital recording, Marietta, GA, September 5, 2012. Unless otherwise noted, all quotes from King date to this interview.

43. Ibid.

44. By financial resources, I refer to what high-income parents bring to booster clubs and school fund drives, not to actual inequalities in school funding, which appears to be consistent across system schools. General Fund Budget, Fiscal Year, 2012, School Board Meeting, May 15, 2012, records available by PDF to the public.

45. Three generations of born and bred Mariettans on at least one side of one's family—"or something like that," Poston said with a laugh. Chris Poston, interview by the author, digital recording, Marietta, GA, October 2, 2012.

46. Clotfelter, "School Desegregation, 'Tipping,' and Private School Enrollment."

47. A list offered by the *Marietta Daily Journal* counts twenty-four private schools in Cobb County (only a few of which are located in the city of Marietta). Of those twenty-four private schools, nineteen are Christian. "Cobb and Marietta Private Schools," *Marietta Daily Journal,* retrieved on March 10, 2013, http://www.mdjonline.com/sites/624/assets/private _schools.pdf.

48. This is, as we know, not strictly true. Certainly it was less diverse when Poston's mother attended—it was still segregated. But when Poston was an elementary school student in the early eighties, West Side was likely at least 25 percent black and low income, due to nearness of Lyman Homes in the mostly black community of Baptistown. Poston's daughter started West Side after local white families were already "tipping in," as Jennifer Stillman calls the process of whites returning to a majority-minority school. *Gentrification and Schools: The Process of Integration When Whites Reverse Flight* (New York: Palgrave Macmillan, 2012).

49. Prior to the redesign of the Marietta City Schools webpages, all the elementary schools featured a similar video on their websites; http://westside .marietta-city.org/, accessed on March 17, 2012.

50. Jeffrey Kane, "Choice: The Fundamentals Revisited," in Peter Cookson, ed., *The Choice Controversy* (Newbury Park, CA: Corwin Press, 1992), 47.

51. Bobby Ryan, interview by the author, digital recording, Atlanta, GA, October 3, 2012. Unless otherwise noted, all quotes from Ryan date to this interview.

52. In 2013, Mableton Elementary was approximately 34 percent black, 27 percent Latino, and 32 percent white, but 62 percent of its students were on free or reduced-price lunch, and the test scores, which Ryan said he uses as his primary reference point, were mediocre. The third- and fifth-grade "met or exceeded expectations" scores on the CRCT for 2011 were 70 and 76 percent, respectively. The scores at his daughter's elementary school, East Side, were 94 and 91 percent, respectively. See Note 26.

53. "Characteristics of the Population, 1970," US Census Bureau, accessed April 10, 2017, http://www.census.gov/prod/www/decennial.html.

54. At the beginning of the desegregation decade in Marietta, there were only 195 black high school students in the city, while there were more than 1,000 white high school students. In 1960, there were only sixty-seven white high school students attending private or parochial schools; by 1970, that number had dropped to thirty-five. "Characteristics of the Population, 1960, 1970," US Census Bureau, accessed April 10, 2017, http://www.census.gov/prod/www/decennial.html.

55. Ronald Reagan condemned a Chicago "welfare queen" in his 1976 presidential campaign, bringing the term into popular use. George Bush's 1988 campaign ran a now infamous ad featuring black convicted felon Willie Horton, who committed rape and assault while released on a furlough program candidate Michael Dukakis ostensibly supported, to skewer Dukakis for being "soft on crime." The ad was seen to pander to stereotypes about black men and criminality held by the white voters Bush was courting. See Dan T. Carter, *From George Wallace to Newt Gingrich: Race in the Conservative Counterrevolution, 1963–1994* (Baton Rouge: Louisiana State University Press, 1996) for the national political context of these examples.

56. Gwendolyn Mink, "Welfare Reform in Historical Perspective," *Social Justice*, 21, no. 1 (1994): 114–31.

57. Ray Buday, interview by the author, digital recording, Marietta, GA, March 7, 2012. Before the 2008 recession, the Housing Authority made millions of dollars selling the land that the projects once occupied for redevelopment; that land may go to "mixed-income" developments, but not to low-income developments. Money from the sales went, for the most part, to the construction of more senior housing and the improvement of existing senior complexes.

58. "About Us," ApolloMD, accessed October 30, 2012, http://apollomd.com/.

59. Erica Frankenberg and Gary Orfield, eds., *The Resegregation of Suburban Schools: A Hidden Crisis in American Education* (Cambridge, MA: Harvard Education Press, 2012), 233.

60. Robert Putnam, "Social Capital: Measurement and Consequence," *Canadian Journal of Policy Research* 2, no. 1 (2001): 41–51.

61. The seminal work on the discourse of respectability among early-twenti-eth-century black reformers is Evelyn Brooks Higginbotham, *Righteous Discontent: The Women's Movement in the Black Baptist Church, 1880–1920* (Cambridge, MA: Harvard University Press, 1994). This is not to say, of course, that Ms. Garman's era saw no radical black activism. Organizing that we associate with the classical Civil Rights Movement was well under way in the 1930s and 1940s among white and black activists in labor unions, communist groups, and socialist groups fighting for voting rights, workers' rights, and educational equality. See, for example, Robert R. Korstad, *Civil Rights Unionism: Tobacco Workers and the Struggle for Democracy in the Mid-Twentieth-Century South* (Chapel Hill: University of North Carolina Press, 2003) and Glenda E. Gilmore, *Defying Dixie: The Radical Roots of Civil Rights, 1919–1950* (New York: W.W. Norton, 2008).

62. Photograph of the class of what was then called the "Harold Street School," undated, Peggy R. Elgin, *Centennial Celebration: Marietta City Schools: 1892–1992* (Marietta, GA: Marietta Schools Foundation, 1993), 79.

63. Diana Rios, interview by the author, digital recording, Marietta, GA, September 20, 2012. Unless otherwise noted, all further quotes from Rios date to this interview.

64. Jon Gillooly, "West Side Lottery Date in Place: In-Demand School to Admit Students Based on Random Drawing's Results," *Marietta Daily Journal,* February 1, 2009. The Spraggins family, for example, disap-pointed by the 2009 lottery, expressed their intention to choose an area private school instead of staying in Marietta City Schools. Jon Gillooly, "School Lottery Stirs Emotions; Parents Cite Unappealing Test Scores, Demographics in Certain Districts," *Marietta Daily Journal,* February 5, 2009.

65. Lembeck became superintendent in 2004, and under her guidance, the high school and city system have seen ups and downs. In 2009, the district won a Title I Distinguished District Award for closing the achievement gap between poor and nonpoor students. Georgia Department of Education, accessed April 10, 2017, http://www.doe.k12.ga.us/External-Affairs-and-Policy/communications/Pages/PressReleaseDetails.aspx?PressView=Archive&pid=132. In 2010 to 2013, MHS made *US News and World Report*'s list of top high schools and was ranked highly by the *Washington Post*'s "Challenge Index," a ranking system reflecting which schools have the most advanced placement offerings and highest scores.

Valerie Strauss, "Challenging Jay's Challenge Index," *Washington Post*, May 20, 2011, http://www.washingtonpost.com/blogs/answer-sheet/post/challenging-jays-challenge-index/2011/05/20/AFzrOz7G_blog.html. "Marietta City Schools 2013–2014 Fact Sheet," Marietta City Schools, accessed April 10, 2017, http://www.marietta-city.org/aboutus/factsheet.php. However, in 2012 MHS was designated ignominiously as a "focus school" in Georgia, due to its 59 percent graduation rate as calculated by the new nationally instituted "adjusted cohort" method. Wayne Washington, "Georgia Releases List of Focus Schools Needing More Attention," *Atlanta Journal Constitution*, March 21, 2012, http://www.ajc.com/news/news/state-regional-govt-politics/georgia-releases-list-of-focus-schools-needing-add/nQSMy/.

66. "Mobility and Stability Statistics Comparison," data kept by the Marietta City Schools and acquired from Thomas Algarin, Director of Communications, via e-mail, February 26, 2013.

67. Valarie Wilson, interviewed by Denis O'Hayer, November 1, 2012, "Charter School Amendment: The Case Against, from Valarie Wilson of the Georgia School Boards Association," accessed April 10, 2017, http://news.wabe.org/post/charter-school-amendment-case-against-valarie-wilson-school-boards-association.

68. The International Baccalaureate (IB) program was developed by a group of teachers in Geneva, Switzerland, in 1968; it emphasizes international education, service, and global citizenship. An IB diploma is internationally recognized as signifying high achievement, and universities in and outside the United States translate IB coursework into college course credit. See Chapter 3 for an extensive discussion of the IB program.

69. MCAA, Marietta Center for Advanced Academics, is the only school in the system where admissions are application based; for that reason, I exclude MCAA when designating West Side as the highest-achieving elementary school. Predictably, MCAA boasts the highest test scores in the city. In 2010-2011, its student body was impressively diverse—15 percent Asian, 31 percent black, and 39 percent white. Latino students, however, are dramatically underrepresented at MCAA. Like West Side, and unlike all the other elementaries, MCAA is a low-poverty school. See Note 26.

70. Lauren Garcia (pseudonym), interview by the author, Skype video call, September 20, 2012. Unless otherwise indicated, all quotes from Garcia date to this interview.

71. Andrew Rotherham, "Why Romney's Big School Voucher Idea Is Really Pretty Puny," TIME.com, June 14, 2012, http://ideas.time.com/2012/06/14/why-romneys-big-school-voucher-idea-is-really-pretty-puny/.

72. Fifty-five percent of the 727 employed black women in Marietta in 1960 worked in "private households." "Characteristics of the Population, 1960," US Census Bureau, accessed April 10, 2017, http://www.census.gov/prod /www/decennial.html.

73. Freedom of choice did not always lead inexorably to dissolution of all-black education systems. In Hyde County, North Carolina, as historian David Cecelski tells it, black community leaders strategically sued for a return to freedom of choice in order to save the two all-black schools threatened by closure during desegregation. *Along Freedom Road: Hyde County North Carolina and the Fate of Black Schools in the South* (Chapel Hill: University of North Carolina Press, 1994), 92.

74. Bill Kinney, "Negro Grammar School, City's Most Modern, Opens," *Marietta Journal,* March 15, 1951.

75. As historian David Cecelski observes, "Between 1965 and 1968, the closing of black schools and attempts to efface their educational legacy became a standard part of school desegregation." He continues, "Neither federal courts nor federal agencies felt obligated to intervene against local school leaders [who were] needlessly and unfairly closing black schools." *Along Freedom Road,* 31–32.

76. Until designated Marietta elementary schools were turned into "junior high centers" in 1965, there was no black junior high in Marietta; black students attended elementary school at Lemon Street or Wright Street until fifth grade, and then for sixth through eighth grades, they had classes in "the annex," a building attached to Lemon Street High School.

77. Daphne Delk, interview by Jessica Drysdale and Jay Lutz, Marietta, GA, November 7, 2009, Cobb NAACP/Civil Rights Series No. 7.; accessible online at Kennesaw State University Oral History Project, http://archon. kennesaw.edu/?p=collections /controlcard&id=202.

78. Margaret Thatcher—the architect of British neoliberal policy—famously insisted that there is "no such thing as society, only individual men and women"; quoted in David Harvey, *A Brief History of Neoliberalism* (New York: Oxford University Press, 2005), 23.

79. Peter W. Cookson Jr., "The Ideology of Consumership and the Coming Deregulation of the Public School System," in Peter W. Cookson Jr., ed., *The Choice Controversy* (Newbury Park, CA: Corwin Press, 1992), 94.

3. Some Kinds of Blue: Tracking at Marietta High

1. Tiffany Turner, interview by the author, Skype video recording, January 11, 2013. Unless otherwise noted, all quotes from Turner date to this interview.

2. Susan Yonezawa, Amy Stuart Wells, and Irene Serna, "Choosing Tracks: 'Freedom of Choice' in Detracking Schools," *American Educational Research Journal* 39, no. 1 (Spring 2002): 39.

3. My discussion of tracking reform draws in part on Tim Loveless's study of the national debate: *The Tracking Wars: State Reform Meets School Policy* (Washington, DC: Brookings, 1999).

4. David Tyack, *Seeking Common Ground: Public Schools in a Diverse Society* (Cambridge, MA: Harvard University Press, 2003).

5. As historians such as Linda Gordon and Nell Irvin Painter point out, "white" was a fluid designation, reliant on region and culture in the United States. In Gordon's *The Great Arizona Orphan Abduction* (Cambridge, MA: Harvard University Press, 1999), in turn-of-the-century Arizona, a furor over a group of Irish orphans, kidnapped by outraged "Anglos" from their adoptive Mexican families, demonstrated how in that place and time, the Irish—on the bottom rung in the Northeast—were "white" in Arizona, and the Mexicans were not. Referring to the same period, Painter cites that according to census records, Mexican Americans were white everywhere but the Southwest. *The History of White People* (New York: W.W. Norton, 2010), 359.

6. In her now classic 1985 study, *Keeping Track*, scholar Jeannie Oakes put it this way: "Those at the bottom of the social and economic ladder climb up through twelve years of the 'great equalizer' . . . and end up still on the bottom rung." Jeannie Oakes, *Keeping Track: How Schools Structure Inequality* (New Haven, CT: Yale, 1985), 5.

7. Ibid.

8. At MHS, "basic" and "college prep" tracks replaced the "scientific" and "classical" tracks in the 1969–1970 school year, the third year of full integration at the high school. David Tyack wryly informs us that in Detroit public schools, when Ford was king, these groups were called "motor, abstract, and abstract-motor." Tyack, *Seeking Common Ground*, 120.

9. Maureen T. Hallinan, "The Detracking Movement," *Education Next* 4, no. 4 (Fall 2004), http://educationnext.org/the-detracking-movement/. Very few districts in the United States have substantially de-tracked, as Hallinan demonstrates, despite the fact that the negative impact of tracking on education equality and minority achievement is an idea undergirded by "a widely accepted research basis" expanded upon and nuanced in the decades since *Keeping Track*. Rosyln Mickelson and Kevin Welner,

"School Reform, Politics and Tracking: Should We Pursue Virtue?" *Educational Researcher* 29, no. 4 (May 2000): 25.

10. Yonezawa and colleagues define tracking "as the grouping of students by presumed ability or achievement into a *series of courses*" and "ability grouping" as "the course by course placement of students by perceived ability or pre-requisites." "Choosing Tracks," 40. Although ability grouping is more accurate, I use "tracking" throughout this chapter as the more familiar term in public discourse.

11. Homogenous social circles in diverse high schools aren't unique to American education. David James and colleagues document that the white middle-class parents they studied in London, Riverton, and Norton chose public schools with the hope that their children would make friends across class and ethnicity, but seldom did the "social mix" produce "social mixing." As in American high schools, the tracking effected by gifted programs kept students socioeconomically, if not ethnically, segregated. David James, Diane Reay, Gill Crozier, Phoebe Beedell, Sumi Hollingworth, Fiona Jamieson, and Katya Williams, "Neoliberal Policy and the Meaning of Counterintuitive Middle-Class School Choices," *Current Sociology* 58, no. 4 (2010): 626.

12. "Downloadable Data," accessed April 17, 2017, https://gosa.georgia.gov /downloadable-data. During this research, all data since 2004 were available through school "report cards" accessible via the Georgia Department of Education website. In 2014, however, all data for school years after 2010-2011 were moved to a new platform, the Governor's Office of Student Achievement, https://gosa.georgia.gov/downloadable-data. For data concerning school years prior to 2010, a data request form must be submitted electronically to http://gosa.georgia.gov/webform/report-card -data-request. IB data were acquired from program administrators. No disaggregated minority data are available for the 2001–2002 IB cohort, and no data at all are available for 2000–2001. "Marietta International Baccalaureate Enrollment, 2001–2002," acquired through e-mail correspondence, February 6, 2013.

13. *Marietta High Pitchfork*, LXX.4 (May 2001).

14. In 1930, the city of Marietta was 29.4 percent black. US Census Bureau, Census of Population and Housing, 1930, http://www.census.gov/prod /www/decennial.html. The black population declined over the next thirty years and began to climb again during the seventies, consistent with trends across the South reflecting what scholars call "reverse migration" which ethnographer Carol Stack documents poignantly in her work, *Call to Home: African-Americans Reclaim the Rural South* (New York: Basic Books, 1996).

15. Christina Thornton (pseudonym), interview by the author, Skype call recording, March 4, 2013. Unless otherwise noted, all quotes from Thornton date to this interview.

16. Black also encompasses the "mixed race" category; dropout totals were calculated from internal documents over two years, 2000–2001 and 2001–2002, labeled "Dropout/Lack of Attendance/Withdrawals by Race," from the files of former faculty member and scholar Adair F. White-Johnson.

17. See Note 12.

18. James Salzer, "State Last in Latino Grads," *Atlanta Journal-Constitution*, November 14, 2001.

19. See Note 12. The education news and research site Education Week offers an interactive map for the graduation rates during the decade between 2000 and 2010, which shows, among other trends, a general upward climb for the whole country and the comparatively abysmal rates in the Deep South. By 2010, the national average had climbed from 67 percent in 2000 to 75 percent, but Georgia still lagged behind with South Carolina, Mississippi, Louisiana, New Mexico, Nevada, and Washington, DC—all with graduation rates below 67 percent. "Graduation Rate Trends: 1999–2000–2009–2010," accessed April 15, 2017, http://www.edweek.org/ew/dc/2013/gradrate_trend.html. It is worth noting that under the No Child Left Behind Act (signed into law in 2001), graduation rates were one of the "indicators" determining whether a school would make AYP (Annual Yearly Progress)—the measure that could doom public schools to closure.

20. "Dropout/Lack of Attendance/Withdrawals by Race."

21. "2012 College Bound Seniors: SAT District Profile Report, Marietta City Schools," released to the public on September 24, 2012. Ken Sprague's personal papers in the author's possession: Ken Sprague, "An Action Plan to Raise the Quality and Accountability of College Preparation for Minority High School Students" (drafted and presented to the Superintendent of Schools in Spring 2005); Ken Sprague, "Restructuring Algebra 1," Memo to Principal Gordon Pritz and Associate Principal Ron Brookins, August 18, 2003.

22. Ken Sprague, interview by the author, digital recording, Marietta, GA, December 28, 2012. Unless otherwise noted, all quotes from Sprague date to this interview.

23. In an article about the birth of Gold's Gym, journalist Paul Solotaroff called Sprague's promotional techniques those of a "showman non-pareil." Sprague himself joked that his activism in Marietta benefitted from his experience in commercials; he knew "to push the beef in the bun forward," that is, how to present an argument for its desired audience effect.

Showmanship had its limits, however, see note 24 below. "The Dawn of Bodybuilding," *Men's Journal,* February 2012, http://www.mensjournal.com/magazine/the-dawn-of-bodybuilding-20121118?page=1.

24. There was little need for Marietta City Schools to censor Sprague, when the readers of the *Marietta Daily Journal* were chomping at the bit. His articles were met with outrage and ridicule, even from colleagues Sprague called friends. (Howard White, "No Policies at MHS to Hold Back Black Students," *Marietta Daily Journal,* May 6, 2004.) Mariettans coming to the defense of the school system (which normally they were quick to critique themselves) were probably the best publicity school leadership could have asked for.

25. Yonezawa, Wells, and Serna, "Choosing Tracks," 54.

26. Ibid., 62.

27. The "old high school" has housed Marietta Middle School since the 2001–2002 school year.

28. Tiffany Turner, "Marietta High Still Segregated, Picture Said," Letter to the Editor, *Marietta Daily Journal,* May 8, 2001.

29. Paul Tarc, *Global Dreams, Enduring Tensions: International Baccalaureate in a Changing World* (New York: Peter Lang Publishing, 2009).

30. "About the IB: Facts and Figures," International Baccalaureate Organization, accessed April 15, 1017, http://ibo.org/about-the-ib/facts-and-figures/. Statistics on the number of IB schools in Georgia, the United States, and the world date to January 2017. Statistics estimating the number of students enrolled in IB programs worldwide date to 2014.

31. In 2013, applicant high schools paid $23,000 (the cost was probably slightly less when MHS applied in 1995) during the two- to three-year application process required to institute the diploma program. After that, IB "world schools" pay annual fees to the organization; if a participating school district has the diploma program, the middle years program, and the primary years program, they pay for each of the three.

32. "IB a Great Opportunity," Editorial, *Marietta Daily Journal,* June 21, 1995; "IBF the Right Step," Editorial, *Marietta Daily Journal,* August 9, 1995.

33. Mickey King, "Partisan School Board Races Key to Stopping IB's Liberal Agenda," *Marietta Daily Journal,* October 16, 2005. Although King is not one to shy away from an unpopular view, he is not totally alone in his criticisms. IB has been accused of "indoctrination not education" and of having a "radical left wing bias" and "a hidden curriculum based on the ideology of Communists." Allen Quist, "The International Baccalaureate Curriculum," *Education News,* March 21, 2007; "The Truth about IB," accessed April 15,

2017, http://www.truthaboutib.com/theibhiddencurriculum.html, a site maintained by "Concerned Citizens of the Unites States of America." Less inflammatory critiques can be found in, for example, the Fordham Institute's questioning of the priorities of IB World History courses and the rigor of IB mathematics. Sheila Byrd, "Advanced Placement and International Baccalaureate: Do They Deserve Gold Star Status?" Fordham Institute, November 2007.

34. Dianne R. Stepp, "'Bad Law' Fight Had $250,000 Plus Tab," *Atlanta Journal-Constitution,* December 21, 2006.

35. Kathryn Dobies, "Traffic Stop Puts KSU Student in Jail as Illegal Immigrant," *Marietta Daily Journal,* May 1, 2010; Kate Brumback, "Student Reluctant Immigration Symbol," May 14, 2011, www.reporternews.com.

36. King, "Partisan School Board Races Key to Stopping IB's Liberal Agenda."

37. Quoted in George Walker, "What Have I Learned about International Education?" Biennial Conference of IB Nordic Schools, September 9, 2005, Stockholm, Sweden, http://www.ibo.org/dg/emeritus/speeches /documents/nordic_sep05.pdf, 5.

38. "Theory of Knowledge" (TOK), a course every IB student takes, described at http://www.ibo.org/programmes/diploma-programme/curriculum/theory -of-knowledge/, accessed April 15, 2017.

39. Paulo Freire, *Pedagogy of the Oppressed* (New York: Continuum, 1970), 72.

40. There seems to no consensus in the research on whether block scheduling is disadvantageous to high school students struggling in core subject areas such as math. However, one recent study of forty-three Virginia middle schools, half on block schedules and half on traditional schedules, showed that black and Latino students on block schedules scored higher on math and reading assessments than those on traditional schedules. Willie Wallicia Allen Gill, "Middle School A/B Block and Traditional Scheduling: An Analysis of Math and Reading Performance by Race," NASSP (National Association of Secondary School Principals) Bulletin 95, no. 4 (2011): 281–301.

41. Unlike "full IB" graduates who leave MHS with an IB diploma, partial IB students take some, not all, IB classes and do not complete all IB exams, fulfill the service hours requirement, or write a final essay.

42. Onyeka Aniemeka and Bella Dima, interview by the author, digital recording, Kennesaw, GA, January 3, 2013. Unless otherwise noted, all quotes from Aniemeka and Dima date to this interview.

43. Adair F. White-Johnson, "'Peas 'N Rice' or 'Rice 'N Peas': Which One Are We Really Ordering? The Plight of African American Male Students Engaged in Education Exchange Processes," *Urban Education* 36 (2001): 351.

44. "Marietta High School: Academics: IB Program," accessed January 20, 2013, http://www.marietta-city.org/files/1213/testing/MHS%20IB%20 ACT%20SAT%202012.pdf.

45. Jan and Bob Davidson, *Genius Denied: How to Stop Wasting Our Brightest Young Minds* (New York: Simon and Schuster, 2005), 4. *A Nation Deceived*, a Templeton Foundation report, led to the creation of the Institute for Research and Policy on Acceleration. The report can be accessed at http://www.accelerationinstitute.org/nation_deceived/.

46. James Baldwin, *The Fire Next Time* (New York: Vintage, 1962), 43.

47. STAR is a program of the Professional Association of Georgia Educators that annually honors exceptional high school seniors and the teachers they select.

48. Savannah and her sister attended The King's Academy, a private Christian hybrid school that offers the option of enrolling as a part-time student, attending classes only two or three days a week; see http://www .thekingsacademy.org/about-us/mission-philosophy.cfm.

49. Savannah King, interview by the author, digital recording, Marietta, GA, December 18, 2012. Unless otherwise noted, all quotes from Savannah King date to this interview.

50. The 2010-2011 eligibility requirement was that players pass four out of six classes. Eligibility at the end of junior year requires an accrued sixteen Carnegie units or credit hours: in order for a student to be promoted from eleventh to twelfth grade, he or she must have twenty units. These were the requirements of the Georgia High School Association, which MHS could have made more strict, but did not. Marietta High School Handbook/Student Agenda, 2010–2011.

51. Caleb Cox, interview by the author, digital recording, Marietta, GA, December 28, 2012. Unless otherwise noted, all quotes from Cox date to this interview.

52. Elizabeth Daigle, "International Baccalaureate Critic Way Off Base," *Marietta Daily Journal,* October 19, 2005.

53. The term's ubiquity in the news media and the blogosphere is not matched in the scholarly literature, but some scholarship on social life and racial separation in school uses self-segregation as its analytical lens. Octavio Villalpando, "Self-Segregation or Self-Preservation? A Critical Race Theory and Latina/o Critical Theory Analysis of a Study of Chicana/o College Students," *Qualitative Studies in Education* 16, no. 5 (2003): 619–46; Troy Duster, "Understanding Self-Segregation on the Campus," *Chronicle of Higher Education* 38, no. 5 (1991): B1–2.

54. Megan Birch, interview by the author, digital recording, Marietta, GA, May 2, 2012. Unless otherwise noted, all quotes from Megan Birch date to this interview.

55. Cesar Verde (pseudonym), interview by the author, Skype video recording, October 25, 2012. Unless otherwise noted, all subsequent quotes from Verde date to this interview.

56. See Note 12.

57. Most students who withdraw are not counted as dropouts; usually, they are presumed to be leaving school with the intention of going back—pregnant students, ill students, and those who are changing schools/districts. The "leaver" calculation method did not require schools to keep track of whether students who withdrew ever returned to school at all; therefore, these students did not count against the graduation rate for their class. For example, the statistics in 2008–2009 and 2009–2010, calculated using the previous method, were, respectively, 81 percent and 76.7 percent of black students graduated; 68 percent and 73.8 percent of Latino students graduated; and 92 percent and 90.7 percent of white students graduated. The 2010–2011 rates demonstrate the difference made by the four-year calculation: 54.7 percent of black students, 39.1 percent of Latino students, and 82.5 percent of white students graduated. In 2010–2011, sixty-nine black students (6 percent) and twenty-four Latino students (5 percent) dropped out, compared to seventy-five black students (6.6 percent) and thirty-four Latino students (7.2 percent) the previous school year. Graduation rates for all groups over the years since 2000 had been slowly rising. Notably the graduation rates for "economically disadvantaged students" have been vacillating between 60 and 70 percent between 2004 and 2011, with no discernible upward trend. See Note 12.

58. Since 1993, there have been only two black members of the school board: Jeanie Carter, a former educator in the Marietta school system, who served from 1993 to 2010, and Jeriene Grimes, who was elected in 2013. Kent A. Miles, "Diversity of Cobb Not Reflected on Boards," *Atlanta Journal-Constitution*, February 8, 2009.

59. A list and calendar of "benchmark" tests are available at http://www.marietta-city.org/curriculum/testing/.

60. Motoko Rich, "'No Child' Law Whittled Down by White House," *The New York Times*, July 6, 2012, http://www.nytimes.com/2012/07/06/education/no-child-left-behind-whittled-down-under-obama.html.

61. LaKenna Andrews (pseudonym), interview by the author, digital recording, Marietta, GA, January 8, 2013. Unless otherwise noted, all quotes from Andrews date to this interview.

62. The Carl D. Perkins Career and Technical Education Act was reauthorized by Congress in 2006, with the intention to energize the Programs of Study (POS) initiative. POS, or Career Pathways, adds components from

previous overhauls—dual enrollment programs, fuller integration of academics and vocational courses—to the effort to connect high school vocational education with postsecondary opportunities and education. Unlike a college prep diploma, a tech diploma required three instead of four credits of math (and no course beyond Algebra II), no foreign language, and five credits in a career area such as Healthcare Science or Architecture and Construction. At MHS, this diploma option was eliminated for all students entering after 2008.

63. At a mentoring seminar I attended, one high school junior said she'd like to be an OBGYN. When asked what those letters stood for, she didn't know, and when asked if she liked science, she replied that she didn't. Another student offered that she'd like to be a psychiatrist, and when asked if she knew that required medical school after undergrad, she was surprised. For students like these two, who are unlikely to enter four-year colleges after graduation, the translation of high school course choices and achievement into graduate school admissions is a confounding one. The various internship programs at the high school, however, are given good reviews by recent graduates. Early incarnations of such programs allowed graduates like Sonia Torres Hill (pseudonym), whose story unfolds in Chapter 4, to enter the high-earning career she wanted—insurance—without even a bachelor's degree, due to connections made during her internship year.

64. Joel Rubin, "High School Vocational Classes Are Stalling Out," *Los Angeles Times*, September 6, 2004, http://articles.latimes.com/2004/sep /06/local/me-voced6.

65. For example, the pathway with highest enrollment every semester is Food Science because, speculated Dr. Brown, non–science-inclined students can take nutrition as a one of their required science credits. "MHS Balanced Scorecard, 2012," accessed February 2, 2013, http://www .marietta-city.org/files/bsc/MHS-balancedscorecard.pdf, 19.

66. Fort Valley has an 11 percent four-year graduation rate, indicating that LaKenna's struggle to balance work and school and maintain momentum toward graduation is not a unique one. Data accessed at https://www .usnews.com/best-colleges/; other sites such as parchment.com and GAfutures.org also offer SAT and GPA averages and four- or six-year graduation rates.

67. Claire Duffie (pseudonym), interview by the author, Skype video recording, December 19, 2012. Unless otherwise noted, all quotes from Duffie date to this interview.

68. The population rose from 268 homeless students in 2008–2009 to 444 in 2012–2013. The population of the city school system hovers around 8,000.

Data acquired from the Marietta City Schools Communications Office, May 28, 2013.

69. Lindsay Field, "Marietta High School Alum Shares Story of Success Despite Homelessness," *Marietta Daily Journal*, July 21, 2013.

70. Lauren Garcia (pseudonym), interview by the author, Skype video recording, September 20, 2012. All subsequent quotes from Garcia date to this interview unless otherwise noted.

71. Will Dean (pseudonym), interview by the author, digital recording, Atlanta, GA, May 21, 2012.

72. Camille Hill, interview by the author, digital recording, Marietta, GA, January 11, 2013.

73. Ryan Henderson, interview by the author, digital recording, Atlanta, GA, January 10, 2013.

74. "MHS IB 2012–2013: IB Diploma and IB Course Students," presentation available at MHS IB DP webpage: http://mhs.marietta-city.org/Page/818; accessed February 2, 2013.

75. Priscilla Graves (pseudonym), phone conversation with the author, January 31, 2013.

76. See Note 12. The spike in black enrollment occurred during the nineties, when the black population of the city of Marietta grew by 10 percent. "Characteristics of the Population, 1990, 2000," US Census Bureau, accessed April 15, 2017, http://www.census.gov/prod/www/decennial.html.

77. Marietta High School IB Diploma Program, Presentation to the Board of Education, November 2010. Power Point presentation available at Board Docs through the "Board Notes" portal on the Marietta City Schools homepage: http://www.marietta-city.org/newsroom/boardnotes/index.php; accessed February 2, 2013.

78. The May 2012 fees for a senior diploma candidate totaled $745 for six tests. Students who opt to take one or two exams in their junior year pay slightly less. (I have estimated here, according to average costs in other districts with the IB program; I was not able to obtain these data from Marietta's IB administrators.)

79. All data acquired from the IB Coordinators' office at MHS. The terminology—i.e., "minority" and "Hispanic"—used in the charts is that of the Marietta IB program.

80. Amy Rocha (pseudonym), interview by the author, Skype video recording, September 10, 2012. Unless otherwise noted, all quotes from Rocha date to this interview.

81. Quoted in George Walker, "What Have I Learned about International Education?"

82. This is an estimate based on 2012 data for seniors enrolled in IB classes; data on full IB graduates (the group of IB candidates who earn an IB diploma through passing the requisite exams and fulfilling a raft of requirements) are not disaggregated by race.

83. Benjamin Derra (pseudonym), interview by the author, Skype recording, June 7, 2013. Unless otherwise noted, all quotes from Derra date to this interview.

84. Bridget Reyes, interview by the author, digital recording, Marietta, GA, May 26, 2013. Unless otherwise noted, all quotes from Reyes date to this interview.

85. Patricia Gándara and Frances Contreras, *The Latino Education Crisis: The Consequences of Failed Social Policies* (Cambridge, MA: Harvard University Press, 2009), 99.

86. The report states: "There were 430 U.S. high schools with at least one Diploma candidate, defined as a student who attempted the full slate of exams for the Diploma Programme. Forty of these schools had at least 20 Diploma candidates who are members of groups that IB identified as underrepresented in the Diploma Programme nationwide: low-income students—measured by eligibility for free or reduced-price lunch (FRPL) through the National School Lunch Program—and / or students who self-identify as African American, Latino, or Native American. Of those 40 schools with at least 20 underrepresented Diploma candidates in 2007, 15 had Diploma pass rates at or above 60% for their underrepresented students." Data are from a 2008 analysis conducted by McKinsey Consulting using 2007 statistics; cited in Jennifer A. Bland and Katrina R. Woodworth, Introduction to "Case Studies of Participation and Performance in the IB Diploma Programme," Center for Education Policy, SRI International, 2009, accessed April 15, 2017, http://m.novi.k12 .mi.us/downloads/hs_ib_docs/case_studies_20120725_132023_4.pdf.

87. "Diploma Gap Study: Project Overview and Main Findings," April 15, 2009, http://blogs.ibo.org/addressingaccess/files/2009/04/dpgap-over-view-apr09.pdf, 3–4.

88. Ibid.

89. Ibid., 9.

90. Jennifer Fischer (pseudonym), interview by the author, Marietta, GA, August 24, 2012.

91. "Rigorous Courses and Increased Achievement for All Students: A Conversation with Arlington Virginia's Superintendent Rob Smith and Assistant Superintendent for Instruction Mark Johnston," document accessed through the Minority Student Achievement Network at http:// msan.wceruw.org/.

92. Yonezawa and colleagues document the failed efforts of a district in which de-tracking consisted only of a "choice" policy wherein advanced and IB courses were theoretically open to all students. But, as the authors show, this nominal openness actually cloaked a system of "hidden requirements" and gatekeeping by counselors, teachers, and even administrators, who were not sure that low-tracked students really could or wanted to succeed in high-level classes. Choice, assert the authors, is not sufficient to encourage low-tracked minority students to venture out of the comfort and familiarity of their previous tracks and courses. "Choosing Tracks," 40.

93. Scholar Tim Loveless (a critic of de-tracking) suggests that parents simply want the best for *their* children while the institution must pursue the best for *all* children. This view, repackaged by a well-known liberal lecturer, Alfie Kohn, suggests that affluent parents (the ones with, traditionally, the most influence in schools) champion ability grouping even at the cost of equity for struggling students. Kohn writes, "The system serves these parents well and their influence is such—or the fear that they will yank their children out is sufficient—that few superintendents (and even fewer school boards) dare to rock this boat on which first class cabins are so clearly delineated from steerage." "Only for My Kid: How Privileged Parents Undermine School Reform," *Phi Delta Kappan* 79, no. 8 (April 1998): 568–77.

94. The number of IB graduates is typically around 10 percent of the entire graduating class.

95. At its inception in 1993, the HOPE scholarship paid for the in-state tuition of students with GPAs of 3.0 or higher taking fifteen credit hours (a full load) per semester at a state college or university. In 2012, as the program faced funding shortfalls, the GPA requirement for a full scholarship was raised to 3.7. Charles Clotfelter, a desegregation scholar whose research also includes work on state lotteries, has commented that the fact that low-income counties buy the lottery tickets that fund the scholarships enjoyed by the students of high-income counties is a "stunning" example of income redistribution. Quoted in Jennifer Levitz and Scott Thurm, "Shift to Merit Scholarships Stirs Debate," *Wall Street Journal*, December 19, 2012, https://www.wsj.com/articles/SB100014241278873244812045781 75631182640920.

96. Statistics at "Georgia's HOPE Program," Georgia Student Finance Commission, gsfc.org.

97. Although it seems logical that middling students should stick to less demanding classes in order to protect their GPAs for the HOPE scholarship, "bonus quality points" awarded for AP and IB classes make it

possible for students to earn a GPA above a 4.0—an important consideration if the student must shoot to surpass 3.7.

98. In my interviews with the principal, the superintendent, and three members of the seven-member school board, the "image" of the schools was a topic we returned to repeatedly.

99. Diane Ravitch, "My View: Rhee Is Wrong and Misinformed," blog post for "Schools of Thought," CNN.com, August 9, 2012.

100. In 2013, North Carolina was the Southern exemplar of regressive education politics. Since the ascendency of a Republican legislature in 2010 and the election of a Republican governor in 2012, teachers have been stripped of pay increases for obtaining master's degrees, classroom caps that were critical in controlling class size, and the protections of "career status" or tenure. One of the activists who orchestrated the 2014 teacher walk-ins protesting these changes, an educator in Durham, North Carolina, offered this assessment, which underscores the connection between rhetoric around "failing schools" and the political assault on teacher pay, rights, and collective action: "All of this is part of a conservative attempt to create a larger narrative that public schools are failing, and that therefore money must be shifted away from public schools into charter schools and voucher programs. Schools are underfunded, teachers are devalued, and students are dumbed down in a system that values test scores over creative thinking. . . . The exciting thing is that, in North Carolina and elsewhere, teachers are uniting with parents to fight back and demand that state leaders do right by our students." Nicholas Graber-Grace, e-mail exchange with the author, February 14, 2014. Allison Kilkenny, "Parents and Teachers Rally to Save North Carolina Schools," thenation.com, November 4, 2013, https://www.thenation.com/article/parents-and-teachers-rally-save-north-carolina-schools/.

4. The New Integrators: Latino Students

1. Although the city of Marietta is Cobb's county seat, Marietta has its own school system—a district about eight thousand students strong. Cobb County Schools are a much larger operation, with an enrollment of more than one hundred thousand students. Marietta City Schools "School District Profile," accessed April 17, 2017, http://www.marietta-city.org/aboutus/schooldistrictprofile.php. Cobb County School District, "About the Cobb County School District," accessed April 17, 2017, http://www.cobbk12.org/aboutccsd/.

2. Daniella Sanchez (pseudonym), interview by the author, digital recording, Marietta, GA, May 17, 2013. Unless otherwise noted, all quotes from Sanchez date to this interview. In this chapter, unless otherwise requested, interviewees' names and identifying details, along with most organization and place names, have been changed to protect those who are undocumented.

3. Mark Noferi, "Deportation without Representation," *Slate,* May 15, 2013, http://www.slate.com/articles/news_and_politics/jurisprudence/2013/05/the_immigration_bill_should_include_the_right_to_a_lawyer.html.

4. William Finnegan, "The Deportation Machine," *New Yorker,* April 29, 2013, http://www.newyorker.com/magazine/2013/04/29/the-deportation-machine.

5. Daniella praised the teen mothers' program at the Cobb school she attended and found much-needed community through it. At Marietta High, there is no such program; however, pregnant students are assigned a "home-bound" tutor who ostensibly guides pregnant and new mothers through the work they miss while on "maternity leave." New mothers can either return to MHS or finish their studies via computer at the Performance Learning Center; free daycare is offered at a nearby church. I obtained details on MHS policies and programs from Mia Howard, who worked with Communities in Schools, an organization that partners with MHS to support students dealing with academic and personal challenges and seeking alternative routes to graduation. Mia Howard, e-mail correspondence with the author, May 29, 2013.

6. In 2011, Georgia's legislature passed a bill, HB 87, much like Arizona's infamous "Show Me Your Papers" law. As the *Atlanta Journal-Constitution* reported on April 15, 2011, "House Bill 87 creates new requirements for many Georgia businesses to ensure new hires are eligible to work in the United States and empowers police to investigate the immigration status of certain suspects." Jeremy Redmon, "Georgia Lawmakers Pass Illegal Immigration Crackdown," Atlanta Journal-Constitution, April 18, 2011. As with Arizona's law, certain provisions of HB 87 were stricken down in court in 2012, but the show-me-your-papers provision was retained. The copycat bill in Alabama, HB 56, also saw its day in court in 2012—similarly, the show-me-your-papers article was retained, while other articles were stricken. In Georgia's bill, a provision criminalizing sheltering and aiding undocumented immigrants was struck down, and in Alabama's, a provision directing public schools to ascertain the immigration statuses of all enrolled students was rejected. "Setback for Rogue Immigration Laws," August 21, 2012, *The New York Times,* http://www.nytimes.com/2012/08/22/opinion/setback-for-rogue-immigration-laws-in-georgia-and-alabama

.html. "Federal Court Blocks Most Provisions of Georgia and Alabama's Anti-Immigrant Laws," National Immigration Law Center, August 20, 2012, http://www.nilc.org/nr082012.html. "Supreme Court Decision on Arizona Immigration Law," extensive analysis, last updated June 26, 2012 at http://www.nytimes.com/interactive/2012/06/26/us/scotus -immigrationlaw-analysis.html.

7. Scholar Alicia Schmidt Camacho argues that increasingly punitive immigration policy and the lack of a path to citizenship "have trapped unauthorized migrants and their kin, a majority of them Latino and of Mexican descent, within an untenable situation of radical vulnerability." Alicia Schmidt Camacho, "Hailing the Twelve Million: US Immigration Policy, Deportation, and the Imaginary of Lawful Violence," *Social Text* 105 (2010): 6.

8. Ibid., 8, 11.

9. Ibid., 10.

10. Cutbacks demanded by the 2013 budget "sequester" affected public schools nationwide. In Georgia, just the cuts to special education, Title I grants, and Head Start funding eliminated an estimated 1,053 jobs and affected more than 59,000 Georgia students. "Impact of Sequestration on Federal Education Programs—State-by-State," National Education Association, accessed April 17, 2017, http://www.nea.org/home /52610.htm.

11. Between 2000 and 2011, the Latino students' share of the Marietta High population doubled from 11 to 22 percent, and the percentage of students on free or reduced-priced lunch rose from 21 to 58 percent. The percentage of white students dropped from 38 to 24 percent during that period. "Downloadable Data," accessed April 17, 2017, https://gosa .georgia.gov/downloadable-data. During this research, all data since 2004 were available through school "report cards" accessible via the Georgia Department of Education website. In 2014, however, all data for school years after 2010-2011 were moved to a new platform, the Governor's Office of Student Achievement, https://gosa.georgia.gov/downloadable -data. For data concerning school years prior to 2010, a data request form must be submitted electronically to http://gosa.georgia.gov/webform /report-card-data-request.

12. Sam Dillon, "Inexperienced Companies Chase US Schools Funds," *The New York Times,* August 9, 2010, http://www.nytimes.com/2010/08/10 /education/10schools.html. Education policy scholar Kenneth J. Saltman's excellent op-ed for truthout.com outlines the dangers of corporatization: "The Failure of Corporate School Reform: Toward a New Common School Movement," December 5, 2011, http://truth-out.org/opinion/item

/5280:the-failure-of-corporate-school-reform-toward-a-new-common
-school-movement. Scholar David Harvey describes "neoliberalization . . .
as a *political* project to reestablish conditions for capital accumulation and
to restore the power of economic elites." David Harvey, *A Brief History of
Neoliberalism* (New York: Oxford, 2005), 19.

13. Scholar David Hursh observes: "Under neoliberalism, individuals are
transformed into equally competent, equally privileged [economic actors]
operating within a marketplace that now includes . . . education." David
Hursh, "Assessing No Child Left Behind and the Rise of Neoliberal
Education Policies," *American Educational Research Journal* 44, no. 3
(2007): 496–97. Researchers Wells, Slayton, and Scott suggest that
proponents of free market school reform "seek a public educational
system that is responsive to immediate demands of the consumers—at
least those consumers with the economic, political, and social efficacy to
make demands." Amy Stuart Wells, Julie Slayton, and Janelle Scott,
"Defining Democracy in the Neoliberal Age: Charter School Reform
and Educational Consumption," *American Educational Research Journal*
39, no. 2 (2002): 338. See also Danny K. Weil, ed., *School Vouchers
and Privatization: A Reference Handbook* (Santa Barbara, CA: ABC-
CLIO, 2002).

14. The National Center for Education Statistics (NCES) estimates the
"status dropout" rate of Latino high school students to have declined from
32 to 15 percent between 1990 and 2010. That dropout rate is still three
times higher than that of white students and almost twice that of black
students. National Center for Education Statistics, "Status Dropout Rates
of 16- through 24-Year-Olds in the Civilian, Non-institutionalized
Population, by Race/Ethnicity: Selected Years, 1990–2010; Fast Facts:
Dropout Rates," accessed September 20, 2014, http://nces.ed.gov
/fastfacts/display.asp?id=16. Marietta High's data indicate that the scores
of Latino students substantially lag behind those of white students, and
their attendance rates are lower than both black and white students.
Throughout the aughts, the Latino graduation rate has been the lowest of
all ethnic/racial groups. However, from a low of 33 percent in 2001–2002,
the Latino graduation rate reached a high of 74 percent in 2009–2010. See
Note 11. Latino students never surpassed black students' graduation rates
(although the gap fluctuated from two percentage points apart to fourteen
points), and black students' graduation rates remained at least ten percentage points behind those of white students in all years for which there
are data published online. "Marietta High Achievement Score, College
and Career Ready Performance Index 2012," accessed April 17, 2017,
http://ccrpi.gadoe.org/2012/.

15. Erica Frankenberg and Gary Orfield, eds., *The Resegregation of Suburban Schools: A Hidden Crisis in American Education* (Cambridge, MA: Harvard University Press, 2012). Frankenberg and Orfield discuss, among other examples, a school choice program in suburban San Antonio and the adoption of the IB program at resegregating schools in a Florida suburb as strategies aimed at attracting affluent families but that are not part of a larger approach to confronting resegregation.

16. School choice in Marietta, which has seven elementary schools but only one middle and one high school, has concentrated affluent white students in the single majority-white elementary, West Side—the only elementary, besides MCAA, which is less than 50 percent low income. The three lowest-scoring, highest-poverty elementary schools have only become more racially and socioeconomically isolated since the instituting of school choice in 2008. Marietta's STEM (science, technology, engineering, and math) academy, Marietta Center for Advanced Academics (MCAA), has a racially and ethnically diverse but very low-poverty student population. For school-related data, see Note 11. See Chapter 2 for a detailed discussion of the politics and impact of school choice in Marietta.

17. The impact of the IB program is discussed at length in Chapter 3.

18. See Note 11.

19. Just between 1990 and 2000, a period of high immigration, the city lost 13 percent of its white population, while its black population grew by 90 percent and its Latino population by 600 percent. "Characteristics of the Population, 1980, 1990," US Census Bureau, accessed April 17, 2017, http://www.census.gov/prod/www/decennial.html; "City of Marietta Comprehensive Plan," Appendix, 158, accessed July 31, 2013, http://www.dca.state.ga.us/development/planningqualitygrowth/programs/downloads/plans/MariettaPlanAppendixParts1to4.pdf.

20. The Immigration Reform and Control Act (IRCA) introduced stricter border control and policing of the employment of undocumented workers. But it was a boon to many undocumented families because it granted amnesty to more than 3 million immigrants who had entered the United States illegally before 1982. Michelle Waslin, "Remembering the Benefits of IRCA, 25 Years Later," ImmigrationImpact.com, November 7, 2011, http://immigrationimpact.com/2011/11/07/remembering-the-benefits-of-irca-25-years-later/. According to a 2011 study by the Pew Hispanic Center, "More Latino children are living in poverty—6.1 million in 2010—than children in any other racial group." Mark Hugo Lopez and Gabriel Velasco, "Childhood Poverty Among Hispanics Sets Record, Leads Nation," September 28, 2011, http://www.pewhispanic.org/2011/09/28/childhood-poverty-among-hispanics-sets-record-leads-nation/. The US Census

American Communities Survey (2007–2011) showed that 30 percent of Latinos living in Georgia live in poverty. For reference, poverty rates in Georgia for black and white residents were below 15 percent. (Georgia's Latinos are the eighth poorest in the country—after those in Pennsylvania, Arkansas, Alabama, North Carolina, Rhode Island, Tennessee, and Kentucky.) Suzanne Macartney, Alemayehu Bishaw, and Kayla Fontenot, "Poverty Rates for Selected Detailed Race and Hispanic Groups by State and Place: 2007–2011," American Community Survey Brief, February 2013, 20, https://www.census.gov/prod/2013pubs/acsbr11-17.pdf.

21. The foremost desegregation research group, the University of California, Los Angeles–based Civil Rights Project, or *Proyecto Derechos Civiles*, has tracked the intensified segregation of Latino students in American public schools. Such reports as "Historic Reversals, Accelerating Resegregation and the Need for New Integration Strategies" by Gary Orfield and Chungmei Lee (August 29, 2007, https://www.civilrightsproject.ucla.edu /research/k-12-education/integration-and-diversity/historic-reversals -accelerating-resegregation-and-the-need-for-new-integration-strategies-1) called attention to deepening resegregation across the country. Their recent regional and state studies, along with the excellent nationwide per-spective provided by Erica Frankenberg and Gary Orfield in *The Resegregation of Suburban Schools* (Cambridge, MA: Harvard University Press, 2012), document resegregation in the West, Southwest, and Southeast. Gary Orfield, Genevieve Siegel-Hawley, and John Kucsera, "Divided We Fail: Segregated and Unequal Schools in the Southland," The Civil Rights Project, March 18, 2011, https://www.civilrightsproject. ucla.edu/research/metro-and-regional-inequalities/lasanti-project-los -angeles-san-diego-tijuana/divided-we-fail-segregated-and-unequal -schools-in-the-southfield; John Kucsera and Greg Flaxman, "The Western States: Profound Diversity But Severe Segregation for Latino Students," The Civil Rights Project, September 19, 2012, https://www .civilrightsproject.ucla.edu/research/k-12-education/integration-and-diversity /mlk-national/the-western-states-profound-diversity-but-severe-segregation -for-latino-students.

22. In Georgia, the 2010–2011 graduation rate for Latino students using the new "adjusted cohort" method was 57.6 percent; black students in Georgia had a graduation rate of 59.8 percent and white students, 75.5 percent. "Race to the Top: Georgia, State Reported APR: SY 2011–2012," accessed September 5, 2013, https://www.rtt-apr.us/state/georgia/2011-2012/sod _4?access=1.

23. The previous "leaver" rate and new "adjusted cohort rate" are discussed at length in Chapter 3. The cohort rate includes students who were enrolled

for any length of time in a given cohort; if a student who transferred schools or left the state couldn't be tracked as having graduated somewhere else, that student counted against the high school's final
numbers. Although many principals, like Marietta High's, felt the new
method unfairly depressed their graduation rates (and twenty-six states
reported lower graduation rates under the new method), the US
Department of Education calls the rates a "more accurate snapshot."
MHS's principal called both the previous rate and the 2011-instituted
rate misleading—one was inflated, she told me, and the other
depressed. Leigh Colburn, conversation with the author, unrecorded,
Marietta, GA, July 18, 2013. "States Report New High School Graduation
Rates Using More Accurate, Common Measure," US Department of
Education, November 26, 2012, https://www.ed.gov/news/press-releases
/states-report-new-high-school-graduation-rates-using-more-accurate
-common-measur.

24. See Note 11.

25. Emily Lembeck, interview by the author, digital recording, Marietta, GA,
March 21, 2013. Unless otherwise noted, all quotes from Lembeck date to
this interview.

26. Brian D. Behnken, *Fighting Their Own Battles: Mexican Americans,
African Americans, and the Struggle for Civil Rights in Texas* (Chapel Hill:
University of North Carolina Press, 2011). "Underclass" is the word used
by Supreme Court Justice William Brennan in the *Plyler v. Doe* [457 U.S.
202 (1982)] opinion that guaranteed noncitizen children the right to a
public K-12 education. The phrase "second-class citizenship" in relation to
immigrants appeared in much of the mainstream media coverage of the
Arizona law SB 1070 and of immigration reform. For example, Arizona
State Senator Steve Gallardo commented, "SB 1070's true intention is to
make second-class citizens of US Latinos." Sandra Lilley, "Arizona Law
Makes Latinos Second Class Citizens, Say Opponents," NBC Latino, April
24, 2012, nbclatino.com; Benjamin Todd Jealous, "No Second Class
Families," *Huffington Post,* May 10, 2013, http://www.huffingtonpost.com
/benjamin-todd-jealous/no-second-class-families_b_3253713.html; Greg
Sargent, "Second Class Citizenship: Not the Answer to the GOP's Problems,"
Washington Post, February 7, 2013, http://www.washingtonpost.com/blogs
/plum-line/wp/2013/02/07/second-class-citizenship-not-the-answer-to-the
-gops-problems/.

27. Leigh Colburn, conversation with the author, unrecorded, Marietta, GA,
July 18, 2013. Colburn's estimate is based on the number of students who
enroll with testing identification numbers, which are issued to students
who don't have Social Security numbers.

28. Patricia J. Williams, *Seeing a Colorblind Future: The Paradox of Race* (New York: Farrar Straus and Giroux, 1997), 17.

29. The 2013 chair of the school board articulated the dominant perception about Franklin Road among Marietta's leadership: "Having a dense, transient population [on Franklin Road] not only increases the likelihood of increased crime, it makes it very hard for kids to receive a quality education and graduate high school, therefore continuing a cycle of poverty." Lindsay Field, "Marietta School Board Talks $35M Redevelopment Bond," *Marietta Daily Journal,* May 22, 2013.

30. An example is the passage of a 2012 amendment to Georgia's state constitution allowing the state to override the decisions of local school boards regarding the establishment of charter schools. A similar initiative won in Washington. In both states, pro-charter groups were funded by wealthy private donors such as the Waltons and by private charter school management companies. In Georgia, such groups raised fifteen times more money than those opposing the amendment. Motoko Rich, "Georgia's Voters Will Decide on Future of Charter Schools," *The New York Times,* November 5, 2012, http://www.nytimes.com/2012/11/06/education/future -of-georgias-charter-schools-on-ballot.html?pagewanted=all&_r=0; Dylan Scott, "Charter Schools Score Victories in Georgia and Washington," *Governing: The States and Localities,* November 7, 2012, http://www .governing.com/blogs/politics/gov-charter-schools-score-victories-in -georgia-and-washington.html. According to the National Center for Education Statistics, 90 percent of children go to public schools. "Projections of Education Statistics 2012," www.nces/ed/gov. One in five public schools is "high poverty" (in the NCES definition: 75 percent or more of students received free or reduced-price lunch) according to a 2013 report from the National Center for Education Statistics. That number represents a 60 percent increase over the period between 2000 and 2010. "The Condition of Education 2013," May 2013, http://nces .ed.gov/pubs2013/2013037.pdf.

31. Jeffrey Canada's brainchild, the Harlem Children's Zone, a holistic educational system for at-risk students that encompasses everything from parent education to dental care, is a celebrated example of a charter school model, as are the KIPP (Knowledge Is Power Program) schools. Both boast high graduation and college acceptance rates for their low-income students. Uniquely, Harlem Children's Zone—technically a ninety-seven -block swath of Harlem—provides support to existing public schools in "the zone" alongside its own charter schools. "The HCZ Project," accessed April 17, 2017, http://www.hcz.org/index.php/about-us/the-hcz-project; "About KIPP," accessed April 17, 2017, http://www.kipp.org/about-kipp.

Voucher programs are magnets for controversy but are expanding in places like Ohio, Florida, and Washington, DC. (DC's "opportunity scholarships" program became a budget bargaining chip in 2011, and Republican supporters of the program prevailed.) This growth suggests that voucher programs are popular with the parents who use them, although it is all too often not the parents of the poorest or most "at-risk" students. Education historian Diane Ravitch attributes the popularity of voucher programs and charter schools in part to the "media regularly pummel[ing] public schools" in cities where these options became available. Diane Ravitch, *The Death and Life of the Great American School System: How Testing and Choice Are Undermining Education* (New York: Basic Books, 2010), 132. Edith Starzyk, "School Voucher Programs Expand, Giving Ohio More Programs Than Any Other State," *Plain Dealer,* July 22, 2013, http://www.cleveland.com/metro/index.ssf/2013/07 /school_voucher_programs_expand.html; Brett Zongker, "School Vouchers: John Boehner Pushes to Revive Program in DC as Model for National Reform" *Huffington Post,* January 26, 2011, http://www.huffingtonpost .com/2011/01/26/john-boehner-dc-school-vouchers_n_814394.html; Kenric Ward, "Florida Leads Nation as School Voucher Programs Expand," *Sunshine State News,* February 4, 2012, http://www.sunshinestatenews .com/story/florida-leads-nation-school-voucher-programs-expand.

32. In his 1900 text *The Education of the Negro* (Albany, NY: J.B. Lyon Co.), Booker T. Washington credited Freedmen's Bureau schools with providing the "basis" of public education in the South (p. 10). Scholar William Troost points out that although he was right, Washington didn't back up his assertion with data. Troost does us that service: he calculates that "counties with bureau schools had literacy rates nearly 40% higher and school attendance rates 200% higher" than counties without bureau schools. The Freedmen's Bureau schools helped shape an infrastructure for Southern public education and laid the groundwork for the schools that anchored black communities until well into the 1960s. William Troost, "Accomplishment and Abandonment: A History of the Freedmen's Bureau Schools" (unpublished dissertation, University of California-Irvine, 2007). On schools as institutions for shaping immigrant children into American citizens, see David Tyack, *Seeking Common Ground: Public Schools in a Diverse Society* (Cambridge, MA: Harvard University Press, 2003).

33. Richard Rodriguez, *Brown: The Last Discovery of America* (New York: Penguin, 2002), 121.

34. In 1990, Marietta's Latinos still made up only 3.2 percent of the whole population. "Characteristics of the Population, 1980, 1990," US Census

Bureau, accessed April 17, 2017, http://www.census.gov/prod/www
/decennial.html.

35. Raymond A. Mohl, "Globalization, Latinization and the Nuevo New
    South," *Journal of American Ethnic History* 22.4 (July 2003): 38.

36. Ibid., 39.

37. "Georgia, Census QuickFacts," US Census Bureau, accessed April 17,
    2017, https://www.census.gov/quickfacts/table/PST045216/13.

38. Some economists suggest that negative effects of neoliberalization and of
    NAFTA are due to uneven implementation and development in North
    and South Mexico—that neoliberalization, essentially, didn't go far
    enough. Lee Hudson Teslik, "NAFTA's Impact," Council on Foreign
    Relations, July 7, 2009, http://www.cfr.org/economics/naftas-economic
    -impact/p15790#p6. But actions like the privatization of 80 percent of the
    nation's banks and all of the previously protected indigenous land render
    that criticism rather flimsy (Harvey, *Brief History,* 103). Across the globe,
    the effect of neoliberal reforms has been to exacerbate, not mitigate,
    income inequality.

39. Raj Patel, *Stuffed and Starved: The Hidden Battle for the World Food
    System* (London: Portobello Books Ltd., 2007), 62. Patel cites that "[In
    1991] the World Bank approved more non-poverty loans for Mexico than
    any other country. Approvals totaled 1.882 billion [dollars]."

40. Harvey further describes structural adjustment as a "program" of reforms
    "administered by the Wall Street-Treasury-IMF Complex" that "control
    [economic] crises and [currency] devaluations in ways that permit accu-
    mulation by dispossession." *Brief History,* 163.

41. Ibid., 103.

42. Roger Bybee and Carolyn Winter, "Immigration Flood Unleashed by
    NAFTA's Disastrous Impact on Mexican Economy," *CommonDreams,*
    April 26, 2006, http://www.commondreams.org/views06/0425-30.htm.
    Patel, *Stuffed and Starved,* 62.

43. Julian Aguilar, "Twenty Years Later, NAFTA Remains a Source of
    Tension," reprinted from *Texas Tribune* in *The New York Times,*
    December 7, 2012.

44. Harvey, *Brief History,* 162.

45. Patel, *Stuffed and Starved,* 67.

46. Ibid., 68.

47. As scholar Linda Green writes, "Immigration [from Mexico to the US]
    can be thought of as . . . a consequence of a complex set of global eco-
    nomic doctrines and geopolitical practices that produce [displaced, 'dis-
    posable' workers] in the global south and low wage, dangerous, and non-
    union jobs in the United States." Linda Green, "The Nobodies:

Neoliberalism, Violence and Migration," *Medical Anthropology* 30, no. 4 (April 2013): 367.

48. The program is facilitated through 287(g), a section added to the 1952 Immigration Nationality Act by the 1997 Illegal Immigration Reform and Immigrant Responsibility Act.

49. Jon Gillooly, "Cobb Keeps Sheriff Warren," *Marietta Daily Journal,* November 7, 2012, http://www.mdjonline.com/view/full_story/20738965 /article-Cobb-keeps-Sheriff-Warren. Fox News's "Toughest Sheriffs" list and slideshow at http://www.foxnews.com/slideshow/us/2010/11/09/americas -toughest-immigration-sheriffs/#slide=3, accessed April 17, 2017.

50. Jon Gillooly, "Sheriff Warren: We Have Always Won on Illegal Immigration," *Marietta Daily Journal,* September 20, 2012, http://www .mdjonline.com/view/full_story/20211840/article-Sheriff-Warren-%E2%80 %88We-have-always-won-on-illegal-immigration.

51. In 2011, Alabama did Arizona one better. Its legislature passed a bill intended to fuel "self-deportation" by "making [the] lives [of immigrants] difficult" to quote one of its sponsors. Among its provisions was the requirement that all public schools in the state had to verify the immigration status of every enrolled student and keep a record of undocumented families in the school system. Many of its most controversial provisions were invalidated by a circuit court in 2012. Campbell Robertson and Julia Preston, "Appeals Court Draws Boundaries on Alabama's Immigration Law," *The New York Times,* August 21, 2012, http://www.nytimes.com /2012/08/22/us/appeals-court-limits-alabamas-immigration-law.html?_r=0; Mark Guarino, "Hispanics Leave School in Face of Alabama's Tough Immigration Law," *Christian Science Monitor,* October 11, 2011, http:// www.csmonitor.com/USA/2011/1001/Hispanics-leave-school-in-face-of -Alabama-s-tough-immigration-law. On any given day, 34,000 people, some of whom are legal residents, are being held in US detention centers. Some of the legal residents who are deported are US-born, minor offenders who are mistakenly swept into the "Deportation Machine," as described in William Finnegan's article of the same name. More than 400,000 people were deported in 2012. Noferi, "Deportation without Representation"; David Grant, "Deportations of Illegal Immigrants in 2012 Reach New US Record," *Christian Science Monitor,* December 24, 2012, http://www.csmonitor.com/USA/2012/1224/ Deportations-of-illegal-immigrants-in-2012-reach-new-US-record.

52. In 2011, thousands of protestors converged on Georgia's capitol building, in Atlanta, to protest HB 87. Bernard Watson, "Undocumented Students Protest Georgia's New Illegal Immigration Law," *CBS Atlanta,* June 28, 2011, http://www.cbsatlanta.com/story/14990349/undocumented; "Georgia

Immigration Law: Thousands Protest for Reform at State Capitol," *Huffington Post,* July 2, 2011, http://www.huffingtonpost.com/2011/07/02 /georgia-immigration-law-protest_n_889271.html. At the level of national immigration reform, undocumented students advocating for the DREAM Act looked to the legislation moving through the Senate the summer of 2013. "DREAM Act Protesters Who Staged Sit-In at Obama's Denver Campaign Office, Call Off Hunger Strike, Vow More Actions to Come," *Huffington Post,* June 13, 2012, http://www.huffingtonpost.com/2012/06 /13/dream-act-protesters-who-_n_1593739.html; "Young Illegal Immigrants Rally in Downtown L.A. to Support Dream Act," *LA Times,* June 15, 2012, http://latimesblogs.latimes.com/lanow/2012/06/young -illegal-immigrants-rally-in-downtown-la-to-support-dream-act.html.

53. Jon Gillooly, "Activists Urge Deal Not to Sign Immigration Bill," *Marietta Daily Journal,* May 4, 2011, http://www.mdjonline.com/view/full_story /13126175/article-Activists-urge-Deal-not-to-sign-immigration-bill.

54. Julia Preston, "National Push by a Local Immigration Activist: No G.O.P. Retreat," *The New York Times,* August 6, 2013, http://www.nytimes .com/2013/08/07/us/national-push-by-a-local-immigration-activist-no-gop -retreat.html?pagewanted=all&_r=0.

55. Rachel Miller, "Public Hearing Set on Bond for Franklin Road Corridor 'Menace,'" *Marietta Daily Journal,* May 29, 2013, mdjonline.com; Lindsay Field, "Marietta School Board Talks $35M Redevelopment Bond," *Marietta Daily Journal,* May 22, 2013; Lee B. Garrett, Joe Kirby, and Otis A. Brumby III, "Cobb at Crossroads: And Franklin Remake the Way to Go, Garrett Says," *Marietta Daily Journal,* May 14, 2013.

56. Frederick Douglass, "The Meaning of July Fourth for the Negro," Corinthian Hall, Rochester, NY, July 5, 1852 (Rochester, NY: Lee, Mann and Co., 1852). Text widely available online including at the University of Rochester Frederick Douglass Project at http://www.lib.rochester.edu.

57. Ibid.

58. Roberto Gonzales, "Young Lives on Hold: The College Dreams of Undocumented Students," College Board Advocacy Report, April 2009, 7, www.nacacnet.org/research/KnowledgeCenter/Documents/ YoungLivesonHoldSummary.pdf.

59. "Sonia Hill" is a pseudonym; I have further disguised her identity by placing her in a different graduating class (chronologically close to her own). The statistics I offer for the class of 1995 are real; only Sonia's place in it is not.

60. The total graduating cohort in 1995 was 282 students; Latino graduates composed 5 percent of the class.

61. In 1996 President Clinton signed the Illegal Immigration Reform and Immigrant Responsibility Act (IIRIRA), which greatly accelerated the rate at which undocumented immigrants were deported and broadened the category of persons vulnerable to deportation. Minor drug possession charges and other crimes were made grounds for deportation, and people who had spent their entire lives in the United States were sent "home" to places where they had no family, employment, or assets. Daniel Kanstroom, "Deportation Nation," *The New York Times*, August 30, 2012, http://www.nytimes.com/2012/08/31/opinion/deportation-nation.html. IIRIRA also made receiving any kind of state benefit an act punishable by deportation and restricted the conditions under which asylum would be granted. Austin T. Fragomen Jr., "The Illegal Immigration Reform and Immigrant Responsibility Act of 1996: An Overview," *International Migration Review* 31, no. 2 (Summer 1997): 438–60.

62. Sonia Torres Hill (pseudonym), interview by the author, digital recording, Canton, GA, November 28, 2012. Unless otherwise noted, all quotes from Hill date to this interview.

63. Sonia Hill and all the graduates I have interviewed of South and Central American descent use the term "Hispanic" to describe themselves. However, I use the term "Latino" because it is inclusive of all Latin Americans, not just those who are Spanish-speaking.

64. These are data from 2009–2010 gathered by the Private School Universe Survey, created and administered by the National Center for Education Statistics. Unlike public schools, private schools do not have to report any data—demographic or otherwise—to federal or state officials.

65. *Bachata* is a dance style associated with the Dominican Republic; it was popularized in the United States in the 1990s by Dominican singer Juan Luis Guerra and the New York–based group Aventura. Its cross-cultural appeal has been enhanced by pop artists like Usher, and among Latino students at MHS, *bachata* music and dance are all the rage. Carly Mallenbaum, "Bachata: The Soulful Music, the Slow Dance," *USA Today*, January 6, 2012, https://usatoday30.usatoday.com/life/music/news/story/2012-01-12/bachata/52400522/1. This conversation with Elena (pseudonym) is from memory and was conducted in a casual gathering not a formal interview setting.

66. Bridget Reyes, interview by the author, digital recording, Marietta, GA, May 26, 2013. Unless otherwise noted, all quotes from Reyes date to this interview.

67. Bridget used "Mexican" and "Hispanic" interchangeably in talking about her peers at the high school. When asked why, she replied that despite the

presence of "a few Salvadorians and Guatemalans," the Hispanic students at MHS are largely natives of Mexico or have Mexican parents. The high school doesn't keep data distinguishing students within the "Latino" category of its demographic breakdown.

68. Statistics suggest that Latino students who graduate from high school are increasingly likely to pursue those college dreams. Seven in ten Latino high school graduates in the class of 2012 went to college, according to a report by the Pew Hispanic Center. Richard Fry and Paul Taylor, "Hispanic High School Graduates Pass Whites in Rate of College Enrollment," Pew Research Hispanic Center, May 9, 2013, http://www .pewhispanic.org/2013/05/09/hispanic-high-school-graduates-pass-whites -in-rate-of-college-enrollment/.

69. Because Ernesto was younger than 16 when he entered the United States, has a GED, and has never been convicted of a felony, he is protected from deportation by Deferred Action for Childhood Arrivals (DACA). In 2012, the Obama administration created DACA, a stopgap program to slow the deportation of young people who were in school, had no criminal record, and/or sought work authorization. Deferred action status lasts for two years and can be renewed—it confers no other rights or benefits, however; it only renders the individual a "low priority" for immigration enforcement and deportation. "Deferred Action for Childhood Arrivals: A Q&A Guide," Immigration Policy Center, accessed April 17, 2017, http://www. immigrationpolicy.org/just-facts/deferred-action-childhood-arrivals -qa-guide-updated.

70. In Chapter 2, I detail West Side's transformation from majority black and Latino in 2005 to majority white by 2011, a result of white parents' activism, the demolition of the Lyman Homes projects, and Marietta's school choice program.

71. One of the most powerful pieces of research on the subject of elementary education and the impact of economic and racial segregation is Susan Eaton's *The Children in Room E4: American Education on Trial* (Chapel Hill, NC: Algonquin, 2007). Eaton documents the trajectories of a class of third graders at one of Hartford, Connecticut's high-poverty elementary schools alongside the trajectory of the famed desegregation court case, *Sheff v. O'Neill. Sheff* was brought to court in 1989 and decided in 1996 in favor of the plaintiffs. The decision recommended no specific course of action, however, and integration efforts were still being adjudicated through agreements between the plaintiffs and the state department of education well into 2016. Matthew Kauffman and Vanessa de la Torre, "With 'Mixed Emotions,' Sheff Plaintiffs Sign New Agreement in Desegregation Case," *Hartford Courant,* June 10, 2016, http://www

.courant.com/community/hartford/hc-sheff-new-agreement-20160610
-story.html.

72. See Chapter 3 for further contextualizing of West Side and of the educational background of MHS students who enroll in AP and IB classes.

73. Paul Gomez (pseudonym), interview by the author, digital recording, Marietta, GA, June 8, 2013. Unless otherwise noted, all quotes from Gomez date to this interview.

74. See Note 11. In the 2011 cohort, 54.7 percent of black students, 39.1 percent of Latino students, 78.6 percent of Asian students, and 82.5 percent of white students graduated from MHS. Again, this rate reflects the changed calculation method; only a year before, Latino and black graduates had graduation rates of 74 percent and 77 percent, respectively.

75. Ted Hesson, "DREAMers Ask to Serve in the Military," *ABC News,* January 25, 2013, http://abcnews.go.com/ABC_Univision/News/dreamers-serve-military/story?id=18313706. In 2009, the military began allowing legal immigrants on visas to enlist in the military, but maintained a ban on anyone in the country illegally. Julia Preston, "U.S. Military Will Offer Path to Citizenship," *The New York Times,* February 14, 2009, http://www.nytimes.com/2009/02/15/us/15immig.html?pagewanted=all.

76. Gonzales, "Young Lives on Hold," 11.

77. Ibid., 12.

78. The DREAM (Development, Relief, and Education for Alien Minors) Act was first introduced in 2001, but as of 2017, it had not been passed by Congress. The "DREAMers"—undocumented youth—and their supporters have long been demonstrating and organizing for a bill that contains provisions for an expedited path to citizenship for young people brought to this country before the age of 16. The Senate's immigration reform bill of 2013 contained such language. Two key resources on the progress of the DREAM ACT are (for youth organizers and activists nationwide) the DREAM Act "portal" at http://dreamact.info/ and, for policy updates and progress on immigration reform at the federal level, the American Immigration Council at https://www.americanimmigrationcouncil.org/topics/legislation.

79. The others are Arizona, Missouri, Indiana, South Carolina, and Alabama. "Undocumented Student Tuition: Overview," National Conference of State Legislatures, accessed April 17, 2017, http://www.ncsl.org/issues -research/educ/undocumented-student-tuition-overview.aspx; Seth Freed Wessler, "Georgia Bans Undocumented Students from Public Universities," October 14, 2010, http://www.colorlines.com/articles/georgia-bans -undocumented-students-public-universities. In January of 2016, undocumented students won a tenuous victory in a suit contesting the legality of

Georgia's ban; Judge Gail Tusan of the Fulton Superior Court wrote of the policy that it "creates a defect of legal justice that has already negatively impacted thousands of Georgia students." Elise Foley, "Judge Sides with Dreamers Over In-State Tuition in Georgia," *Huffington Post,* January 4, 2017, http://www.huffingtonpost.com/entry/georgia-daca-tuition_us _586d1d1ae4b0de3a08fa5bb4.

80. Sara Hebel, "Georgia Regents Ban Illegal Immigrants from Selective Public Colleges," *Chronicle of Higher Education,* October 13, 2012, http:// chronicle.com/article/Georgia-Regents-Ban-Illegal/124903/. South Carolina and Alabama have passed similar bans. Alene Russel, "Policy Matters: State Policies Regarding Undocumented College Students: A Narrative of Unresolved Issues, Ongoing Debate and Missed Opportunities," A Higher Education Policy Brief, American Association of State Colleges and Universities, March 2011, 4, http://www.nacacnet.org/research /KnowledgeCenter/Documents/UndocumentedCollegeStudents.pdf.

81. Laura Diamond and Kristina Torres, "Senate Votes to Ban Illegal Immigrants from Georgia's Public Colleges," *Atlanta Journal-Constitution,* March 5, 2012.

82. Kennesaw State University, "Undergraduate Tuition Fall 2013–Spring 2014," https://financialservices.kennesaw.edu/bursar/sites/financialservices .kennesaw.edu.bursar/files/Regular%20Tuition%20Fall13%20SP14.pdf.

83. Kathryn Dobies, "Traffic Stop Puts KSU Student in Jail as an Illegal Immigrant," *Marietta Daily Journal,* May 10, 2010, http://www.mdjonline. com/news/traffic-stop-puts-ksu-student-in-jail-as-an-illegal/article _1be79cbd-baea-5e76-9318-f563fe6f99bc.html. Because, in part, of the national scorn heaped on local law enforcement, Colotl was not deported; in 2013 her "courtroom odyssey" ended when all charges against her were dropped. Andria Simmons, "Charge Against Jessica Colotl Dropped," *The Atlanta Journal-Constitution,* January 10, 2013, http://www.ajc.com/news /charge-against-jessica-colotl-dropped/yj5PpLBUAcWiIIol2HengK/.

84. As noted in Chapter 3, where Lauren is also quoted, the name is a pseudonym.

85. The term dates to a 1988 article by famed sociologist James S. Coleman, "Social Capital in the Creation of Human Capital," *American Journal of Sociology* 94 (1988): S95–120. Sociologists have variously defined and applied the term, but it was brought into popular discourse in part by the scholarship of political scientist Robert Putnam. John F. Helliwell and Robert D. Putnam, "Education and Social Capital," *Eastern Economic Journal* 33, no. 1 (Winter 2007): 1–19.

86. Patricia Gándara and Frances Contreras, *The Latino Education Crisis: The Consequences of Failed Social Policies* (Cambridge, MA: Harvard University Press, 2010), 115.

87. Bridget paid to become a "client" of a group called College Admissions Assistance LLC, a private company offering "expert college planning" in the form of tutoring and aid with the college application process ("Who We Are," accessed April 17, 2017, http://www.caaconnect.com/who-we-are/). When I asked her about the company, Bridget wrote me the following: "I think they got us because after my junior year we didn't know anything about college. My parents literally did not know what to do and they convinced them that they would help." Although the company reviewed some of her college application essays, Bridget judged their services "not worth" the $2,000 her parents paid for her membership. She wrote, "The price would have been lower [but] we had to do payments [and] interest was just a lot." Referring to the scholarships she won in the months before graduating, she added, "I'm happy that I don't need to ask my parents for any more money." Bridget Reyes, e-mail correspondence with the author, July 13 and 14, 2013.

88. See Chapter 3; the IB diploma cohorts of 2011 and 2012 were 12 and 13 percent Latino, respectively. In cohorts of around fifty students, this percentage equates to no more than six or seven Latino graduates each year.

89. Lauren Garcia (pseudonym), interview by the author, Skype video recording, September 20, 2012. Unless otherwise noted, all quotes from Garcia date to this interview.

90. Joel Spring, *American Education,* 15th ed. (New York: McGraw-Hill, 2012), 85. Spring discusses "human capital" as an idea originally espoused by nineteenth-century educational theorist and reformer Horace Mann.

91. Paul E. Peterson, Ludger Woessmann, Eric A. Hanushek, and Carlos Xabel Lastra-Anadón "Are U.S. Students Ready to Compete?" *Education Next* 11, no. 4 (Fall 2011): 51–59, accessed April 17, 2017, http://educationnext.org/are-u-s-students-ready-to-compete/.

92. Spring, *American Education,* 99.

93. Grace Lee Boggs, *The Next American Revolution: Sustainable Activism for the Twenty-First Century* (Berkeley: University of California Press, 2011), 139.

94. Ibid., 157.

95. Ibid., 143.

96. Institutions like the left-leaning Center for American Progress and the more conservative Heritage Foundation come to predictably opposite conclusions. "Weighing Economic Pros and Cons of Legalizing Undocumented Workers," segment, *PBS News Hour* Series, "Inside Immigration Reform," aired June 5, 2013, transcript, pbs.org.

97. Raul Hinojosa Ojeda and Sherman Robinson, "Adding It Up: Accurately Gauging the Economic Impact of Immigration Reform," Immigration Policy Center, May 7, 2013, http://www.immigrationpolicy.org/just-facts

/adding-it-accurately-gauging-economic-impact-immigration-reform; Steven A. Camarota, "The Fiscal and Economic Impact of Immigration on the United States," Center for Immigration Reform, Testimony Prepared for the Joint Economic Committee, May 8, 2013, http://www.cis.org /node/4573.

98. Adam Davidson, "Do Illegal Immigrants Actually Hurt the Economy?" *The New York Times Magazine*, February 12, 2013, http://www.nytimes .com/2013/02/17/magazine/do-illegal-immigrants-actual-ly-hurt-the-us-economy.html. A study by the conservative think tank the Cato Institute showed that "the overall financial cost of providing public benefits to non-citizen immigrants and most naturalized immigrants is lower than for native-born people." Leighton Ku and Brian Bruen, "Poor Immigrants Use Public Benefits at a Lower Rate Than Poor Native-Born Citizens," Cato Institute, Economic Bulletin No. 17, March 4, 2013, https://www.cato.org/publications/economic-development-bulletin/poor -immigrants-use-public-benefits-lower-rate-poor.

99. Benjamin Derra (pseudonym), Skype recording, June 7, 2013. Unless otherwise noted, all quotes from Derra date to this interview.

100. AH! is a pseudonym, as are the names of the founders. This is to protect the identity of involved students who requested anonymity.

101. Rosa Villabos and Miguel Carerro (pseudonyms), interview by the author, Skype recording, November 9, 2012. Unless otherwise noted, all quotes from Villabos and Carerro date from this interview.

102. Laura Keefe, interview by the author, Skype call recording, February 20, 2013. Unless otherwise noted, all quotes from Keefe date to this interview.

103. Wendell Berry, "The Idea of a Local Economy," *Orion*, Winter 2001, https://orionmagazine.org/article/the-idea-of-a-local-economy/.

104. Kim Freedman (pseudonym), conversation with the author, unrecorded, Marietta, GA, April 17, 2013.

105. Miller, "Public Hearing Set."

106. Jon Gillooly, "Franklin Road Makeover Is the Main Goal of $35M Plan," *Marietta Daily Journal*, March 26, 2013.

107. Robin Montgomery's identity has not been disguised. Rachel Miller, "Lots of Controversy as the Public Gives Their Opinions on Franklin Road Proposal," *Marietta Daily Journal*, May 9, 2013, http://mdjonline.com/ view/full_story/22512615/article-Lots-of-controversy-as-the-public-gives -their-opinions-on-Franklin-Road-proposal-?instance=home_lead_story.

108. Mobility percentages index the movement of students in and out of a school during one academic year: for example, MHS was 22 percent mobile in 2011–2012; that is, 22 percent of students who began the year at the high

school didn't finish it there. "Mobility and Stability Statistics Comparison," data kept by the Marietta City Schools and acquired through Thomas Algarin, Director of Communications, via e-mail, February, 26 2013.

109. Leigh Colburn, conversation with the author, unrecorded, Marietta, GA, July 18, 2013.

110. Colburn designed and distributed two surveys to the class of 2013 during their graduation practice sessions. One survey asked students about their educational histories (schools attended in Marietta and years spent in the system), scholarships won, and college plans. The other survey solicited information about the students' "greatest challenges" and "favorite parts" of their MHS experiences. Colburn shared the surveys with me (with identifying details obscured) during the week of July 18–24, 2013.

111. There were fifty-two Latino students in the senior class of 2013, according to the enrollment totals for the fall of 2012. Such numbers for the senior class would suggest a rather paltry Latino enrollment. But many Latino students who begin high school at MHS don't finish it there or finish at all; for example, according the same data, "FTE October 2012," the Latino enrollment for the ninth grade in 2012–2013 was 225, for tenth grade it was 147, and for eleventh grade, 81. Enrollment data acquired from Leigh Colburn, via e-mail, July 18, 2013.

112. The term originated in Scotland in the 1990s and was used to describe poor communities' lack of access to nutritious food. Steven Cummins and Sally Macintyre, "'Food Deserts'—Evidence and Assumption in Health Policy Making," *BMJ: British Medical Journal* 325 (2002): 436–38.

113. Ruth Wilson Gilmore, *Golden Gulag: Prisons, Surplus, Crisis, and Opposition in Globalizing California* (Berkeley: University of California Press, 2007), 28–29.

114. H. Patricia Hynes, *A Patch of Eden: America's Inner-City Gardeners* (White River Junction, VT: Chelsea Green Publishing, 1996); Monica White, "Sisters of the Soil: Urban Gardening as Resistance," *Race/ Ethnicity: Multidisciplinary Global Contexts* 5, no. 1 (Autumn 2011): 13–28; Richard Reynolds, *On Guerilla Gardening: A Handbook for Gardening without Boundaries* (New York: Bloomsbury, 2008).

115. American Community Gardening Association, "Bi-National Community Garden Database," accessed April 17, 2017, https://communitygarden.org/.

116. Scholar Yvonne Hung interviewed the youth interns of the East New York Farm. The interns reported the abilities and dynamics I list, but they were paid to work at the farm and take their produce to market—so those youth also reported learning business and money-management skills during their internship period. Yvonne Hung, "East New York Farms: Youth Participation in Community Development and Urban Agriculture,"

Children, Youth and Environments 14, no. 1 Collected Papers (2004): 56–85.

117. Scholar Joy Dryfoos has deeply researched the community schools movement in the United States. Joy Dryfoos, Jane Quinn, and Carol Barkin, eds., *Community Schools in Action: Lessons from a Decade of Practice* (New York: Oxford University Press, 2005).

118. Novella Z. Keith, "Whose Community Schools? New Discourses, Old Patterns," *Theory into Practice* 38, no. 4 (Autumn 1999): 226.

119. Boggs, *Next American Revolution,* 119.

120. A fact sheet produced by the Center for Information and Research on Civic Learning and Engagement (CIRCLE), based at Tufts University, defines service learning as "a response to real community needs over a sustained period of time, youth decision-making and participation in the design of the project, and regular reflection and analysis (through journals, group discussion, and papers) to assist students in drawing lessons from the service." Allison Stagg, "Service Learning in K–12 Education," July 2004, http://www.civicyouth.org/PopUps/FactSheets/FS_ServiceLearning.pdf.

121. John Dewey, *Democracy and Education* (New York: McMillan, 1916), 98.

122. William Mathis, "Research-Based Options for Education Policymaking: Twenty-First Century Skills and Implications for Education," Brief for the National Education Policy Center, May 2013, http://www.greatlakescenter .org/docs/Policy_Briefs/Research-Based-Options/08-Mathis-21stCentury .pdf, 1.

123. Ibid., 2.

124. Ibid., 3.

125. John Charles Boger and Gary Orfield, eds., *School Resegregation: Must the South Turn Back?* (Chapel Hill: University of North Carolina Press, 2005); Charles T. Clotfelter, *After Brown: The Rise and Retreat of School Desegregation* (Princeton, NJ: Princeton University Press, 2004); Gary Orfield and Chungmei Lee, "Historic Reversals, Accelerating Resegregation and the Need for New Integration Strategies," A Report of the Civil Rights Project, UCLA, 2007. Researcher Roslyn Mickelson's 2011 testimony to the Minnesota Education Commission Task Force on Integrated Schools illustrates the trend in social science research on the effects of racial segregation and desegregation of connecting improved academic outcomes to social and cultural outcomes—that is, how students fare in a "diverse" workforce. "What Social Science Research from the Last 20 Years Says About the Effects of Integrated Education on Achievement Outcomes," Remarks to the Minnesota Education Commission Task Force on Integrated Schools, December 20, 2011, http://www.school-diversit .org/pdf/Mickelson_Minnesota_testimony_12-20-11.pdf.

126. The range of "integration" options now seen as feasible in public education are displayed in the "Integration Report," which emphasizes the
funding of magnet schools, open-enrollment or "interdistrict" programs,
and the monitoring of federally funded charter schools to ensure race and
income diversity. "The Integration Report: A Monthly Update on the
Status of Integration in Our Nation's Schools," A Report of the National
Coalition on School Diversity, Issue 28, January 19, 2011, http://www
.school-diversity.org/full_text.php.

127. Quoted in Leigh Raiford and Renee Romano, eds., *The Civil Rights
Movement in American Memory* (Athens: University of Georgia Press,
2006), 180.

Conclusion: Reclaiming *Brown:*
Integration Is Not a Policy Goal—It's a Movement

1. Sociologist Douglas Massey's well-known work documents the impact of
race and class isolation on the opportunities of low-income children.
Douglas S. Massey, "American Apartheid: Segregation and the Making of
the Underclass," *American Journal of Sociology* 96 (1990): 329–57. Other
recent work on the issue includes: Russell Rumberger and Gregory
Palardy, "Does Segregation Still Matter? The Impact of Student
Composition on Academic Achievement in High School," *The Teachers
College Record* 107, no. 9 (2005): 1999–2045; and Gary Orfield and
Chungmei Lee, *Why Segregation Matters: Poverty and Educational
Inequality* (Cambridge, MA: Civil Rights Project, Harvard University,
2005). In the wake of the 2007 Supreme Court ruling in *Parents Involved
in Community Schools v. Seattle School District No. 1,* which dramatically
restricted the use of race in districting and student assignment, some districts sought income-based strategies to replace previous racial desegregation plans. However, a growing body of research suggests that income
integration will not necessarily produce racial integration in public
schools; both class- and race-based desegregation strategies are necessary
to produce educational equity. Sean F. Reardon, John T. Yun, and Michal
Kurlaender, "Implications of Income-Based School Assignment Policies
for Racial School Segregation," *Educational Evaluation and Policy
Analysis* 28, no. 1 (2006): 49–75.

2. Deanne Bonner, president, Cobb County NAACP, digital recording by the
author of statements at public hearing before City Council, May 8, 2013.
This discussion of the public hearing blends both of my own records—
digital and written—with the account provided by Rachel Miller's May 9,

2013, article for the *Marietta Daily Journal:* "Lots of Controversy as the Public Gives Their Opinions on Franklin Road Proposal."

3. Robin Montgomery, digital recording by the author of statements at public hearing before City Council, May 8, 2013.

4. Miller, "Lots of Controversy."

5. "Potential Redevelopment Targets," published with text, Jon Gillooly, "Marietta to Detail $35M Plan Tonight," *Marietta Daily Journal,* May 1, 2013.

6. Lance Lamberton, president of the Cobb Taxpayers Association, statements at public hearing before City Council, May 8, 2013.

7. Burt Reeves, digital recording by the author of statements at public hearing before City Council, May 8, 2013.

8. Robin Montgomery and Cheryl Stevenson, digital recording by the author of statements at public hearing before City Council, May 8, 2013.

9. Attendance Zone map; accessible at the Marietta City Schools website, http://www.marietta-city.org/files/district/AttendanceZoneMap.pdf.

10. Leigh Colburn, interview by the author, digital recording, Marietta, GA, July 30, 2013.

11. Jon C. Teaford, "Urban Renewal and Its Aftermath," *Housing Policy Debate* 11, no. 2 (2000): 443–65; Mindy Fullilove, *Root Shock: How Tearing Up City Neighborhoods Hurts America, and What We Can Do about It* (New York: Random House, 2004); Jeff Crump, "Deconcentration by Demolition: Public Housing, Poverty, and Urban Policy," *Environment and Planning* 20, no. 5 (2002): 581–96.

12. The bond got 54 percent of the vote. Jon Gillooly, "68M Redevelopment Bond Passes," *Marietta Daily Journal,* November 6, 2013.

13. Nikki Wiley, "First Complex Bought in Wake of Franklin Road Vote," *Marietta Daily Journal,* January 13, 2014. At a town hall meeting I attended on February 18, 2014, Marietta's economic development director addressed plans for Woodlands Park. City leaders' responses to questions from the students of YELLS and from Franklin Road residents demonstrated that the city would not offer YELLS assistance in relocating its programs. When asked about future plans for the sites, the economic development director replied that there were no concrete plans for the properties and admitted that, as yet, there weren't any interested investors or developers either. The only other property the city had ever purchased on Franklin Road, a thirteen-acre complex acquired in 2010, was still sitting vacant and overgrown in 2014, and the park Franklin Roaders were promised would occupy that site still had not materialized. Jon Gillooly, "Park Plan Moves Ahead," *Marietta Daily Journal,* February 4, 2010. At

the town hall meeting, residents of Franklin discussed both the broken promise of the park and their imminent displacement from their homes as reflective of the failure of city leaders to represent and listen to the people of Franklin Road. The economic development director and the city council member who represents Franklin responded with assurances about how redevelopment was, in fact, an effort to address the concerns of Franklin Roaders and better serve the citizens of the corridor. Finally, in the fall of 2016, the city broke ground on the promised park, which will offer playing fields, walking trails, and concession stands. Anthony White, "Marietta Celebrates Groundbreaking of $10.9 Million Sports Park," *Marietta Daily Journal,* October 18, 2016, http://www.mdjonline.com /news/marietta-celebrates-groundbreaking-of-million-sports-park/article _6f4d5844-95a1-11e6-bdbf-af5d5bab3763.html.

14. Scholar Ruth Wilson Gilmore calls redevelopment that targets low-income communities "a geographical solution that purports to solve social problems by removing people . . . and depositing them somewhere else." Ruth Wilson Gilmore, *Golden Gulag: Prisons, Surplus, Crisis, and Opposition in Globalizing California* (Berkeley: University of California Press, 2007), 14.

15. *Green v. County School Board of New Kent County* 391 U.S. 430, 438 (1968) (majority opinion).

16. Lindsay Field, "New National Calculation Method Submarines Graduation Rates in Cobb, Marietta," *Marietta Daily Journal,* April 11, 2012, http://www.mdjonline.com/view/full_story/18194684/article-New -national-calculation-method-submarines-graduation-rates-in-Cobb --Marietta. In 2011, 39 percent of Latino students, 55 percent of black students, and 83 percent of white students graduated. In 2010, using the former method, those rates were 74, 77, and 91 percent, respectively. "Downloadable Data," accessed April 17, 2017, https://gosa.georgia.gov /downloadable-data. During this research, all data since 2004 were available through school "report cards" accessible via the Georgia Department of Education website. In 2014, however, all data for school years after 2010-2011 were moved to a new platform, the Governor's Office of Student Achievement, https://gosa.georgia.gov/downloadable-data. For data concerning school years prior to 2010, a data request form must be submitted electronically to http://gosa.georgia.gov/webform/report-card -data-request.

17. Leigh Colburn, interview by the author, digital recording, Marietta, GA, July 30, 2013. Unless otherwise indicated, all quotes from Colburn date to this interview.

18. Field, "New National Calculation Method."

19. Question and answers excerpted from a survey given by Leigh Colburn to the graduates of the class of 2013; only the first names of the writers were disclosed to me, and I anonymized them here.

20. "Superintendent Welcomes Employees—Kicks Off Graduate Marietta," Marietta City Schools, Press Release, August 5, 2013, http://mhs.marietta -city.org/site/default.aspx?PageType=3&DomainID=18&ModuleInstanceID =2309&ViewID=047E6BE3-6D87-4130-8424-D8E4E9ED6C2A&Rende rLoc=0&FlexDataID=5386&PageID=29. Video link at: http://player .multicastmedia.com/player.php?p=zkw388b7.

21. Juan Gonzalez and Amy Goodman, "Arizona Students Protest New Law Banning Ethnic Studies Classes," *Democracy Now,* May 14, 2010, http:// www.democracynow.org/2010/5/14/arizona_students_protest_new_law _banning; Valerie Strauss, "Georgia Students Fight Segregated Proms," *Washington Post,* April 5, 2013, http://www.washingtonpost.com/blogs /answer-sheet/wp/2013/04/05/georgia-students-fight-segregated-proms/.

Epilogue

1. Carolyn Cunningham, "Marietta Embarks on Franklin Road Revitalization," *Atlanta Journal-Constitution,* June 2, 2015.

2. Brittni Ray, "City Razes Second Apartment Complex on Franklin Road," *Marietta Daily Journal,* July 13, 2015.

3. Cunningham, "Marietta Embarks on Franklin Road Revitalization."

4. "The International Baccalaureate," accessed April 17, 2017, http://www .ibo.org/en/programmes/find-an-ib-school/.

5. Joe Cortright, "Why Aren't We Talking about Marietta, Georgia?," *The City Observatory,* July 14, 2015, http://cityobservatory.org/why-arent-we -talking-about-marietta-georgia/.

6. Ibid.

7. Eric Jaffe, "Troubling Echoes of Urban Renewal in an Atlanta Suburb," *City Lab,* July 15, 2015, http://www.citylab.com/housing/2015/07 /troubling-echoes-of-urban-renewal-in-an-atlanta-suburb/398582/.

8. Cortright, "Why Aren't We Talking about Marietta, Georgia?"

9. Ibid.

10. I applaud Cortright's righteous anger and his attention to demographic change: he helpfully charts the Franklin Road corridor's transformation over the years between 1980 and 2010 from 95 percent white to nearly 85 percent black and Latino. However, just because Cortright and Eric Jaffe can't hear a full-throated critique of redevelopment on Franklin doesn't mean there isn't one. The only local critic of redevelopment Cortright

cites is a white citizen who lives in an affluent neighborhood in downtown Marietta.

11. Erica Frankenberg and Gary Orfield, *The Resegregation of Suburban Schools: A Hidden Crisis in American Education* (Cambridge, MA: Harvard Education Press, 2012).

12. Alice Walker, *In Search of Our Mothers' Gardens: Womanist Prose* (Orlando, FL: Harcourt, 1983), 198.

13. "Home Depot Opens 200,000-Square-Foot Technology Center," *Atlanta Business Chronicle,* October 7, 2015, http://www.bizjournals.com/atlanta /morning_call/2015/10/home-depot-opens-200-000-square-foot -technology.html.

14. David Wickert, "Atlanta United Scraps DeKalb Site in Favor of Marietta," *Atlanta Journal-Constitution,* November 6, 2015, http://www.ajc.com /news/local-govt--politics/atlanta-united-scraps-dekalb-site-favor-marietta /d2uOPiloMlrAeMGHzvCIiP/.

15. I was present at the forum, but the structure, questions, and other logistics are drawn from a document, "Mayor Town Hall Meeting Agenda and Questions," shared with me by Laura Keefe; quotes specifically from the forum are drawn from my video recording and transcribing of the proceedings.

16. Carolyn Cunningham, "Marietta's Franklin Road to Be Franklin Gateway," February 11, 2016, *Atlanta Journal-Constitution,* http://www.ajc.com/news /local/marietta-franklin-road-franklin-gateway/cEg5IX8eau1o1q WWWYxvUO/.

17. I draw here on Peter McLaren, *Life in Schools: An Introduction to Critical Pedagogy in the Foundations of Education*, 6th ed. (Boulder, CO: Paradigm, 2015), 147.

18. Ben Brasch, "Groundbreaking Held for Atlanta United's Franklin Gateway Complex," *Atlanta Journal-Constitution,* October 19, 2016, http://www.myajc.com/news/local/groundbreaking-held-for-atlanta -united-franklin-gateway-complex/9S8etkRqXKVi2bTgbxy1dP/.

ACKNOWLEDGMENTS

Perhaps it is apparent that without the willingness of Mariettans to share their reflections and resources with me, there would be no book. I began this research in 2011, and in the years since then, so many of Marietta's students, teachers, and elected leaders gave to me of their time and energy. My erstwhile informant and now friend Bridget Reyes, a 2013 Marietta High School graduate, was instrumental both in the practical matters of this project, such as identifying interviewees, and in those less tangible. Bridget's openheartedness, her commitment to her community, and her indefatigable optimism left a lasting mark on me and on this work. Former MHS faculty member Joan Harrell was a mentor to me (as well as the source of decades' worth of MHS yearbooks); she too connected me with graduates who may not have otherwise entrusted their stories to an unfamiliar researcher, and non–Blue Devil to boot. Former principal Leigh Colburn and former superintendent Emily Lembeck offered me their perspectives and their time; they are tireless warriors for public education and the students of Marietta City Schools. My academic mentors, Kathryn Dudley, Jonathan Holloway, and Glenda Gilmore, were sources of rich intellectual and moral support, and I'm deeply thankful to them. Kate Dudley encouraged me to discover my questions in the field. She is a wonderful reader, teacher, and ethnographer. Tom Scott, historian and friend, was incredibly generous with his resources and his contacts. Alberta Cook, MHS Class of 1971 and one of my very first interviewees, welcomed me to the Class of 1971 reunion, a crucial entrée for me. I remain thankful for her insight and encouragement at the project's wobbly beginning. Andy Horowitz, Zen master of zooming out, always provided the big picture that eludes the writer in the weeds. He's a great scholar and an even greater friend. More so than anyone else, Wende Elizabeth Marshall's intellectual imprint is on these pages. She shaped this book by shaping the way I see this world and the capacity for justice in it. I also am indebted to and inspired by the students and staff of Marietta YELLS—all of whom taught me a great deal. The interpretations and analysis in this book do not, however, represent YELLS or its leadership. Bringing the book into being took the insight, patience, and wisdom of Andrew Kinney and his colleagues at Harvard University Press. I also thank Stephanie Gilmore of the *Oral History Review* for publishing my previous work on Marietta. Finally, I acknowledge the infinite forbearance and support of my parents, John and Dede Yow, and my partner in all things, Benjamin Shirley— they've read every word, many times over. Surely they dread the next project, but all they show me is pride and love. I'm grateful to and humbled by all these folks—the big community of this book—and hope I have done some justice to their ideals, work, generosity, and passion.

INDEX